M000035033

A Woman's Guide to the
Earth Traditions

Vivianne Crowley

Thorsons

Thorsons
An Imprint of HarperCollins*Publishers*
77–85 Fulham Palace Road
Hammersmith, London W6 8JB

The Thorsons website address is: www.thorsons.com

Published by Thorsons 2001

1 3 5 7 9 10 8 6 4 2

©Vivianne Crowley 2001

Vivianne Crowley asserts the moral right to be
identified as the author of this work

A catalogue record for this book is
available from the British Library

ISBN 0 00 711699 3

Printed and bound in Great Britain by
Creative Print and Design (Wales), Ebbw Vale

A Woman's Guide to the
Earth Traditions

Contents

To Chris who walks with me, and to all those
with whom I have danced the Spiral Dance.

Foreword

The second half of the twentieth century has seen an upsurge of books about Pagan Earth Traditions. There are books on the myths of the Celts, Germanic, and Native American peoples. There are books on African-inspired teachings such as Santeria and Voudon, and teachings of newer Traditions such as Wicca that draw on ancient European heritage. Many books can explain specific paths. This book aims to draw together the philosophies that underlie them and to answer the questions of what do these beliefs have in common; what does it mean to practice an Earth Tradition; how can the beliefs of the past make sense in the twenty-first century?

The Pagan Earth Traditions are not single entities, but they share underlying similarities. The first edition of this book was focused solely on Earth Traditions that have derived from European culture, but many people in North America and in Europe also feel drawn to Native American spirituality and to African-derived Traditions; particularly if these are part of their own cultural heritage. In this new edition for the new millennium, I have included chapters on these Traditions so that readers can see that they share much in common with the pre-Christian Traditions of ancient Europe. All these Traditions venerate the Earth, and accept that to portray the full Divine reality, we must have goddesses as well as gods, and deities that are present in Nature and the Earth as well as in some distant Heaven. This book describes mainly Traditions practiced within Europe and North America, but Earth Traditions all over the world are undergoing an unprecedented revival as people come to value and respect once more their traditional cultures, cultures that have often been suppressed and which people have been taught were 'primitive', 'superstitious' or 'inferior'. In Africa, Traditional Religion can now be studied as a school matriculation paper.

This book is a personal view of the Earth Traditions. It does not speak for all who practice Earth-centered Pagan spirituality, but is the outlook of one person who has been a practicing Pagan for many years. In writing about Paganism, I must generalize, but Pagans are individualists who have a wide variety of religious opinions. I cannot convey all the richness and beauty of the spectrum of the Earth Traditions in this one volume. For those of you who are new to these spiritual paths, this book can be the starting point of your personal quest and for those who are already followers of an Earth Tradition, I hope it will give you new insight into the beauty of your heritage.

Vivianne Crowley, Spring 2001

Introduction

Beginning a book is always difficult. Perhaps it is the Celt in me which must always begin with a vision; for all things come to me first in pictures, then in poetry (for what is a poem but a picture in words?), then in understanding, and finally back into the words of prose, the language of explanation; and that is always the hardest thing. So, I will begin with what was for me the beginning.

When I played in the stream in the woods as a child and plunged my legs up to my thighs in its soft clay mud and baked them dry beneath the sunlight, lying on my back on the bank and watching the clouds sail by above, I merged a little with the Earth. And when I made for myself garlands of ivy and climbed a tree to the highest point that would bear my weight, and entwined myself in its swaying branches and rode with it upon the wind, listening to the mysteries whispered by the rustling leaves, then I forgot for a while which was tree and which was I.

I had much freedom as a child, much more than is possible to many now, and from the age of six I would spend hours at a time in the woods, returning only to eat and to give adults the reassurance I knew they needed that all was well. Sometimes if my friend was with me, we would be out all day and would take our lunch and eat it in the tree-tops; but more often than not she could not come, for she lived too far away, and our nearest neighbor was a Gypsy woman who lived in a caravan in the copse, with 30 cats and a daughter who was wilder than I. Not even I played with her.

And being alone, I did not wish to be disturbed; so when people came to walk in the wood, I would hide myself so that they did not see. I learned to walk silently and to merge with leaf and tree and sometimes to 'disappear myself', so I could be neither heard nor seen. I also learned to see, and this was a different kind of seeing which came first by night. For it seemed to me that sometimes I left my body and went back to the woods, which were bathed not in their night-time darkness but with golden light; and there were beings there who had no substantial shape, but seemed to me those presences whom I sensed by day, but could not see. And after a time, the memory of this seeing stayed with me, and leaves, tree and flower were no longer solid but crystals of colored light. And when I touched the pink ragged robin that grew by the edge of the marsh, I felt that I touched the garment of the universe and my fingers tingled with the softness and the beauty of it. And so it was that I spent the early part of my child-hood in a kind of waking dream.

But some things penetrated the dream and one was this. I was returning one afternoon from the woods and walking up the steep road home to the farm. The tarmac was hot and haze shimmered on the road and I was tired. Then shining on one side of the road, I saw what I thought was an egg. I stopped and picked it up and it was warm in my hand and heavy. It was a stone. I turned it over and there was that stopping in time and space that occurs when we first see the one we are to love, or when there is great danger; for on the other side of the stone was the face of a goat. I took the stone home and it seemed to me a sacred thing, a thing of power. I made an altar for it in my bedroom and covered the altar with a cloth and brought a vase of wild flowers and sat and looked at the stone until it was evening.

When I was nine, I tried to write a poem for a competition. A stag appeared to me and in his antlers he bore the Sun, and he looked at me as though to speak, but we had no common language and could not. I wrote a poem and I called him 'Majesty'. It was the first poem I wrote which did not rhyme, but it was a failure and I lost it; for I could not capture in words what I had seen.

Then for five years, I sought to worship the man who was a god; until one day I saw in my vision a tall red-haired chieftain with a golden torc about his neck and gold upon his brow. His cloak was of many colors and he rode the land on a white horse, whose bridle shone with silver. The chieftain's standard-bearer rode before him and his banner was an eagle on a green field; for he honored the Green Lady of the meadows; though later his banner was the black mourning of the Morrigan, for he was an exile from his own land. Behind the chieftain rode a band of warriors clad as brightly as he. They fought many battles to free the native people from a great oppression and tore down the halls of the rulers who had abused their power. But these were not his people and he was a stranger amongst them. He, in his majesty, seemed to them a god and they bowed down before him as though to worship him. But this was not what he sought.

'I am no god,' said he,
'I am the voice of my people,
and your voice too, if it be your will.
In your temples, worship the Great Spirit,
the sky and the wind, that unite both gods and men,
turn not your worship to a mortal king.'

So first they took him for their king but, when he died, they forgot that he was not a god and they worshipped him.

It seemed that he and the stag were the same, and for a long time I could not understand what this meant. Then it came to me that no man should be worshipped and I could not find my god in prophets or in human form. Then a woman came to me in a dream and her hair was black and straight and hung to her waist, and her eyes were the gray-green of the sea, and she came out of the North, walking towards me across waves and ice floes, and glittering and terrible were the jet pupils of her eyes. As Goddess she came to me, and I knew fear and awe.

So it was the God who came to me first, and I found him in trees, then in stone, then as Cernunnos Antlered One, coming out of the warmth of the Southern Sun, and then as man, and then as none of these; for he was to me then as the breath of the Universe, and the spaces between things, and that which binds the molecules and sets them free. My God came at last as spirit, but within the world was He. And She who came out of the coldness of the North, the Goddess of the Sea, I heard her voice upon the waves and within the silence that rings with sound. And still if I do not know the answer to a thing, I will go and sit by the edge of the sea and the answer will come to me, brought in upon the waves.

All this is simply to say that the Old Ones had awoken for me and I have sought throughout my life to know their ways. And it seems to me that, in this journey of the spirit, I and others still walk that steep uphill road where I found my goat-headed stone. We reach the summit only to find that there in the distance a hill still higher beckons, and for all the wisdom we have sought, the understanding that we gain is always less than a child's. And all our religious edifices, which serve first as staffs to help us on our way, in the end become crutches that we must discard. For there is more wisdom in the leaf on the tree than in the leaves of books that contain the thoughts of woman or of man. And the doctrines we espouse and which we hold dear are only shining stones we pick up from the road and place in our baggage. With each new dogma and doctrine, the baggage grows heavier, until we discard these pebbles, one by one, leaving them on the roadside for others to find and to carry a little further. And in the end, we need neither doctrine nor creed, or to name that which we worship: it is beyond all images and words. And who but a fool carries stone to a mountain?

Impossible contradiction,
how shall we name Thee?
Unknowing, but rejoicing still,
we hymn Thy greatness and Thy boundless will.
Do what Thou wilt shall all the Law be,
and Thine the Law that we obey.
O Lady of the Night most Timeless,
we, Thy children, ever seeking Thee,
searching for Thy elusive shadow,
through the woven dream of matter,
until at last we do become Thee,
at-one-ment in eternity.

From *Goddess Hymn*, Vivianne Crowley, Yule 1977

What are the Earth Traditions?

The Earth Traditions are the ancient pre-Christian Pagan traditions of our planet that venerate the Divine in the world of Nature as well as in the world beyond. If you say you are a Pagan, people may not understand what you mean. Some people think you are joking; others that you have no religion or that you are anti-Christian. Paganism is not a word that our ancestors would have used to describe their religions and, in many ways, it was derogatory. The word Pagan is derived from Latin. Pagans were those who worshipped the deities of the *pagus* or locality, rather than the new solo male god. When Christianity was first brought to Europe, it was a religion of the cities, or more specifically of *the City* – Rome. To be called a Pagan implied that you were backward-looking, preferring peasant tradition to the modern Christian urban faith. Outside Europe, people often reject the term Pagan and see it as an example of Western colonialism denigrating their traditional beliefs. In West Africa, practitioners of indigenous spirituality prefer to call it African Traditional Religion. Elsewhere, the term Earth Tradition is often used. In our new millennium, we are seeing a spiritual Renaissance, a reflowering of these ancient spiritual traditions.

Each Earth Tradition venerates its own deities, but the common denominator is that the Earth Traditions follow a Nature-based spirituality and reverence deities who pre-existed the monotheisms of Judaism, Christianity and Islam. People may venerate the deities of a particular ethnic group such as the Celts, Germanic peoples, Finns, Balts, Yoruba or Lakota. They may also reverence their deities through traditions that draw on a number of sources. Many contemporary Pagans take an eclectic approach to their spirituality, drawing on a number of different Earth Traditions to evolve their own spiritual practice, rather than subscribing to one pantheon and a set ritual approach. Others follow a distinct path such as Celtic druidry, Ásatrú based on Scandinavian deities, Santeria based on African Yoruba deities who have fused with Catholic saints, and Wicca, the religion of witchcraft, which worships the Great Mother Goddess and Horned God as representations of all Goddesses and Gods that the human heart has worshipped. Many people are attracted to the Earth Traditions because the Divine is found in the form of Goddess as well as God. In an era when the equality of the sexes is taken for granted, to worship deities made in one sex's image and not the other seems archaic and counter to people's everyday experience.

There are traditional names by which particular Earth Traditions know their deities. In Wicca, the most familiar Goddess names are Aradia and Cerridwen. In Scandinavian Tradition, the Goddess is worshipped as Freya and Frigga. To those following a Celtic path, She may be Bride. Many people venerate the Goddess under her Egyptian name of Isis. She is Changing Woman or Estsanatlehi among the Navajo, White Buffalo Calf Woman among the Lakota, and Erzulie in Voudon. For their male deities, Celtic Pagans and Wiccans may use the name Cernunnos, the stag god, or Lugh, the Light-Bearer. Scandinavian tradition venerates Odin, King of the High Gods. Voudon invokes the name of the serpent god of the Dahomey, Damballah. Some people prefer not to name their deities at all, but to refer to them as 'the Goddess' and 'the God' or 'the Lady' and 'the Lord'. Sometimes the Goddess is called She-Whose-Name-May-Not-Be-Spoken and the God is The-Hidden-God-who-ever-yet-Remains.

How are Earth Traditions organized?

Few Earth Traditions proselytize or seek converts. The Earth Traditions believe that people will find and remain on these paths if they are called by the gods. As they are not seeking converts, there is not the same need for organizations to 'propagate the faith'. Earth Traditions differ from most religions in that they are loosely organized. There are no central authorities and each individual, group and community organizes itself. Among traditions of European origin, there are organizations that represent particular paths such as druidry, Wicca, Ásatrú or the spirituality of particular ethnic communities. There are also umbrella organizations that serve the needs of the wider Pagan community. However, these are networking bodies rather than bodies that control what their members do or believe. In Europe, the major organization is the Pagan Federation, which provides information about European Earth Traditions and helps people get in touch with individuals and groups in their locality. The Pagan Federation also organizes conferences, workshops, magazines and religious gatherings. In North America, organizations such as Circle Network and the Covenant of the Goddess are networking bodies that link many groups and individuals who have Pagan beliefs.

Most Native American traditions are part of the culture of their peoples, but one organization, the Native American Church, has sought to bring Native Americans together to create a pan-Indian spirituality that can appeal to all those of Native American heritage. Increasingly ideas are being shared among Native American peoples, and practices such as vision quests are being taken up by peoples who did not originally observe them. In Santeria and Voudon, each local community is autonomous, but groups may meet together for major ceremonies.

Why do people practice Earth-centered spirituality?

People come to Earth Traditions from all backgrounds. Some are born into an ancestral tradition that has been practiced by their families for hundreds or thousands of years. Some are returning to ancestral traditions that have been suppressed through conquest, colonialization, or forced emigration. Others are coming anew to the ancient wisdom of the Earth Traditions. They may discover them through reading the myths of their ancestors and discovering that a tradition they thought dead is now active and growing. Many people of European origin will find that if they dig deeper into their family history they will find an ancestor who had a reputation for knowing folk medicine, village witchcraft, a bardic tradition, or farming customs that venerated pre-Christian deities. In many cultures, overt Christianity has co-existed with ancient Pagan ideas that have remained an ingrained part of traditional folk culture.

Some people become interested in Earth Traditions because they experience a sense of the Divine in Nature – a feeling that spiritual forces inhabit trees, forests, fields and hills. Some find that their inner response to the Divine is not to a male god but to a female deity, the Great Goddess. Sometimes people participate purely by chance in a Pagan festival, ceremony, wedding, conference or workshop. Through such meetings, we may find that we share common ground with those who describe themselves as 'Pagans' or followers of a particular Earth Tradition. We may choose to join an organization or to celebrate festivals with others on a regular basis, but no one needs to join with others to worship ancient deities or to practice Paganism. Some Pagans belong to formal structured groups or organizations. Others may come together on an ad hoc basis with friends. Worshipping with others has many joys and benefits and can bring deep spiritual awareness, but such awareness may also come from silence and solitude in the privacy of a quiet room or outside in Nature. No special ceremonies are needed to make us Pagans. We are Pagans if our beliefs match those of Pagan thought and we consider ourselves Pagans. Particular Earth Traditions may have entry through a dedication ceremony, initiation or adoption into a family or clan; but these offer gateways into their own paths only. People can be pagans without any of these ceremonies.

Dogma

Unlike most religions, the Earth Traditions do not claim a monopoly on religious truth. There is no one revelation of the right way to approach the Divine. The Pagan Earth Traditions see their path as one of the many. The choice of spiritual path is one of individual preference. Earth Traditions can be non-intellectual, even anti-intellectual. They are spiritual traditions born of the heart and inspiration; of deep inner knowing rather than complex theological doctrines. The openness of contemporary Pagan thinking can be disorienting. Those who are following revived Earth Traditions rather than being brought up in an ancestral or tribal tradition are often accused of having diffuse beliefs that are all things to all people, but this prejudice arises from the idea that religion must have rigid dogma and uniformity. This idea is more noticeable in the West than in the East and is derived from the philosophies of the monotheisms that have dominated Western society for the past two millennia. Followers of the Indian traditions that have come to be called Hinduism have no difficulty in dealing with a multitude of deities and a wide span of beliefs. In Indian Tradition, the various versions of Ultimate Reality offered by diverse spiritual teachings are seen not as separate truths, but as different ways of looking at reality. Just as different deities are myriad facets of the Divine, so religious teachings are different pathways by which people in different places and times have attempted to communicate with the Divine. Indian tradition teaches:

> To dispute the religion (*Dharana*) of another is the mark of a
>   narrow mind.
> O Lord! O Great Magician!
> With whatsoever faith or feeling we call on Thee,
> Thou art pleased.[1]

Similarly, around a thousand years ago, a Scandinavian priestess who has become known in history as Sigrid the Proud explained to the foreign missionaries who sought to convert her to Christianity:

❧   I must not depart from the faith that I have held,
    and my ancestors before me;
    on the other hand, I shall make no objection
    to your believing in the god that pleases you best.[2]

The Earth Traditions teach religious tolerance. The Divine has manifested in different ways at different times to suit different peoples. The truth is revealed to each of us from deep within ourselves. It is found through meditation and inner reflection. The images by which we worship our deities are simply that – images. To kill, maim and torture other human beings in order to convince ourselves that one human image of Ultimate Reality is superior to that of another is absurd; that which we worship is beyond the limitation of all images and words.

The Earth Traditions are based on myths, teachings and practices that are our inheritance from our ancestors over thousands of years. Those myths that have endured convey universal and eternal truths. They are important because they contain the spiritual wisdom, not of one individual, but of many people over great periods of time. The respect that the Earth Traditions have for ancient myth is different from the attitude of the monotheisms to their scriptures. The monotheisms believe that their sacred texts are the unchangeable word of God, but in reality these texts are the spiritual insights and histories of human beings. They are filtered through the cultural and religious background and personalities of those who record them. In translating abstract truths into human thought, we clothe them in images drawn from our experience. In nineteenth-century Catholic Italy, a simple peasant girl might see a vision of the Divine feminine and believe that she saw the Virgin Mary. Two thousand years earlier, in Pagan Italy she would have seen the huntress goddess Diana. This does not mean that either vision was false, that there was no spiritual encounter; but in order to understand what we have seen, we turn to images familiar from myth and religious teaching. How else are we to interpret them?

The teachings of Earth Traditions were expressed in symbolic language and speak to intuition and feeling rather than to intellect. They were never codified because they were transmitted through oral traditions. Celtic bards, Scandinavian skalds and Native American holy men could convey ethics, philosophy and spiritual teachings all the more powerfully because they gave their teaching indirectly through image, metaphor, symbol and allusion. In the same way as a powerful piece of fantasy literature, song or poetry can speak to the unconscious, so did oral traditions feed their peoples' psyches. An African explains this in connection with African Traditional Religion.

> It is the religion which has been handed down from generation to generation by the forebears of the present generation of Africans. It is not a fossil religion (a thing of the past) but a religion that Africans today have made theirs by living it and practicing it. This is a religion that has no written literature, yet it is 'written' everywhere for those who care to see and read. It is largely written in the people's myths and folktales, in their songs and dances, in their liturgies and shrines, in their proverbs and pithy sayings. It is a religion whose historical founder is neither known nor worshipped; it is a religion that has no zeal for membership drive, yet it offers persistent fascination ...[3]

The many deities, myths and rituals of the Earth Traditions can be interpreted in many ways according to our level of understanding. We must study, meditate upon and grow familiar with our myths and traditions in order to discern, behind their stories, the eternal values and virtues that teach us how to live.

Many and one

Humans in some of our earliest cultures were polytheists who saw their many deities not as all-powerful, but as super-powerful beings who could control some aspects of Nature and destiny, but who were themselves subject to destiny and often to higher gods. It made sense to worship different deities for different purposes, appealing to them for mediation in their particular sphere. Some contemporary Pagans are polytheists and see different deities as individual entities – powerful beings who pre-existed humanity. Others believe that goddesses and gods are images that represent different facets of the Divine life force. They point to the multitude of forms in which deities have been worshipped in different cultures and at different times, but which, at the same time, often have similar characteristics to those of other times, places and peoples. To these Pagans, the deities are aspects of a Divine force that is 'all-pervading, all-powerful, changeless, eternal'[4] rather than separate beings. Dion Fortune expressed this beautifully in her book *The Sea Priestess*.

❦   The Temple of Isis is built of black marble and hung with
         silver,
     and She Herself sitteth veiled in the innermost.
     She is all goddesses that men's hearts have worshipped,
     for they are not many things, but one thing under many
         forms.[5]

If some Earth Traditions believe that deities are different aspects of an underlying reality, why do they not adopt monotheism and worship a single goddess or god? To Pagans, to reject the deities who have sustained humanity through the millennia is a mistake. The forms or archetypes through which we worship the Divine are ways and channels for the human mind with its limitations to perceive and communicate with the infinite that is beyond our understanding. Deities can be thought of as incarnations, avatars or personalities through which the Divine unity manifests in order to help us understand and communicate with it. These images are a mutual creation of deity and worshipper. Our human minds, which think in words and images, receive the abstract message of the Divine and translate it into pictures and symbols based on our culture, knowledge and experience of the world around us. The archetypes of the deities are manifestations of the underlying spiritual force that gives rise to them – the Great Spirit that permeates all. The archetypes of the deities are mysteries that reveal layers of meaning and wonderment that take us many lifetimes to understand and unravel. Some of their power is in their mysteriousness. Dr Arwind Vasavada, an Indian psychotherapist, writes:

❦   The more puzzling the archetypes, the nearer are we to the
     Unknown, because it is telling us something important: stop
     knowing.[6]

The archetypes help us, because the true reality is beyond the comprehension of the human mind. Dion Fortune explained that 'because we are imprisoned upon the world of form':

❦   ...we can only conceive the Formless
     as far as minds habituated to form can imagine it.
     But we who are men and women
     and who want to know God as He manifests in Nature –
     we see the luminous countenance of the Eternal

in the beautiful forms of the gods.
And in this way we learn more, and can do more,
than if we strive after abstract essences that elude us.[7]

The idea that the forms of the deities are human images of reality, rather than reality itself, can be threatening to people who fear the reduction of religion to 'mere psychology'. However, as anyone who has encountered powerful archetypal forces will know, deities cannot be treated as though they are not 'real'. Once we are in the grip of these forces, once we have awakened them and they have taken an interest in us, then we are indeed at the mercy of mysterious and ineffable beings much stronger than ourselves.

Deity archetypes originate in that repository of images that is the collective unconscious of humankind. They are immensely powerful but not all-powerful. Many of our Pagan ancestors believed that if deities were not worshipped, they would die – an idea that fantasy humorist Terry Pratchett has taken up in his novel *Small Gods* in the Discworld series. Traditional witchcraft teaches that:

> The gods are not all-powerful. They wish men well, but to aid man, they must have his help.[8]

If we do not keep ourselves open to our deities, if we neglect their worship and forget them, then the channels of communication between us may be lost. This will not mean that the deities have died, but our route to them may be forgotten. We are in danger of losing the maps of the cosmos, which the myths of our ancestors revealed to us, to be set adrift, floating aimlessly in the starry seas of the universe, orphaned of gods.

The Divine within us

The twenty-first century is one of individuality. Each person finds his or her own interpretation of the Divine and we can argue and debate with others, but we should not seek to impose our worldview on other people. Power and authority must reside within the individual and not be imposed from outside. In Wiccan lore, there is a saying:

❦　　If that which thou seekest, thou findest not within thee,
　　thou wilt never find it without thee;
　　for behold: I have been with thee from the beginning,
　　and I am that which attained at the end of desire.[9]

This is an important statement that has many levels of meaning; one of which is that spiritual knowledge is something that unfolds from within us; from accessing that deeper layer of the mind that is the collective unconscious containing the full repository of all human knowledge – past, present and that which is yet to be revealed. Access to this timeless zone comes from learning the techniques of meditation and finding an interior stillness within ourselves where we commune with the Divine and hear the voice of the spirit penetrating the veil between the conscious and unconscious mind. It is achieving this connection with the deeper level of the Divine self within us that is the root of our Earth-centered spirituality.

In the last millennium, we were content to follow the voice of authority – the mouthpieces of the established religions. If people believed something different from those hallowed sources, they were wrong and evil. Increasingly, we are beginning to see the limitations of dogmatic ideas about the infinite and the shadow side of the rigid power structures that have dominated religions for so long. Issues of power, control, and domination of human beings by others are important to Pagans. People no longer want to be told by an elite power group what to think and believe. In part, this is due to the effect of the media. Our leaders – political, religious, and social – have been exposed to the glare of contemporary publicity and have been found wanting. The average young person is more likely to respect the views of a football or rock star than those of the religious or political establishment. When the voice of authority is not respected, it is difficult to convince people to follow hierarchical leaders. Instead, we must find new sources of authority by developing links with the voice of our own inner Divine core and recovering the wisdom deep within us. This weakens the authority of organized religion and leaves people in a less certain and secure world, but this may be no bad thing. A British Christian minister comments:

❦　　There is, in any case, something to be said for the view (not
　　confined to Wiccans) that any religion in power is, *ipso facto*,
　　a debased and a dangerous religion. Once any religion gets
　　power, it is more likely to suppress than to try to refute those
　　with whom it disagrees.[10]

Although for contemporary Paganism, a re-rooting in ancient traditions is important, the ideas that inspire us to be Pagans today are also contemporary ideas about human potential, spiritual growth and the search for the Divine within everyone. These ideas were found in earlier centuries in those aspects of religion which people called 'mystical' or 'esoteric'. In Paganism, these mystical currents were found in the mystery cults, above the doors of whose temples were carved the words 'Know Thyself'. A major aim of the ancient mystery religions was to teach us about our inner being and our true relationship with the Divine. This understanding of our place in the scheme of things enables us to function as whole human beings.

A new era

In our new millennium, the yearning for the Mysteries has revived. This millennium is under the astrological rulership of Aquarius, one of the few zodiac signs to be represented by a human image. Dion Fortune, a leading figure in the revival of the European Pagan Tradition, wrote about the change from the Age of Pisces to our own era of Aquarius.

> The great Sun, moving in the heavenly houses,
> has left the House of the Fishes for the House of the
>   Water-Bearer.
> In the coming age shall humanity be holy,
> and in the perfection of the human shall we find
>   the humane.
> Take up the manhood into Godhead,
> and bring down the Godhead into manhood,
> and this shall be the day of God with us;
> for God is made manifest in Nature,
> and Nature is the self-expression of God.[11]

The Earth Traditions honor the deities of the past, but we are not living in the past. We live in the present and our religions must meet our current needs and those of the future. Once every two thousand years, the position of the signs of the zodiac appears to change in relation to the Earth. This means that the sign that appears against the eastern horizon at dawn on the spring equinox is no longer that of Aries, as it was four thousand years ago when our present zodiac system was devised. The zodiac signs appear to move slowly anti-clockwise around the Earth so the sign on the dawn horizon at spring equinox is now Aquarius. Aquarius is a sign of intellectual curiosity and challenge. We are not content to follow the thought of others. We must and do question. This questioning spirit gave birth to the scientific age. The psychologist Carl Jung saw the Aquarian Age as a turning point in the development of human consciousness. All changes of Age are important, but the change to the Age of Aquarius may be doubly so. It is time for humankind to come into full maturity with an awakening of consciousness. With all changes of Age, old ideas are overthrown, but under Aquarius we shall see this happening to a much faster and greater degree. In 1956, Carl Jung wrote:

> We are living in what the Greeks call the *kairos* – the right moment – for a 'metamorphosis of the gods', of the fundamental principles and symbols. This peculiarity of our time, which is certainly not of our conscious choosing, is the expression of the unconscious man within us who is changing. Coming generations will have to take account of this momentous transformation if humanity is not to destroy itself through the might of its own technology and science.[12]

Aquarius has ushered in a new eon and evidence of its influence is everywhere. Aquarius breaks the boundaries of scientific knowledge and uses rationality to create new discovery. As we approached Aquarius in the twentieth century, we began the era of quantum physics, space travel, electronics and computing. Change brings danger and turmoil, both in outer society and within individuals. A change of Age is a time of psychological upheaval. Our most cherished beliefs and certainties are destroyed and must be rethought and rebuilt. Society can live or die, succeed or fail utterly at such a time. For society to move successfully forward into the new era, Carl Jung considered it essential that as many people as possible should be in touch with the change of thinking and philosophy required by the transition into Aquarius and able to make what he called the 'psychic connection' between past and future.[13] To achieve this, we must rediscover those things that were lost to us – our ancient deities and our ancient ways – and must reintegrate them into our lives in a new dispensation. At this point, a change of religion would be expected to occur. Christianity, the religion of the fisherman and the fish, was the great breakthrough in thought of the Piscean Age. Religions that recognize the Divine within human beings are the religions of the 21st century. As Dion Fortune once pronounced: '... this is the Revelation of the Eon'.[14]

Honoring the Divine within all

If we become aware of the Divine within us, we must also become aware of the Divine within others. To find the Divine in other human beings is not easy. It requires a certain optimism about our fellow humans that can be difficult to sustain. When we look around at our world, we see much to cause despair – war, hatred, ethnic strife, poverty, economic decline, and a disintegration of the fabric of society, as people raised without a coherent spiritual or philosophical belief turn to crime and violence as ways of satisfying their needs. Finding a spiritual philosophy that can help us make sense of our lives and understand our place in society and in the greater universe is essential to human happiness and well being. In earlier centuries, dominant power groups could impose whatever religious or political creed suited their convenience. Today, we are no longer isolated. The internet and satellite television mean that we are constantly exposed to other viewpoints, other visions, other races and other creeds. Now we must make our own choices as to the path we will follow and what is right and wrong.

Many creeds argue that social problems are due to people ignoring the message of their particular brand of religion. Practitioners of Earth Traditions believe that society's problems come not from ignoring the teachings of a particular creed, but from ignoring the underlying messages that all spiritual traditions share. Contemporary Paganism teaches that religious differences are the product of our attempts to interpret great truths, but our common human experience means that all societies are struggling for answers to similar problems and in the end the answers that our different belief systems find are also similar. We cannot live selfishly and if we do, we will destroy ourselves; human beings are social animals and it is only through mutual aid that we can create and maintain the complex societies in which we live. The world will be best served if people recognize their mutual interdependence. We must concentrate on the ideals that we share, rather than ideas that divide us. This can only come about when we recognize and respect one another's beliefs, faiths and individuality; together with our need to establish a common core of ethics and honorable living that can help us to live with one another and the world around us.

The Earth is our Mother

Practitioners of Earth Traditions worship many different deities, but a common characteristic that distinguishes the Traditions from monotheistic religions is where they place their deities. In many religions, the Divine is separate and removed from the Earth and humankind. Gods and goddesses live 'out there', in some insubstantial realm of the beyond; a heavenly realm that disdains the inferior world of matter and is unpolluted by it. The religions that originated in the Middle and Near East – Christianity, Islam and Judaism – conceived of the Divine as an anthropomorphic male being who created the world at a particular moment in time. This gives rise to dualism – the created universe is separate from its Creator who has given human beings dominion over it to exploit it to their heart's content. These religions also emphasize a distinction between spirit and flesh, soul and matter. In contrast, most Earth Traditions have elements of pantheism – the Divine is found everywhere. It is the ground of everything and may be contacted in all places, in all things and through many forms. The Earth Traditions believe that the Divine is immanent or in-dwelling in the universe. It is:

> the Soul of Nature who giveth life to the Universe
> ... the beauty of the green Earth,
> the white Moon amongst the stars
> and the mystery of the waters.[15]

All Earth-centered spiritualities respect the Earth and the Divine in Nature. Some believe that the Divine, while present within material creation, also transcends it in a realm beyond the material universe. Theologians call this idea panentheism. To panentheists, the Divine is both immanent and transcendent, within the world of Nature yet existing beyond it.

The notion of immanence is not always easy to understand. How can the Divine be present in matter, even though we do not see it? In the Indian sacred texts, *The Upanishads*, Svetaketu is a young spiritual seeker who wishes to understand the nature of reality. His father tells him to place a lump of salt in some water and to come back the next morning. The next morning his father tells him to retrieve the lump of salt, but Svetaketu says that he cannot because it has dissolved. His father then tells him to taste the water. Svetaketu tells him that it is salty. His father has made his point:

❧ In the same way as salt was dissolved in the water,
an invisible and subtle essence pervades the whole universe.
That is spirit. That is reality.
That is truth, and you are it.[16]

To Pagans, the Earth is not different in substance from spirit. Spirit permeates every particle of our cosmos. Dion Fortune explains:

❧ The ignorant and impure gaze upon the face of Nature,
and it is to them darkness of darkness.
But the initiated and illumined gaze thereon
and see the features of the Divine.
Be ye far from us, O ye profane,
while we adore the Divine made manifest in Nature.[17]

Whereas Middle and Near Eastern religions emphasize dualism, Pagans see life as a continuum of energy in different forms. In a similar way to Hindu tradition, they see no division or split between spirit and instinct, mind and matter.

In the mysticism of many spiritual traditions is the idea that there is a single immanent Divine and unifying force at the heart of all matter. In recent centuries, this idea has been found more often in the teaching of Eastern traditions; but it is also found in the Earth Traditions. Many contemporary scientists have come to share similar views. Margaret Stutley in her book *Hinduism: The Eternal Law*[18] points out that molecular biologists have discovered the underlying unity of all forms and that the fundamental molecules of cabbages, flies or bacteria are the same as those of human beings. In India, spiritual insights from the past have led to scientific insights in the present. The Nobel Prize winning scientist Sir Jayadish Chandra Bose based his scientific investigations on the ancient teaching that whatever can be found in man and animal would also be found in vegetal life. The crystallographer CV Raman, another Nobel Prize winner, based his work on the teaching that inanimate stones are imbued with the mysterious force of Brahman, the Divine source of all things, the giver of life. Since all life is subject to the processes of creation, formation and decay, he made the hypothesis, now proven, that crystals, having assumed a certain shape, would undergo continuous change from growth to decay.

Green spirituality

A distinctive feature of the Earth Traditions is their concern with ecological issues. To live in harmony with Nature rather than to dominate it is one of the three Pagan principles that many practitioners of Earth Traditions follow. While organized religions have often shown little respect for the Earth, mystics of all faiths have recognized the importance of living in harmony with Nature. Christian mystical poet Thomas Traherne in his *Centuries of Meditations* praises the planet.

> ❧ The Earth itself is better than gold,
> because it produceth fruits and flowers ...
> You never enjoy the world aright,
> till the sea itself floweth in your veins,
> till you are clothed with the heavens,
> and crowned with the stars ...[19]

In the Hippy era of the late 1960s and 1970s, the Incredible String Band revived these words and they became an anthem for many of the flower-child generation who returned to ways of worship that honored the Earth.

To the Earth Traditions, humans are not a superior form of life that should have limitless power over other life forms, but part of a Divine creation. With our intelligence and skills, we are capable of destroying the life of the creatures that share our planet. We have already destroyed a large percentage of the ozone layer, that invaluable part of the Earth's atmosphere that protects animals, plants and ourselves from the harmful constituents of the sun's rays. The sun is necessary for our survival but, like all forces, in excess it will destroy us. Harmful chemicals manufactured by the West in pursuit of material comfort and wealth have seriously damaged the ozone layer. Other parts of the world are now reluctant to relinquish these 'blessings' of modern civilization. The challenge is for us not to destroy, but to maintain our Mother the Earth; to take responsibility for Her and to act as Her stewards, for our own benefit, for that of other species, and for those that follow. A chant often used at festival gatherings reflects this attitude.

> ❧ The Earth is our Mother,
> We will take care of Her,
> The Earth is our Mother,
> She will take care of us.

The future of our planet is important to all human beings (though governments are only now beginning to wake up to this fact); but it is particularly important to practitioners of Earth-centered spirituality. To Pagans, the Earth is not only an ecosystem that sustains the physical life of humankind, She is also a living entity – Gaia, the Great Mother. The Divine is all around us – within us and in the world around us. It permeates, impregnates, and makes sacred and holy the Earth and all living beings upon it. The Christian ethic that has dominated the West in recent centuries has its virtues; but it has had a disastrous effect on our environment. The Reverend Michael Perry, formerly Archdeacon of Durham, in his book *Gods Within: A Critical Guide to the New Age*, sees the Biblical view of humanity having dominion over the earth as having had 'the direst of results in the way in which we have felt justified in treating the material creation.'

'Be fruitful, and multiply, and replenish the Earth, and subdue it: and have dominion over the fish of the sea, and over the fowl of the air, and over every living thing', it went in the King James Version so familiar to our forebears. We heard the word 'subdue' and forgot the word 'replenish', and we heard the word 'dominion' and forgot that the ruler who had dominion over his subjects also had responsibilities towards them. That allowed us to take and take and never give back; to squander the fossil remains of forests which had taken a million years to build up, and burn them in a generation; to make dustbowls out of wheat fields and deserts out of fruitful ground; and to believe that, as lords of creation, we were not only allowed but divinely commanded to do so.[20]

The Earth Traditions believe not that human beings are superior, but that the Great Mother finds all her creation pleasing. All of us, humans, animals and plants, have a role to play in the scheme of things. The other forms of creation are there for us to live with in harmony, not to exploit. We are at a unique period in human history where we have enormous knowledge, but have not yet gained the insight and wisdom to use it well. Life has changed at a pace that would have been unthinkable a hundred years ago and unbelievable two hundred years ago. Many people come to the Earth Traditions because they have no faith in current Western philosophies and spiritual systems to solve the problems which face our planet today. Michael Perry comments that as we teeter towards 'a wasteland of rampaging pollution in sea, earth, and ozone layer' the present spiritual bankruptcy of Western technology is evident. To those who honor the Earth, her sacredness is not just an abstract and mystical ideal. Practitioners of Earth Traditions take an active role in environmental campaigning. Campaigns to save historically and ecologically important sites have been led by Pagans all over the world; sometimes under a Pagan banner, but often as part of other groups such as Greenpeace and Friends of the Earth. The Earth Traditions have also taken an important role in campaigning for fairer world trade.

Notes

1	Vasavada in Spiegelman and Vasavada, *Hinduism and Jungian Psychology*, page 38.
2	Odinist Committee, *This is Odinism*, page 5.
3	Awolalu, 'Sin and its Removal in African Traditional Religion', page 275.
4	Bourne, *A Witch Amongst Us*, page 205.
5	Fortune, *The Sea Priestess*, page 121.
6	Spiegelman and Vasavada, *Hinduism and Jungian Psychology*, page 21.
7	Fortune, *The Sea Priestess*, page 91.
8	Unpublished Wiccan material.
9	From the Wiccan *Book of Shadows*, quoted in Crowley, *Wicca: The Old Religion in the New Millennium*, page 191.
10	Perry, *Gods Within*, page 68.
11	Fortune, *The Sea Priestess*, page 173.
12	Jung, 'Gegenwart und Zukunft' in *Collected Works 10*, paras 585, 586.
13	Hillman, 'Senex and Puer: An Aspect of the Historical and Psychological Present' in *Puer Papers*, page 4.
14	Fortune, *The Sea Priestess*, page 92.
15	From 'The Gerat Mother Charge', quoted in Crowley, *Wicca: The Old Religion in the New Millennium*, page 191.
16	*Chandogya Upanishad*, Chapter 6, verses 13.1–13.3.
17	Fortune, *The Sea Priestess*, page 124, language updated.

18   Stutley, *Hinduism*, page 11.
19   Perry, *Gods Within*, page 79.
20   Perry, *Gods Within*, page 78.

Reviving the Earth Traditions

In caverns deep, the old gods sleep,
but the trees still know their Lord,
and it's the Pipes of Pan that call the tune,
in the twilight in the wood.
The leaves they dance to the Goat God's tune,
and whisper his name to the winds,
and the oak tree dreams of a god with horns,
and knows no other king.

Vivianne Crowley (1969)

The Earth Traditions are the oldest forms of religion. Their roots lie in the earliest forms of human spirituality. How can we know how our early ancestors regarded the spiritual forces that inhabit the universe? We can never fully know, but they have left us evidence of their beliefs, which we find in vibrant images of beautifully-drawn wild animals in cave paintings and rock art. We see figures of women, pregnant and fertile. We find pictures of shamans dressed in animal skins with horned headdresses. We can see that our early ancestors were aware of the forces of Nature and eager to contact and work in harmony with them. They worshipped those deities who most affected their lives – the deities of each animal species that sent good hunting and deities that made women fertile and pregnant. Later, as we learned to cultivate crops, human beings began to worship the deities of sun, rain, wind, and earth that determined whether we would have favorable weather that would bring good harvest.

As societies grew more sophisticated, they developed complex pantheons. Ruler deities were distinguished from deities of war, love, agriculture, music, healing, and other important aspects of human life. We know much about these more complex pantheons from the memorials that their worshippers have left — their deity statues, images, temples and prayers.

The rise of monotheism

In early societies, when peoples clashed, it was also a war of their gods. The people with the most powerful deity were sure to win. This thinking is evident in many of the myths of our ancestors and in recent history. The missionary religions of Christianity and Islam attacked the sacred groves and deity statues of those they sought to convert to demonstrate to the credulous the superior power of their own religion. 'Look, we have toppled your idols and destroyed your sacred groves and the wrath of your deities has not descended upon us. Our god is more powerful than yours.' From 'our god is the best god', it was an easy step to 'our god is the only real god', the horrors of religious persecution and the 'shadow' side of religion. Monotheism can be a dangerously intolerant and rigid spirituality. If there is only one god, those who do not view the Divine in the same way are enemies of that god. They are evil and must be punished and dissuaded from their erroneous views. The misery of the Inquisition is a logical result. Monotheism also has considerable disadvantages for women. The patriarchal societies that created monotheisms created images for their powerful deities. In societies ruled by men, these images were male. The Divine was made in man's image and not in woman's. It was to be ever God and never Goddess.

The struggle of old and new

One of the reasons for the success of monotheism is that it offers simplicity. 'Believe in our god and all your problems will be solved,' is the message. The Pagan cultures that monotheisms encountered contained many great teachings; but they were cultures where spirits inhabited trees, stones and other natural phenomena. To some, this made Nature sacred and holy; to others it made Nature fearsome and strange, for onto these entities human beings projected their inner fears. Many spirits were seen as helpful, but others were seen as mischievous and malicious forces that must be propitiated. Christianity and Islam removed many of these fears. They did so by removing spirit outside the material realm. There were no longer dark forces in rock and tree. There was no longer a multiplicity of deities with different priorities, a minefield where pleasing one might offend another. In monotheism, there was order, simplicity and safety.

Monotheism was successful partly because it offered people simplicity in the face of the complexities of reality, but also because it did what other religions had not – it engaged in spirited marketing of its new 'product'. With the adoption of Christianity by the Emperor Constantine in 324 CE as the official religion of the Roman Empire, the new faith harnessed an efficient distribution system for its wares. With its road network, regular shipping routes and central position dominating Europe, North Africa and the Asian countries of the Eastern Mediterranean, the Roman Empire was ideally situated to spread Christianity. Many new religious movements have come to relatively satisfactory accommodations with older religious forms, but monotheisms could not. The attitude was uncompromising and missionaries such as Augustine preached definite views about the Pagan religions: the worship of Pagan deities was the worship of devils. The fate of some deities was kinder than that of others. Many were absorbed into the new system in the form of sanctified human beings – saints. It was no longer possible to make offerings to the god Apollo or the goddess Bride, but people could pay honor to St Apollinarius or St Brigid. Other deities were relegated to the status of demons. The deities of the Old Religion were made into the devils of the new. People were no longer to worship under sky and wind which unite the Divine, human and Nature, but under roofs made by human hands and in buildings controled by the state-approved religion.

Over the next eleven hundred years, Christianity gradually became the dominant religion of Europe, having lost its hold over its own Near Eastern birthplace in the birth throes of the newer monotheism, Islam. In some areas, people willingly embraced the new beliefs. Elsewhere, this was not the case. The new monotheism set an example for its successor Islam of conversion at the point of a sword. In Scandinavia, St Olaf made his subjects choose between conversion or death. In Germany, Charlemagne or Charles the Great conducted forced mass baptisms of Saxons by driving them at sword point through rivers that had been blessed further upstream by his bishops. This forced allegiance was never anything but nominal. Others, such as King Redwald of the East Saxons, compromised and kept two altars, one for the new god and one for the deities of his ancestors.

Although late versions of the myths were recorded during the Christian era, apart from the religions of Greece and Rome with their well-developed literary traditions, much has been lost of the religions of Pagan Europe. We can learn something, however, from the practices which Christianity found it necessary to forbid and suppress. Old ways died hard and bishops produced a steady flow of books denouncing Paganism. In the seventh century, Archbishop Theodore of Canterbury condemned celebrating the New Year by appearing as a stag or bull god, sacrificing to Pagan gods and goddesses and feasting in Pagan temples. In the eighth century, it was the turn of Archbishop Ecgbert of York to condemn making offerings to Pagan deities, witchcraft, divination, swearing vows at wells, trees or stones, and gathering herbs with non-Christian incantations. In the tenth century, King Edgar continued in the same vein, forbidding well worship, man worship, spells, and consorting with trees and stones. Trees and stones were definitely Pagan and suspect. These lists of forbidden practices are instructive. It is evident that the Earth Traditions involved 'man-worshipping', ie revering a deity incarnated in a priest or priestess for the purposes of the rite, and the worship of the Divine immanent in Nature, especially in evocative objects such as wells, trees and standing stones. The Church itself was not immune to the lure of Paganism. In the late-thirteenth century, a priest in Inverkeithing in Scotland appeared before his bishop accused of leading his flock in a fertility dance around a phallic figure of a Pagan deity. The bishop's reaction seems to have been rather mild, for the priest kept his parish.

Paganism awakes

Although the Church was wary of the Pagan deities, the memory of the deities of the Mediterranean lived on in the classical works which all educated men were required to study. These were the same works that young men had studied under Paganism, such as the writings of Plato, Socrates, Plotinus, and Pliny. Knowledge of Pagan thought was stimulated by the Crusades. Ironically, these expeditions to preserve Christianity in the East brought Eastern and Classical Pagan thought into the West. Many Classical Greek texts – scientific, philosophical and religious – that had been lost or destroyed by the Christian Church were preserved in what was then the much more enlightened intellectual climate of Islamic societies. The marauding crusaders were eager to plunder these treasures and bring them home to Europe. This learning spread to Western intellectuals and inspired a Renaissance, or rebirth, of Western culture. The most learned men of the day, churchmen, began to decorate their walls with paintings of Pagan deities. In the bosom of the Church, Pagan thought was cherished and nurtured so that it could not die. The Renaissance also stimulated developments in intellectual thinking that led people to question the dogmas of the Church. This process was hastened by ecclesiastical corruption. For some of the disaffected, the solution was to adopt one of the burgeoning new brands of Christianity and a reformation of the excesses of Catholicism swept Northern Europe. For others, who were looking for something that orthodox Christianities could not offer, there were other avenues to explore.

The study of magical and Pagan texts became common amongst men of learning and Pagan ideas began to awaken. Some of these ideas went too far for their thinkers' own good. Depending on one's perspective, one of the more inspired or foolhardy of the Pagan revivalists was the renegade Dominican monk Giordano Bruno. He developed a spiritual system based on ancient Egyptian religion which he believed would redeem the corruption into which Christianity had fallen. With a naivete verging on lunacy, Giordano Bruno attempted to convince the Pope of the merit of his new ideas and to enlist him as head of the new religion. Under torture, he recanted his heresies, but there was a recalcitrant streak of stubbornness in Giordano Bruno. The torture over, he recanted again, this time back to Paganism. On February 16, 1600, Giordano Bruno paid the price for his impetuosity and was burned at the stake as a Pagan martyr.

Despite the efforts of the Inquisition, the Church was fighting a losing battle in trying to hold back those developments in human thought which led, on the one hand, to that empirical study of the world around us which is contemporary science, and on the other to a questioning of the dogmas of Christianity. By the eighteenth and nineteenth centuries, there had been a revival of interest in Pagan religion amongst those who had access to education. The Pagan pantheons became common knowledge amongst the educated and such study led inevitably to a reappraisal of Christianity's place in the scheme of things. This was stimulated by affluence. From the eighteenth century onwards, a higher standard of living for the rich meant that young aristocrats and the sons and daughters of newly rich industrialists could go on extended holidays to the Mediterranean to study the culture of the Pagan Greeks and Romans. They brought back with them statues of classical deities to grace the gardens of their country houses. English country winters must have been rather a shock to the average Roman deity and even more of a shock to the Egyptian goddess Sekhmet, whose ancient statues were installed in the nineteenth century in the gardens of the English stately home Chatsworth House. The nineteenth century also saw the opening of the great museums. In the cities of the Western world, people could now see for themselves the images of the ancient deities of the Pagan world.

The Pagan land

The eighteenth century onwards also saw a revival of interest in the Paganism of our Northern European ancestors. As well as failing to suppress Pagan thought, the Church had failed to suppress Pagan landscape. In England, ignorant Puritans arranged Sunday outings to go 'stone bashing' and destroy Neolithic stone circles, but the landscape was littered with them. Across Europe, the sacred sites of our ancestors pointed to earlier lost beliefs. Monuments such as Carnac in Brittany, Avebury and Stonehenge in Britain, New Grange in Ireland, the Externsteine in Germany, and the landscape itself, marked by burial mounds and sacred tracks, pointed to a past in which our ancestors believed in the sacredness of stone and star, and the mysteries of the Earth. These sanctuaries beneath the open sky evoked a feeling different to that of the churches that replaced them. Here was no exaltation of a deity in human form, but a spirituality that spoke of the sacredness of the natural world. Developments in historical scholarship and the science of archeology were important for the revival of Paganism. Archeological advances and developments in the historical dating process led to the inevitable conclusions of the evolutionists – that the Christian version of history was wrong.

There was a new romanticism about Europe's Pagan past and drawings depicting Stonehenge in its original glory went into circulation. These celebrated stones were thought to be the work of druids and much speculation began about druid practices. Druidry began to excite interest not only in Wales, where it was part of a Welsh cultural revival, but also in England. These druids did not necessarily see themselves as deserting Christianity, but they believed that they would find wisdom in the works of their Pagan ancestors. Translations of Celtic myth and legend began. Unfortunately, the little that had been historically verified about the druids was supplemented by a great deal of seventeenth- and eighteenth-century romanticism. The druids were variously credited with building Stonehenge, founding Cambridge University and being Chaldean magicians. Although historically inaccurate, these romantic visions represented a yearning for a genuine Pagan spirituality.

Folk movements in Ireland, Scotland, Wales, Scandinavia, Germany, the Baltic countries, and the Balkan countries began to collect and revive ancient myths, lore and traditions that were the remnants of Pagan religion. The middle and upper classes, who had been content to speak English, French, or German rather than their native languages, began to learn them and rushed to record traditional myths and lore before industrialization swept them away for ever. Woman began to play an important role in this revival. Earlier generations of women had been denied an education and had less access to the revived Pagan learning than their brothers, but in the nineteenth century ideas about education for girls began to change and women became leading writers. Lady Charlotte Guest brought together for the first time an English translation of the Welsh Celtic myths in the *Mabinogion*. In nineteenth-century Ireland, a similar resurgence of interest in national culture began. This was not only amongst Irish speakers. Prominent Anglo-Irish families, such as those of Yeats and Oscar Wilde, were leading lights in the movement. Lady Wilde, Oscar Wilde's flamboyant Irish Nationalist mother, compiled *Ancient Legends, Mystic Charms, and Superstitions of Ireland*. In Scotland, Alexander Carmichael began compiling his collection of Scots Gaelic folklore, drawing on the oral memories of women who had preserved Celtic hymns, prayers, charms, and spells. It revealed a Christianity that was fused with Celtic Pagan spirituality. His collection was published at the turn of the century as the *Carmina Gadelica*.

Across the seas in the New World, Thomas Bullfinch, not a scholar but an accountant in a Boston bank, labored after his long hours at the office to compile *Bullfinch's Mythology*, one of the most comprehensive overviews of mythology ever attempted at the time. This introduced many thousands of Americans to the cultural heritage of their European ancestors and still makes fascinating reading today. The nineteenth century also saw a change in American attitudes to the environment. Henry David Thoreau and other New England Transcendentalists began a love affair with Nature that saw spirituality in woods rather than in churches. The great nineteenth-century American thinker Ralph Waldo Emerson wrote in his essay 'Nature':

> In the woods is perpetual youth. Within these plantations of God a decorum and sanctity reign, a perennial festival is dressed, and the guest sees not how he should tire of them in a thousand years. In the woods we return to reason and faith. There I feel that nothing can befall me in life, — no disgrace, no calamity (leaving me my eyes), which nature cannot repair. Standing on the bare ground — my head bathed by the blithe air, and uplifted into infinite space — all mean egoism banishes. I become a transparent eye-ball; I am nothing: I see all; the currents of the Universal Being circulate through me: I am part or particle of God.[1]

In the beauty and variety of the American landscape, there was endless stimulation for wonder in and contemplation of Nature. This meant going out into Nature. As pioneering America gave way to middle-class America, people could afford the time for trekking in the wilderness or simply taking walking holidays in the woods. Henry D Thoreau, in his essay 'Walking' written in 1863, wrote:

 When I recreate myself I see the darkest wood, the thickest and most interminable, and, to the citizen, most dismal swamp. I enter a swamp as a sacred place, — a *sanctum sanctorum*. There is strength, the marrow of Nature. The wildwood covers the virgin mould, — and the same soil is good for men and for trees. A man's health requires as many acres of meadow to his prospect as his farm does loads of muck.[2]

The landscape of North America has produced the same response in some of its newer immigrant peoples as it had in Native Americans — Nature is alive and for our spiritual and psychological health, we must be aware of this and love and venerate Nature. Awareness that the wilderness, wildness and beauty of the landscape could easily be lost in the face of competing priorities from mining, logging, and agriculture led to the founding of the National Parks movement to protect and preserve the extraordinary diverse and spectacular environment of North America for future generations. A leading figure in the parks movement was John Muir, a Scottish immigrant to Wisconsin. After an accident at work, he took a long break and traveled to California. Here he discovered the wonders of the Yosemite Valley, which became his personal paradise and personal mission, leading to creation of the Yosemite National Park and the Sierra Club.

Goddess revival

Veneration, wonder and exultation in Nature is one important foundation of the Earth Traditions. Another is their attitude to the feminine. Since the nineteenth century, many people in the West have believed that society was declining because of an over-emphasis on the masculine at the expense of the feminine. This imbalance was encouraged by monotheistic, male-dominated religious thinking that distorted the worldview of society. From the late eighteenth century onwards, rapid industrialization and the destruction of Europe's natural scenery and resources led many people to feel that the time was 'out of joint'; that common sense was being sacrificed for material progress, with potentially disastrous results. This feeling increased after the horrors of the First World War. Throughout the 1930s, there was a desire for a return to the reverence of Nature that manifested in a growing interest in the naturist movement, the founding of hiking and rambling societies, and the spread of Scouting and Guiding organizations. All these groups took people out of grimy cities and sterile suburbs into the countryside, to commune with Nature and to learn the skills of woodcraft and outdoor living that our ancestors took for granted.

The return to Nature led to a desire amongst many people for a Nature-oriented religion. One of its flowerings was modern Pagan Witchcraft, which saw in the remnants of traditional village wisecraft a basis on which to graft more sophisticated Pagan thought derived from ancient Egyptian, Greek, Roman, Celtic, and Germanic revivals. This resulted in Wicca, a religious system based on initiation into a mystery tradition which practiced rites based on the seasonal cycle, out of doors, often skyclad or in naturist fashion, and honoring the female aspect of the deity — the Goddess. Other Goddess traditions and druidry also underwent a revival. Writers such as Dion Fortune, whose novels described the religion of the Great Goddess and Horned God, wove the spirituality of Paganism into literature for public consumption. Wicca and witchcraft were given new impetus with the feminist movement of the 1970s on, which had an enormous impact on the religious beliefs of women and men. Feminism led many people to turn to Goddess spirituality in a desire for religious forms that gave greater expression to feminist ideals. Some of these women identified with the label 'witch', which they saw as a power word for women and a way of manifesting latent female energy. Others saw themselves simply as Goddess-worshippers.

Pluralistic societies

The period before World War Two saw the brief emergence of an undesirable variety of Paganism. In the German-speaking world, the Nazis saw the opportunity to prop up their political ideas with religion. The 'back to Nature' movement was subverted into a cult of physical perfection and the interest of German scholars in national culture and traditional religion was used to justify an aggressive warrior cult fronted by ancient Pagan symbols. This Nazi shadow has, until recent years, blocked the development of a true understanding of the Germanic deities and the wisdom of the *Eddas*. Despite this setback, the period after World War Two saw a substantial growth in Nature-based spirituality. The horrors of the two World Wars had also created a climate in which people questioned authority and unilateral political and religious systems. The West saw its future lying in plurality and tolerance between races and creeds. Immigration into

Europe from other parts of the world changed the face of European society forever. Gone was the isolation of the white race. Other peoples brought their religions and deities to Europe. European cities were no longer the province solely of Christian churches. Mosques and Hindu temples now graced the city streets. In this climate, the notion that there was only one religion and one way of viewing God inevitably changed. The Christian Churches themselves had to make adjustments. Aware of the racialist horrors that European ethnocentricity could unleash, they bent over backwards to accommodate the religious expressions of the immigrant peoples. Europe was now a multicultural and multi-faceted society. Those brought up in the post-World War Two period were raised in a different religious climate from that of their parents and grandparents. Comparative religion was taught in schools and increasingly people were aware that religious adherence was as much a matter of ethnicity and parental influence as Divine inspiration. In a climate where young people were taught to question the wisdom of their elders, many began seeking their own forms of religious expression.

From East to West

Many of those who have chosen Paganism as their spiritual path have also explored Eastern traditions such as Buddhism. In the 1960s and 1970s, there was a movement towards Eastern mysticism fostered by the passing fad of rock stars such as the Beatles for paying visits to gurus. Rich Western youth no longer went on Grand Tours of the Mediterranean but overland to India, to sit at the feet of the Mahariji-Ji, the Mahariji Mahesh Yogi and the Bhagwan Shree Rajneesh. The fashion for guru-cults was short-lived. The Western mind is not truly guru-oriented, pop culture moved on, and, more importantly, there was increasing disillusionment with gurus, as people became aware that their teachers, like all human beings, had feet of clay. The teachings of the Earth Traditions also became more accessible. As more books were published and Paganism became more public, people began to turn westwards for their spiritual inspiration.

Throughout the late twentieth century, there was a growing interest in the Earth Traditions. Interest in Native American and Afro-Caribbean spirituality spread far outside their original communities. Writers such as Caitlín Matthews, Elsa-Brita Titchenell, Freya Aswynn, and Marian Green made accessible Celtic and Germanic spirituality that had previously only been available to scholars and those in specialist historical, mythological and spiritual groups. All over Europe and North America, people met to enact the rituals of revived druidry. As the fear of the Nazi past receded, there was also a growing interest in runic lore and the teachings of the Germanic tradition. Both large organizations and smaller eclectic groups were formed to explore the ways of our ancestors and to enact seasonal celebrations. Similar organizations were also founded in Soviet-dominated Europe, often meeting in secret and sometimes persecuted and imprisoned for their attempts to revive Pagan spirituality. The Earth Traditions were emerging from the past.

Notes

1   Ralph Waldo Emerson (1836) 'Nature' in *Selected Essays*, pages 38–9.
2   Henry D Thoreau (1863) 'Walking' in *Norton Book of Nature Writing*, pages 181–8.

3

Celtic Roots

If we wish to practice an Earth Tradition in the twenty-first century in the West, we cannot recreate ancient traditions in their ancient form. We must create them anew in contemporary forms that meet the needs of today. To know what to recreate, we must know something of the origins of the Earth Traditions that are active in the world today. We must understand where we are rooted and how we can nurture the plant of our spirituality. Many revived Earth Traditions draw on the heritage of the Celts. Economic difficulties in the far west of Europe from the eighteenth century onwards mean that there has been an enormous Celtic diaspora. Millions of us on both sides of the Atlantic, white and black, have some Scottish, Welsh and particularly Irish ancestry. You have only to see the multiracial Irish national soccer team to see how Celtic ancestry has dispersed itself. The Celts have always been a migrant people.

Where did the Celts originate? Their ancestors are thought to have been the early Indo-European peoples who lived around 4000 BCE near the Black Sea that separates modern Turkey from the former Soviet Republics. Some peoples migrated west to Greece. Others migrated north. Others migrated eastwards over the Himalayas to India, taking with them spiritual traditions that became part of the basis of Hinduism. In Slovakia, there are artifacts around 3000 years old of a proto-Celtic civilization known as Urnfield culture because of the people's distinctive use of urns to inter the remains of their dead. Urnfield culture began to evolve into the peoples we call the Celts around 800 BCE. Over the next six hundred years, this culture spread eastwards to modern-day Bulgaria and Turkey, westwards into Austria, Germany, France, Spain, Portugal, and across the water to Britain and Ireland.

The Celts were tribal peoples, ruled by a chieftain chosen from among the kinsmen of the previous chief. Usually leaders were men, but where there was no male heir, women might inherit. Women had the right to own property; something that was taken away when the Celts became Christian. They might also be warriors and lead their people in battle. In England, the most famous

Celtic people is the Iceni who, led by Queen Boudicca, mounted the last con-
certed rebellion in the British Isles against the invading Romans. Boudicca's rebellion failed and had come too late to prevent the integration of Celtic and Roman
cultures. Roman influence stopped at Hadrian's Wall and did not cross into
Scotland; nor did the Romans ever invade Ireland, but in southern Britain, Roman
and Celtic deities fused and Celts adopted the Roman practice of venerating their
deities in roofed temples. Before this, the sacred spaces of the Celts were sacred
groves of trees whose branches lifted to the stars. It was in these natural cathe-
drals that their druid priesthood led their worship. The word druid may derive
from the word *drus* or oak tree.

Celtic religion

We do not know if there were any Celtic myths of creation, although it seems
likely that there would have been; for people in all times and places have sought
to explain their origins. Unfortunately, we have only fleeting commentaries from
Roman writers such as Strabo, who wrote that the druids of Gaul taught that
human souls and the universe are indestructible, although one day fire and water
would prevail over the world.[1]

Although our information is limited, we know that the Irish Celts thought of
the universe as comprising four realms symbolized by the four treasures of
Ireland, brought there by the High Gods, the Tuatha de Danann. The Spear
of Victory, representing the heavenly realm of light, symbolized the realm of
Findias. The Sword of Light, representing the heavenly realm of heat, symbolized Gorias. Murias' symbol was the Cauldron of the Dagda, the Cauldron of
Plenty, representing the watery underworld. Falias' symbol was the sacred stone
Lia Fail, representing the realm of Earth. The Earth was considered round but flat,
a disc rather than a globe, which floated on the waters of a great sea. Water was
important in Celtic spirituality and was believed to have magical and healing
properties. Compared with some of the other races in Europe at the time, the
Celts had remarkably advanced ideas of physical hygiene – they washed. The
landscape of the Celtic world, Ireland and Brittany in particular, is littered with
sacred springs that serve the same purpose today as they did in earlier times – to
bring the sacred waters of life to the people.

Celtic cosmology

The concept of the Otherworld, in Irish Tir na N'Og, was important in Celtic myth. Wells brought healing and they were entrances to the Otherworld. It was also possible to reach the Otherworld by sea. The Celts had come across the great landmass of Europe to the isles and coasts of the West. To them, the sea was a moat around the land. In Ireland, the west coast is still referred to as 'the edge of the Western world' and it seems natural to think of the Otherworld as lying just beyond the western horizon. No one who has been to this ethereal landscape, where gray wave fades into mist, and mist into sky, can fail to be impressed with a sense of standing at the edge of time and space. It seems a border country where it is easy to step out of the everyday world into some other reality.

In Celtic Tradition, the Otherworld is a beautiful realm of warmth, of Nature in abundance, a perpetual early summer, heady with the smell of flowers and blossom, filled with the sound of bird song and tinkling streams. Nothing ages and there is no disease. The Otherworld was also called the Land of Fairy. To enter the Otherworld is to enter Paradise – a brighter, more beautiful version of the mundane world. In contrast with the mythology of other peoples, the Celts had a joyful, often ecstatic approach to existence. There is no preoccupation with evil and no concept of sin and punishment. When the dead pass into the Otherworld, there is no doubt that they are going to a better place. In death, there is nothing to fear. The Celtic Otherworld seems similar to the Otherworld of shamanic cultures all around the world. It is inhabited not only by dead human beings, but also by spirits and otherworldly beings.

The souls of the young and the sick were thought to be in danger of wandering into the Otherworld, never to return. It was also possible to fall in love with otherworldly beings and to be enticed away. There are many stories in Celtic Tradition of people who go to dwell for a while in the Land of Fairy. The Scottish story of Tam Lin is one of the better known, having been popularized in recent decades by folk groups. Tam Lin is a knight who is captured by the Queen of Fairy when he falls off his horse. He becomes her consort in the Otherworld and seems happy with his role until he comes near to the end of his seven-year term of office, at the end of which he is to be sacrificed to renew the fertility of the Earth. Fortunately for Tam Lin, he has a human lover, Janet, whose maidenhead he demanded when she was unwise enough to venture alone to the woods. He has made Janet pregnant and she is keen to rescue Tam Lin from his fate so that she can take him home to do his husbandly duty. The enterprising Janet stages a rescue at Samhain, the festival of the dead, when the gates between this world and the Otherworld are open and the Fairy Queen likes to ride abroad with Tam Lin at her side. Janet pulls Tam Lin down from his horse and, despite a series of frightening shape-changing spells by the Fairy Queen that turn him into fierce animals and a piece of burning wood, she holds onto him until the Queen gives up. In this human and otherworldly encounter, the human woman emerges the victrix.

Celtic deities

Witches, druids and revivers of Celtic spirituality venerate Celtic deities. Given that they are so honored in the Pagan revival, remarkably little is known about them. Much has been lost to us because Celtic peoples relied primarily on an oral tradition to transmit their sacred legends and lore. Celtic deities are more diffi-cult to classify than those of other Pagan peoples. As far as we know, the Celtic deities do not seem to have undergone the rationalization process, familiar to us from the Greek, Roman and Germanic pantheons, whereby male and female deities were paired into married couples and other deities became their children. There are some family relationships between the deities of Celtic mythology; but no coherent story of a divine genealogy has been handed down to us. The difficulty is compounded by the fact that the Celts were not one nation, but a number of peoples spread across Europe, who shared similar languages and culture. They had many deities and there are likely to have been many local vari-ations. Identifying the Celtic deities is not helped by the fact that the Celts were reluctant to reveal the true names of their patron deities. In magical thinking, to know the name of something or someone is to have power over it. Caitlín Matthews comments in *Elements of the Celtic Tradition* that in every recorded story of Celtic tradition people refused to name their deities, simply saying:

🌿   I swear by the deities that my people swear by ...[2]

One battle strategy amongst warring Celts was to pit their tribal druids against one another to divine the name of the other side's deities. They would then call these out in battle to make the opposing peoples tremble with fear.

In the written collections of the Celtic myths and legends, such as that of the Welsh *Mabinogion*, deities do not figure as such. The stories purportedly describe the deeds of heroes and nobles; for by a process called euhemerism Christian scholars turned deities into human beings. Euhemerus himself was a Greek philosopher who argued that deities were originally men and women who had been deified for their achievements. It seems that the Christian scribes who first committed the myths to writing preferred (or found it safer) to describe their ancient deities as humans, in the same way as the Medieval Icelandic scholar Snorri Sturluson describes Odin as a descendant of King Priam of Troy! However, the attributes and magical powers of the figures in the legends betray their divine origins.

Irish deities

Irish deities can be divided into three groups – the High Gods or Tuatha de Danann, tribal and local goddesses associated with particular peoples or areas of land, and other perhaps older deities. The goddess Dana is the Mother of Tuatha de Danann. The principal god is the Dagda or 'Good God'. The Dagda is known as All-Father, Eochaid Ollathair, and is considered wise and knowledgeable. His weapon is a club. He also possesses a magical cauldron that can never be emptied. There are suggestions that the chalk image of a giant phallic figure with a staff which is carved into the hillside at the village of Cerne (ie horn) Abbas in South West England is an image of the Dagda or his English equivalent, but contemporary scholars are uncertain as to the image's antiquity. Lugh is another god who appears frequently in myth. He is the brilliant and many-skilled god whose weapon is the spear. Lugh claims to be a harper, hero, poet, healer, and magician. His name was given to one of the main Celtic festivals – Lughnasadh, or the Games of Lugh, a festival at the beginning of August to celebrate the grain harvest.

Three important female deities in Ireland were the goddesses of the battlefield – Morrigan, Badhbh and Nemhain – often referred to collectively as The Morrigan. Perhaps not surprisingly, given their love of carrion, their symbol is the crow or raven. The Morrigan is said to mate with the Dagda every Samhain, October 31. This is traditionally the Festival of the Dead when the Gates between this world and the Otherworld are open and the dead may converse with the living. The goddess Brigid is a less darksome goddess. She had her chief shrine in Kildare where her vigil fire was kept perpetually burning, tended by a group of unmarried priestesses known as Inghean an Dagha, Daughters of Fire. With the Christianizing of Ireland, Brigid became St Brigid and her holy offices were taken over by nuns. The nuns continued to tend the sacred flame until the late thirteenth century, when the Bishop of Kildare decreed that the custom should be suppressed because it was Pagan, as indeed it was. However, it was not until the sixteenth century that the flame was finally put out – but not for long. Irish religious sisters based in Kildare have revived the custom and are holding celebrations on Brigid's feast day at the beginning of February as part of an annual conference on justice. Conference delegates of all spiritual traditions and local people attend the Brigid rituals.

Brigid is a bridge now as in earlier centuries between the Nature-venerating Pagan world and the Christian world. In her, the legends of a pre-Christian goddess have fused with those of a fifth-century Christian saint, until it is hard to discern where history ends and myth begins. Brigid in both her saintly and her goddess forms is patron of poets, blacksmiths, healers, dairymaids, cattle, fugitives, midwives, women in labor, and newborn babies. When Scotland became Christian, Scottish Celts linked their version of Brigid, who in Scots Gaelic is Bride, to Christ by creating a legend that she was the Virgin Mary's midwife. Christ was then known by the beautiful title of Dalta Bride bith nam beannachd, the foster-son of Bride of the Blessings. In the Western Isles of Scotland, the festival of St Bride was celebrated until recent times with the making of a bed by the fireside so that she might enter the house and rest there. Bride was seen as a protectress and by praying to her daily, her followers could be kept from harm.

> 🦋   Every day and every night,
> that I say the genealogy of Bride,
> I shall not be killed,
> I shall not be wounded ...
> no fire, no sun, no moon shall burn me,
> no lake, no water, nor sea shall drown me.[3]

The goddesses of the land had a strong relationship with the people who lived there. In Celtic myth he who wins the hand of the Goddess has control over the land, so the relationship between goddesses of the land and the holder of worldly power, the king, is an important theme in Celtic mythology. The Irish texts suggest that a king might be married to his tribal goddess. This would take place as a sacred marriage with a priestess. Professor Ronald Hutton in *Pagan Religions of the Ancient British Isles* suggests that the number of royal husbands accredited to Maeve Queen of the Irish province of Connacht indicates that she was a goddess rather than a mortal queen. Once the sacred marriage was performed, the continued health of the king was important for his people. Many legends point to disaster befalling the land if the king is injured.

Welsh deities

In Welsh myth, one of the most important goddesses is Rhiannon. She appears dressed in brilliant gold clothing riding a magical white mare. Her name can be equated with 'Divine Queen' and she may have been the same goddess who was worshipped in France as the horse goddess Epona and whom Roman soldiers saluted as 'Regina' – Queen. Arianrhod or 'Silver-Wheel' is the mother of the Welsh equivalent of the Irish god Lugh. Caer Arianrhod, the Castle of Arianrhod, is placed in the Northern heavens and is associated with the pole star. It is also the home of dead heroes. Caer Arianrhod is considered particularly sacred in some Wiccan traditions as the shining beacon that guides our spiritual destiny and figures in much ritual prose and poetry.

The relationship between goddess and land is also found in Welsh myth. A recurring theme throughout Welsh myth is that of two god-like figures fighting for the hand of a goddess. Pwyll and Gwawl contend for Rhiannon, Bran and Mallolwch for Branwen, and Owein and the Knight in Black for the Countess of the Fountain. There are suggestions[4] that the two rivals represent the gods of summer and winter contending for the eternal Goddess.

Cernunnos and Cornelly

Another Celtic deity is Cernunnos, the Horned Lord of the animals who was found in Britain and continental Europe. Today, he is revered primarily in Wicca. As Herne and Cern, all derivatives of the word 'horn', his name figures in many place names in the British Isles. Two images of the horned god appear in Celtic Europe – one of Cernunnos as a stag god and the other of a god with cattle horns. One of the few representations of Cernunnos in Britain, on a silver coin dug up in Petersfield in southern England, shows him as a stag god with a sun-wheel between his antlers. The image of a stag crowned with the sun appears frequently in dream, poetry and myth across many cultures as an image of positive male energy. Cernunnos is also depicted in Celtic imagery as a dispenser of wealth, an attribute often associated with fertility deities. In France, the cult of the horned god of the cattle was absorbed by Christian missionaries and he was turned into Saint Cornelly, or Cornelius in the Latinized form, patron saint of horned beasts. The cult of St Cornelly is still widespread in Brittany, most notably in Carnac, one of the most prominent Pagan sacred sites in Europe. Horned animals decorate Saint Cornelly's churches and, until recently, people brought live animals to the churches for annual blessing by the village priest. Old customs were slow to die.

Sun

Veneration of the sun seems to have been important amongst the Celts. The eight-spoked wheel, which has been adopted by druids and Wiccans in the twentieth century as a symbol of their seasonal festivals, appears often upon Celtic altars and may represent the Sun. The Christian missionary St Patrick condemned 'those who adored the Sun' to perish eternally and insisted that Christ was the 'true Sun'. A number of Celtic festivals involved fire. Fire was brought from the Sun by a sacred bird – a swallow, wren or swift. The red markings and forked tail of the swallow were thought to be a result of scorching by the Sun's rays. Fire was used as an element of purification. At the festival of Beltane or Bright-Fire, at the beginning of May, all the fires in Ireland were extinguished. The sacred flames were then rekindled by the druids who performed a ceremony of driving the cattle between two fires to protect them from disease. This custom of making a new fire at Beltane continued into the nineteenth century in the Highlands and Islands of Scotland, as did the custom of making the Sun 'dance', an image that appears often in Celtic poetry. This involved reflecting the Sun's light into a bowl of water and then shaking it so that as the water rippled, the sunlight danced about the room. The light of the Sun could be brought into the darkness of the tomb in this way. In a contemporary Celtic spring rite, the priestess says:

> The tides of Spring are upon us,
> when the Sun shall dance,
> when water shall merge with fire,
> when the Maiden is made Mother.
> In the name of the Two and the One,
> we shall seek the mystery of unity.

To see the dancing of the Sun was thought to bestow great blessings. In traditional witchcraft, the Moon is drawn down using a bowl of water in the same way.

Song of Amairgin

Other insights into Celtic deities can be found in the *Song of Amairgin*, said to have been brought to Ireland by the Sons of Mil. The Sons of Mil were probably invaders who overcame the previous settlers whose deities were the Tuatha de Danann. The earlier peoples retreated to the hills and wild places to become the Little People of Irish legend. When the Sons of Mil first attempted to land in Ireland, the druids of the Tuatha de Danann sang spells against them and raised a magic wind to carry them far out to sea; but after many trials and tribulations, the Sons of Mil succeeded in making a landing and Amairgin made a declaration asserting his power.

> I am a wind on the sea,
> I am a wave of the ocean,
> I am the roar of the sea,
> I am an ox of seven combats,
> I am a hawk above the cliff,
> I am a shining tear of the Sun,
> I am fair amongst flowers,
> I am a boar in boldness,
> I am a salmon in the pool,
> I am a lake on the plain,
> I am the hill of poetry,
> I am a battle-waging spear,
> I am he who sets the brain afire.
> Who but I knows the mystery of the unhewn dolmen?
> Who but I knows where the Sun shall set?
> Who but I foretells the phases of the Moon?
> Who calls the cattle from the House of Tethra?
> Whom will the fish of the laughing ocean make welcome?
> For whose troop does the Maker-God conjure
> enchantments about a spear, enchantments of winds?[5]

Potentially the whole of creation is found in Amairgin and he is capable of all things. Amairgin is described by the Christian Medieval scribes as a poet and judge of the Sons of Mil and brother of the King; but his declaration of thirteen statements and six ritual questions indicates that he was originally a god. His qualities are similar to those of other deities. Alwyn and Brinley Rees suggest that Amairgin's utterance is similar to that of the Indian god Krishna in the *Bhagavad-Gita*.

> I am the radiant Sun among the light-givers ...
> among the stars of night, I am the Moon ...
> I am the ocean among the waters ...
> I am the wind ...
> I am the dice play of the cunning,
> I am the strength of the strong ...
> I am the silence of things secret,
> I am the knowledge of the knower.[6]

Druids

Knowledge was one of the highly prized possessions of Celtic society and knowledge was transmitted by one of the highest classes of society – the druid priesthood. There were three grades of druids, representing three levels of training. Druids were the most advanced and had full command of all the druidic arts, artistic, intellectual, and magical. Vates or uates performed magic and divination, and bards were poets and musicians. Most druids appear to have been male, but women acted as prophetesses and priestesses of particular goddesses. These were called veledas or ueledas amongst the Celts of continental Europe and by titles such as banfhili, female seer, by the Irish. Veledas often lived in sacred caves or groves, similar to those of Greek prophetesses at the famous oracle of the god Apollo at Delphi. People from kings to commoners would come to the veledas' sanctuaries to seek their wisdom. Veledas exerted considerable political influence and with the conquest of the Celts by the Romans, they became advisers at the courts of Roman emperors.

Druids, vates, and bards were teachers, doctors, historians, astronomers, and poets. They controled the legal system, acted as judges, and supervised executions of criminals. Murder was common among the quarrelsome Celts, but despite Roman propaganda that depicted the Celts as bloodthirsty savages, a strategy used by all colonial powers to justify their activities, executions were probably relatively rare. The Celtic criminal justice system operated differently from the contemporary Western systems. Murder was usually punished by a hefty fine payable to the victim's family by the family of the perpetrator.

Intellectually, druids were living libraries famous for and admired for their prodigious memories. The Celts developed the use of the Ogham alphabet for writing inscriptions and the Roman Emperor Julius Caesar recorded that they used the Greek alphabet for writing letters, but the druids scorned the use of the written word for sacred and poetic thought. Each druid was required to learn by heart the whole of their law, teachings, poetry, story, myth, religious observance, astronomy, astrology, medicine, genealogy, and tribal history. This could take up to twenty years. A boy would begin his apprenticeship in early childhood and this would continue until he was considered proficient. While this is a powerful way of transmitting an oral tradition, it is disastrous if the culture is conquered. With the Roman suppression of the druids, most Celtic teachings were lost and a great treasure of Western culture destroyed.

The druids practiced some techniques that seem shamanic in origin. To find the answer to a question, they would eat raw bull's flesh, drink the blood, and sleep wrapped in its hide. The answer would then come during sleep. There are indications that the Celts knew of the use of bodily posture in prayer and meditation to stimulate mystical visions. The Celtic god Cernunnos is depicted sitting in a meditative position reminiscent of the Buddha. He holds a snake in one hand, an image often used for energy rising up the spinal column from the muladhara chakra at the base of the spine. The tenth-century Irish text *The Cauldron of Poesy* describes two positions conducive to prayer and one to ritual incubation, whereby a bard would lie in darkness in order to receive poetic inspiration. This involved lying flat on one's back weighed down on the stomach with stones to prevent movement. This state of darkness and stillness caused sensory deprivation during which dream and vision would come. Shamans practice similar techniques. As well as being seekers and interpreters of visions, druids had a fearsome reputation as magicians. They were reputed to have the ability to raise storms, winds and mists, and to make the sun stand still in its course.

Despite the intellectual demands required to become a druid, as a career, it had a lot going for it. Druids were both respected and feared. In the middle of war, they could command the opposing factions to lay down their arms. Given the fiery temperament of the Celts, this service was probably frequently in demand. Druids, vates and bards were exempt from military service and almost immune from attack. Murder in Celtic society was a crime not just against the victim, but also against his or her family and clan. Clans were jointly responsible for the behavior of their members and financial compensation or 'honor price' was payable by the relatives of the murderer, with the price for victims of high social status being costly indeed. The Irish hero Fionn, after avenging his father's death by slaying his killer, says that, 'He dared not remain in Ireland unless he undertook poetry, for fear of the sons of Uirghriu and the sons of Morna.'[7] As a bard, he would be relatively safe. The honor price of a bard was so enormous that nobody could afford to kill one. If Druids, vates and bards were not quite worth their weight in gold, they were approaching it.

Contemporary druidry

Today, druidry is active all over the Western world, but particularly in the British Isles, Brittany and North America. Not all druid orders have returned fully to their Pagan roots. Some are more akin to freemasonry and some are Christian-oriented. In Britain, druids lead the cultural festival of the Welsh eisteddfod, where Bards appear in blue robes, Vates in green and Druids in white robes and headdresses. Druids also lead Pagan religious festivals at ancient pre-Christian religious sites such as Stonehenge and Avebury. Some contemporary druid groups scorn the use of white robes, believing these originate in eighteenth-century romanticism. From a practical point of view, white does not marry well with life in muddy villages full of thatched huts. In fact, it is known that color in clothing was an important mark of social status amongst the Celts. The higher people's social status, the more colors they were permitted to wear at any one time. Kings could wear up to twelve colors and druids up to ten. The everyday dress of the druids is likely therefore to have been Celtic plaid. However, there may have been differences between everyday and ritual dress. Independent sources from the Roman writer Pliny to the Christian monastic book *The Tripartite Life of St Patrick*[8] comment that druids wore white robes on ceremonial occasions. Amongst the colorful plaid of the nobles, the white dress would have been a distinctive and useful focus when conducting large ceremonies and white is often used in a religious setting to denote purity. In *The Tripartite Life of St Patrick*, we are also told that the druids had a tonsure, ie the center of the head was shaved from forehead to back. This is thought to be the reason why the monks of the early Celtic Church had a different-shaped tonsure from the round bald patch now familiar to us from the Roman Church. Some kind of visible sign of priesthood, such as shaving the head, is common amongst many cultures.

The practices of contemporary druids vary between the different orders. Some teach a wide curriculum of esoteric lore. Others encourage the development of spiritual understanding through the creative arts such as music and poetry. Contact with the land is important in druidry. Druids prefer to celebrate their rites outside with their feet standing upon the Earth. Pilgrimages to sacred sites and spending time outside communing with Nature are encouraged as a way of contacting the spirit of the land and learning to live in harmony with it. Walking, trekking and camping in the wilderness and other sites of natural beauty are opportunities to remind ourselves that we are part of the world of Nature. Environmental campaigning has also become an important part of druid activity. In Europe, druids are frequently asked to conduct rites during environmental protests.

Honoring the sacred times and tides is considered important. Most druids celebrate the same seasonal cycle of festivals as witches. The celebration of the seasonal cycle allows druids to synchronize their lives with Nature. Some druids draw on Celtic spiritual tradition of retreating to places of natural beauty to meditate and pray. Spiritual retreats with periods of silence and meditation in beautiful natural surroundings act as food for the spirit. Philip Carr-Gomm, head of the Order of Bards, Ovates and Druids, writes that time is often seen as our enemy in contemporary society. We live frenzied lives in which we constantly 'race against time'. He advocates 'befriending' time and learning both to make use of it and to find time each day or week for meditation and inner tranquility. This is not self-indulgence, but helps us attune ourselves to the needs of our world. Druidry is concerned with service to the environment and also with service to humanity. Meditation can help people discern the spirit of the times and see what their role can be. Each period of history has an agenda in relation to the evolution of consciousness. Certain individuals have become great innovators and agents for the advancement of humanity, 'because they have been aware of the needs of the time and have succeeded in articulating what was already fermenting in the collective psyche'.[9] This should be the endeavor of each one of us. In the Order of Bards, Ovates and Druids, the role of druid as teacher and spiritual counselor is strongly emphasized. This encourages people to be of service and open to those seeking the wisdom of the Earth Traditions:

Let Unity, Harmony and Beauty be your watchwords.
May you abundantly share in the Illumination.
Be you ready to hear the voice of those crying out
   for Wisdom.

Listen at the Portals – for the world is large and many
    are seeking.
Open the Gates for them and portal after portal shall open
    unto you.

Notes

1   MacCrossan, *The Sacred Cauldron*, page 110.

2   Matthews, *Elements of the Celtic Tradition*, page 14.

3   Carmichael, trans, *Carmina Gaedelica*, quoted in Matthews *Elements of the Celtic Tradition*, page 14.

4   Gantz, trans, *The Mabinogian*, pages 15–16.

5   Based on the Macalister translation of *Lebor Gabala Erenn, V*, page 114–7.

6   From the *Bhagavad-Gira*, quoted in Rees and Rees, *Celtic Heritage*, page 99.

7   From O-hogain, *Fionn Mac Cumhail*, quoted in Matthews *Elements of the Celtic Tradition*, page 14.

8   Hutton, *Pagan Religions of the Ancient British Isles*, page 171.

9   Carr-Gomm, *The Elements of the Druid Tradition*, page 90.

Heathen Roots

'Pagan' is a term often used to describe practitioners of Earth Traditions. This refers to the Earth Traditions' link with the *pagus*, the land. Those who venerated the pantheon of Germanic deities often prefer to call their practice Heathenism. 'Heathens', like Pagans, were the country dwellers, the 'people of the heath', those who followed the old ways. The deities of Germanic peoples were worshipped all over Northern and Western Europe as Germanic peoples spread south, west and north. Goths settled in many parts of Italy. Angles, Saxons and other Germanic peoples came to make their homes in Britain in the tumultuous years following the withdrawal of the Roman armies from Western Europe around 400 CE. A few hundred years later, they were followed by Scandinavians of Germanic descent who became known as Vikings or the Norse. Germanic families whose ancestors had migrated to Scandinavia were now seeking pastures new and a quick route to fortune and glory. They looked southward to the more hospitable climate of eastern Scotland and England. These invading peoples came first with warriors and swords, but later they brought their families to settle and farm. They pushed the Celts and their deities into the West, where their descendants, the Welsh and the Cornish, live today. Counties in England still bear the names of the Germanic peoples that settled them. There is Essex of the East Saxons, Sussex of the South Saxons, and the former kingdom of Wessex, which has been divided into smaller counties. The British monarchy is proud of its descent from the Kings of Wessex, of whom Alfred was the most famous, who claimed descent from the god Odin or Woden. When Prince Edward married in 1999 he and his wife Sophie took the titles Earl and Countess of Wessex.

We usually think of Ireland as a Celtic country, but Viking settlements were founded in the ninth and tenth centuries and became some of Ireland's major cities. Dublin was a Viking port, as were Limerick and Waterford. Vikings also built many of the ports along the northern French coast and France's name comes from a Germanic people, the Franks or Bold Ones.

American Vikings

Political unrest in ninth century Norway forced many Viking noble families to do what their ancestors had always done – to seek new land to colonize. The Icelandic sagas tell of how a group of Scandinavian families left Norway in large cargo boats called 'knorrs' to settle in Iceland. The Irish had got to Iceland before them and established monasteries and the Vikings may have learned about Iceland through relatives settled in Ireland. Iceland proved popular. By the early tenth century, there were 30,000 settlers and the fertile land around the coast was running out. Some of the more adventurous settlers began to wonder what lay further west. The discovery of Greenland was opportune for overcrowded Iceland. Soon there were 3,000 Vikings in Greenland and they were only 500 miles from the Labrador coast of North America, and around 300 miles, a little over two days' sailing, from Baffin Island. The first sighting of the North American coast was made by accident when a ship was blown off course. A few years later, the first landing was made in Newfoundland. The excavation of the first Viking settlement at L'Anse aux Meadows in Newfoundland was made in the 1960s following an extraordinary intuitive leap by a Norwegian novelist who examined the descriptions of voyages recorded in the sagas and pinpointed the location. The excavations discovered jewelry in the form of Thor's hammer, a Heathen symbol, and the Christian cross, indicating that the two religions were co-existing during the Medieval period, which practitioners of the Heathen Tradition often refer to as the period of 'Dual Faith'. The Newfoundland settlement was not a success. The indigenous inhabitants proved hostile and the climate inhospitable. The settlement at L'Anse aux Meadows was abandoned and it was to be hundreds of years before Scandinavians once again became immigrants to North America.

The World-Tree

Like all the Earth Traditions, Germanic peoples relied on an oral tradition. Their myths and religious lore were not written down until after the coming of Christianity. However, they were recorded much earlier in the Christian period than the Celtic myths and show less Christian influence. In about 1220, the Icelandic scholar Snorri Sturluson, concerned to preserve his people's traditions, wrote down what he knew in a collection of works known as the *Prose Edda* to distinguish it from the *Poetic Edda*.

From the *Eddas*, we learn that the Germanic peoples believed that the cosmos was a multiverse of nine worlds that together make up the World-Tree, Yggdrasil. Ygg is another name for Odin, King of the High Gods, and Yggdrasil means Odin's Steed. Yggdrasil is vast and has three roots. The first is in Asgard, the home of the High Gods, and is watered by the spring of Urd, which is the spring of Fate. It is by the Well of Urd that the High Gods hold daily council. The second root of Yggdrasil is in Jotunheim, Giant-Home. Under this root is the well of the giant Mimir in which is hidden wisdom. The third root is in Niflheim, Cloud-Home, and is watered by Hvergälmer, the origin of all life-giving waters. A number of important animals live on the Tree. Ratatosk the squirrel runs up and down communicating between the eagle or sacred cock at the crown and the serpent Nidhögg, Gnawer-from-Below, at its base in Niflheim. The squirrel Ratatosk is an image of the seeker of knowledge. He climbs to the heights of consciousness and down to the depths of the unconscious in order to come to awareness.

The chief god of the Aesir is Odin in Scandinavian languages or Woden in Anglo-Saxon. His name was given to Wednesday when the Anglo-Saxons adopted the Roman system of the seven-day week. The Romans attributed this day to Mercury, god of mental agility, and there are aspects of Mercury that can be equated with Odin. Odin is Alfadhir, the All-Father. He is also a god of wisdom, knowledge and communication. Elsa-Brita Titchenell in *The Masks of Odin* equates Odin's name with Odr or Universal Intelligence. Odin possesses a magical ring that produces eight more like itself every ninth night. These can be seen as images of the cycles of creation. Elsa-Brita Titchenell points out that the image of the endless cycles of the spiral is found among plants and animals throughout Nature, 'from the atomic worlds to the great sweeping movements of stars and galaxies in space'.[1]

Frigga, the wise mother of the High Gods, is Odin's wife. She can see into the future and is described as the one who 'knows every being's fate, though she herself says naught'.[2] Frigga and Odin's son is Baldur the Beautiful. He is wise and merciful and his death marks the beginning of the disintegration and destruction of the world of Asgard. Loki is Odin's foster-brother and the son of a giant. He brings the forces of chaos and disorder into Asgard. The battle goddesses, the Valkyries, assist Odin in times of need.

Other important figures are the three Norns or Fates, who weave the Web of Wyrd. The Norns were still in folk memory in sixteenth-century Britain but by then they were thought of as three witches. It was in this guise that they appear in William Shakespeare's play *Macbeth*. Although Odin is leader of the Aesir, ultimately he too is bound by the threads of Wyrd. Within the Germanic

Tradition, the gods are not all-powerful. There are forces within Nature and destinies that are beyond control. Urd is the chief of the Norns. She rules the past. Her name means Origin and she is the cause of the present and future. The second sister is Verdandi or Becoming, who represents the present – that which is coming into being. Together, the two sisters create a third sister, Skuld or Debt who represents the future. Skuld is depicted as wearing a veil, for while past and present are known, the future has yet to be revealed. Skuld is the result of the actions of past and present and is akin to karma. She cuts the thread of life, when our time ends. Together the Wyrd Sisters spin the web of destiny that affects all things – deities and humans. In the *Völuspá* or *The Sibyl's Prophecy*, the functions of the Norns are described.

> A tall ash-tree stands by name of Yggdrasil,
> watered daily by white icicles,
> that drip the dew that drops in the dells.
> It stands ever green above Urd's well.

> Thence come three Maidens who know much,
> from that bower beneath the tree:
> one is named Origin, the second Becoming;
> these two fashioned the third, named Debt.
> They established law that determines the fates,
> of the children of ages and the lives of men.[3]

Asgard, the home of the High Gods, forms the first of three upper worlds of Yggdrasil. The others are Vanaheim and Alfheim. Vanaheim is the home of the Vanir, deities of peace and plenty. Many believe that the Vanir were the deities of the Bronze Age, whose followers came into conflict with the invading Iron Age Indo-Europeans and their warrior gods. The myths describe how a war was fought between the deities of the two pantheons. Peace was negotiated when the two sides exchanged hostages, a common practice amongst peoples of the time. The goddess Freya and her father Njörd were given as hostages to the Aesir. The giant Mimir and his brother Hoenir were given to the Vanir. The wily Aesir got the better of the bargain. The Vanir found Hoenir was useless unless advised by Mimir. Outraged, they cut off Mimir's head and returned it to Asgard, where Odin used it to learn hidden lore.

Chief among the Vanir are Freya, 'The Lady', and her brother Frey, 'The Lord'. Their father Njörd is a sea god, who sends winds to seafarers and protects them on their voyages. He is also associated with the planet Saturn and can be seen as Father Time. Freya is the patroness and protectress of the human race. She is also associated with the sea and one of her names is Mardoll, derived from mar, sea.

Alfheim, Elf-Home, also known as Ljössalfheim, Light-Elf-Home, is the world of the light elves who are responsible for the growth of vegetation. This world was given to Frey as his teething gift. Alfheim represents the natural world of fertility, plants and animals. It is similar to the deva kingdoms in Eastern traditions and the Fairyland of the Celts. Frey is distinguished by his erect phallus and has similarities to other Nature deities such as Cernunnos, Pan and the Egyptian Bes. At Ragnarök, the time of the destruction of the phase of creation we are currently in, the link with the Horned God is again apparent when Frey uses a pair of antlers to fight the destroyer Surt.

One of the four middle worlds, Jotunheim, Giant-Home, is a hostile realm inhabited by the giants, whose energies when unchecked can bring chaos. One of Yggdrasil's roots is in Jotunheim. Nidavellir is the home of the dwarves. Dwarves are useful, but can be greedy, treacherous and unfriendly. They care primarily for their own. The dwarves rule the treasures of the inner earth. Svartalfheim, Black-Elf-Home, is home to the troublesome black elves. The fourth middle world is Midgard, Middle-Earth, which will be familiar to readers of JRR Tolkien's *Lord of the Rings*. This is the human world, which is ruled by the god Thor, who is friend of farmers and workers. Thor, or Thunor in Anglo-Saxon, whose name was given to Thursday, is Odin's son by the giantess Jord or Jorth who represents the Earth. Thor travels the world in a chariot drawn by goats. He is immensely strong and one of his greatest treasures is his hammer, Mjölnir, which can slay giants and shatter rocks. His worship was widespread and when Saxons were converted to Christianity, he was one of the three deities they were specifically required to renounce. Like the Celtic 'Good God', the Dagda, Thor is an earthy, pleasure-loving deity. He has a zest for life and an enormous appetite for food and drink. He can literally drink his hosts dry. Midgard is connected to Asgard, the realm of the High Gods, by Bifrost, the Rainbow Bridge. Bifrost is guarded by the Heimdall, the White God who is the son of nine maidens.

Muspellheim, or Fire-Home, is one of the two lower realms of the Tree. This is a world of creative and destructive fire, a world of pure energy in expansion. It is ruled over by Surt, who leads the destruction at Ragnarök, the time of the destruction of creation as we know it. Muspellheim is balanced by Niflheim, Cloud-Home, a world of creative and destructive frost and ice that represents energy in contraction. It is controled by the serpent Nidhögg. Hel, the realm of the dead, is in Niflheim. Hel does not carry the negative connotations that Christianity later placed upon it. This world is ruled by the goddess Hel, daughter of Loki, and consists of many realms both pleasant and unpleasant. From Niflheim, Nagelfar the ship of the Dead, which is built of dead men's nails, will sail forth at Ragnarök with Loki at its helm. The nails of the dead have been seen to have magical power because they continue to grow after death.

Hel was not the destiny of all who died. Warriors were received into Asgard to dwell in Valhalla, the Hall of the Slain, and to feast with the High Gods. Later Valhalla came to be seen as the resting place of all men and women dedicated to Odin, not just the battle-fallen. Snorri Sturluson tells us that Odin, who established this rite, received all those whose bodies were cremated. People looked forward with joy to dwelling with their god. The chieftain Earl Ragnor says before his death:

> It gladdens me to know that Baldur's father
> makes ready the benches for banquet.
> Soon we shall be drinking ale from the curved horns.
> The champion who comes into Odin's dwelling
> does not lament his death.
> I shall not enter his hall with words of fear upon my lips.
> The Aesir will welcome me.
> Death comes without lamenting ...
> Eager am I to depart ...
> The days of my life are ended.
> I laugh as I die.[4]

Death was not the end, but a transition to a new life. It could also be a resting place between lives prior to reincarnation. When Odin's son Baldur is killed, he can be restored to life, but only if everything on Earth will mourn him. The evil Loki, who has engineered Baldur's death, disguises himself as an old woman and refuses to mourn so Baldur is forced to remain in the world of the dead. There is also evidence that the Germanic peoples believed in reincarnation down the ancestral line. The *Flateyjarbok,* or *Book of Flatey*, a fourteenth-century Icelandic text found on the island of Flatey, tells us that when king Olaf the Holy was born, there was great anxiety because his mother was in such long labor. The birth came about safely when a sword and a ring were taken from the burial mound of one of his ancestors, Olaf of Geistad, and presented to the child. In adult life, Olaf was believed to be the reincarnation of Olaf of Geistad. He was questioned about this on one occasion when he rode past his ancestor's burial mound.

🐝　　　'Tell me, Lord, ... were you buried here? ... They say that
　　　when you came to this place before, you said, 'Here we were
　　　once, and here we fare now.'[5]

Olaf, who had adopted Christianity, strongly denied that he ever said such a thing.

Jotunheim, or Giant-Home, is a hostile realm inhabited by the giants, the forces of chaos. It is a world in constant motion, which seeks to oppose anything that resists it. It acts in opposition to the creative forces of Vanaheim. The role of the giants is an interesting one. The deities are often equated with the highest form of consciousness present in existence, whereas the giants are seen as its opposite, all that acts against the thrust of evolution. Freya Aswynn, author of *Leaves of Yggdrasil*, believes that the giants represent some of the earliest deities of animistic Stone Age peoples who inhabited Northern Europe.[6]

In Heathen cosmology, human beings are only one of the conscious creations inhabiting the World-Tree. All the different orders of creation see the same Sun, planets and stars, but they perceive them from different perspectives. Their views of reality are not quite the same. The same data is interpreted differently and represents different things. In the *Allvismál* or *Song of Allwise*, the dwarf Allwise seeks the hand of Thor's daughter. Thor tests Allwise on his knowledge of all aspects of creation to see if he lives up to his name. Thor asks him, 'What is the Moon that people see in every world?' Allwise answers:

🐝　　　It is 'Moon' to humans, to the Aesir 'The Ball',
　　　'Turning Wheel' in the House of Hel;
　　　giants say, 'Hastener', dwarfs call him 'Shine',
　　　elves they name him 'Measure of Time'.

Thor then asks, 'What is Night, Daughter of Dark, named in each world?' Allwise answers:

🐝　　　Men call her 'Night', Gods say 'Dark',
　　　the Aesir say 'Disguiser';
　　　giants say 'Unlight', elves 'Joy-of-Sleep',
　　　dwarfs call her 'Dream-Spinner'.[7]

As in many of the poems of the *Eddas*, the purpose is to instruct the audience, who learn that there are a number of worlds with different orders of being that have different viewpoints. The song also has another salutary message – that it is unwise to force the hand of the High Gods. Although Allwise has answered Thor's questions correctly, Thor is wilier. Unwilling to give his daughter to a dwarf, he has kept Allwise talking to dawn and the sun turns him to stone.

Creation and destruction

Unlike Celtic mythology, the creation myths of the Germanic Tradition were preserved. From the *Eddas,* we learn that the universe as we know it comes about through the interaction of cosmic forces that result in the creation of the nine worlds that together comprise Yggdrasil. In the beginning is darkness and silence, Ginnungagap or Yawning-Void. The *Eddas* call this the time of the Fimbulvetr, Mighty-Winter, the long cold night of Non-being. Fimbul-Winter is not a complete void. Two opposing polarities exist – Fire and Ice – Muspellheim, Fire-Home, and Niflheim, Cloud-Home. Matter is created when the two polarities interact – the heat of Muspellheim melts the ice of the cold world of Niflheim, thus creating vapor in the Yawning-Void. If you think about modern descriptions of the creation of our universe, you will realize that these, although expressed more poetically than modern scientific descriptions, were along the right lines. The vapor of the Yawning Void is Ymer the Frost Giant, from whom the deities will create our world of Middle-Earth. The world of giants is a world of chaos. They create matter, but they do not know how to order it, categorize it, and separate one thing from another. They are not fully conscious beings. Ymer commences the process of creation, but this first stage alone is not sufficient to establish the manifest universe. There is no soil, sea, or wind. The potential for life has been created, but not Nature as we know it.

> Sun turned from the south, sister of the Moon,
> her right arm rested on the rim of Heaven;
> she did not know where her place was,
> or Moon what powers he had,
> or the stars their constellations.[8]

For the processes of creation to develop, the active intervention of more evolved conscious beings is needed. At this stage, Buri, Bur and the sons of Bur are created. These are the ancestors of the Aesir, the High Gods, and have the power to bring order into chaos and to establish Middle-Earth – the world as we know it.

> Gaping abyss alone – no growth,
> until Bur's sons raised the lands,
> and brought forth magnificent Midgard.
> From southwards Sun warmed the cold earth;
> and green grass sprung from the fertile soil.[9]

It is from further interplay between order and chaos that creation comes. Both are necessary: there cannot be one without the other. Each reaction has an equal and opposite reaction. This balance between opposing forces is more reminiscent of Eastern thought than recent Western thought. It can be found in Indian tradition in the interaction of the god Shiva and the goddess Shakti, the force of destruction and the force of creation, and in Chinese philosophy in the balance of female Yin and male Yang. In Heathen myth, destructive forces are not evil in the dualistic sense. Both creative, building forces and destructive, breaking-down forces – anabolism and catabolism – have their role to play. The human world, Middle-Earth, is at the center of creation. We are mediators between the chaos giants, the forces of destruction, and the world of the creator deities.

Now that form has been created and ordered, in the second stage of creation, the High Gods create time.

> The High Gods gathered in council,
> to confer in their Hall of Judgment.
> They gave names to night and dusk;
> they named the morning and midday,
> and with Midwinter and Midsummer
> they divided the year.[10]

Time is a measurement of change and in Heathen Tradition, creation is not a once-and-for-all-event, but ever-renewing cycles and spirals of evolution and becoming. The universe that we see today will pass and fade, beings will live and die. The forces of creation and destruction are ever at work. In the same way that crystals are formed and then decay, so too does our world, Middle-Earth, reach culmination and then begin to decay from within. This is the pattern of all things – our bodies, our societies, our religions, the planet itself. The process of

52

ecological erosion is graphically conveyed in the description of Yggdrasil. The serpent Nidhögg gnaws through one of Yggdrasil's roots, four stags nibble at the leaves and two goats at the bark, all gradually undermining and destroying it. Despite this continuous process of destruction, the Germanic Tradition is optimistic. Richard Wagner's opera cycle *The Ring of the Nibelungen* has created a mistaken impression that the *Eddas* convey a pessimistic spiritual philosophy in which the High Gods are overcome by the forces of evil. The myths describe the end of the world, but the Wagner operas stop at Ragnarök, the time of destruction. What the operas do not show is what happens after Ragnarök. In the *Vaftrudnismál* or *Song of Illusion*, Odin in his guise as Gagnrád, Gainful-Counsel, questions the giant Vaftrudnir about the end of the world. Interestingly, the giants of chaos are portrayed as knowing more of the future than the King of the High Gods. Odin asks Vaftrudnir which human beings will survive the Fimbul-Winter?

> Life and Survivor are hid in the Tree,
> morning dew their food will be,
> and from them will be born,
> generations to come.

Odin then asks what will be the source of life, when Fenris-Wolf has swallowed Elf-Wheel, the Sun.

> One daughter alone Elf-Wheel bears,
> before Fenris-Wolf devours her;
> Radiant-Mane shall gallop her mother's roads
> when the powers of the old gods perish.

Elf-Wheel or Alfrödul is the soul of the Sun. The visible orb itself is often called Dvalin's Toy. Fenris-Wolf is Loki's son by the giantess Angrboda. From Vaftrudnir, we learn that a man and a woman, Lif and Lifthrasir, or Life and Survivor, will come through the destruction by hiding in the leaves of Yggdrasil. The Sun will reappear in the form of her daughter Radiant Mane. Many of the High Gods will be destroyed, but some will survive to found a new dynasty.

> Vidar and Vale shall have the old gods' shrines,
> when the flames of Surt have subsided.
> Mode and Magne shall have Mjölnir
> when Vingner is overthrown.[11]

Surt is the destroyer of the worlds. Mode (Force) and Magne (Might) are two sons of Vingner, another name for Thor. Mjölnir is Thor's hammer. In *Odens Korpgalder* or *The Song of Odin's Corpse*, we are told how the phase of destruction will end. As the smoke of Ragnarök dies away, the Fenris-Wolf and the other destructive forces will retreat to their lairs. Their work is done. The surviving deities will rise up. Heimdall the White, the watcher who keeps guard upon the Rainbow Bridge of Bifrost, blows the horn of alarm at the beginning of Ragnarök and is there to announce that the destruction is over. His clarion call announces the dawning of a new day. In Heathen mythology, there is no irreversible finality. The cosmos has seasons and cycles, even as does the planet itself. The phase of destruction is followed by Fimbul-Winter, a period of dormancy, and then by a new creation.

Seidr

Women played an important role in Germanic Traditions as volvas and seidkonas. They had magical and divinatory powers and carried out healing under the patronage of the Goddess Eir. The word volva means prophetess. Seidkonas had a similar function and practiced seidr or prophecy. A description of a volva is found in the *Saga of Erik the Red*. She has gloves made of cat fur and a cloak with a cat fur-lined hood. The goddess Freya, whose chariot is drawn by cats, is patroness of seidr. Freya taught seidr to Odin, but it was primarily a female art. Seidr involved entering a trance in order to communicate with the Otherworld. The priestess was seated on a platform surrounded by other priestesses who performed ritual chants to help induce and maintain the trance. The seeresses traveled about the country visiting different settlements to give advice and prophecy. They would be called upon to assist with any community problems, from identifying the causes of sickness to solving crimes and giving advice on political matters. The Roman historian Tacitus writes that the German peoples believed:

> There resides in women an element of holiness and a gift of prophecy; and so they do not scorn to ask their advice, or lightly disregard their replies.[12]

Prophecy was associated particularly with the Vanir deities. While Freya is the patroness of seidr, prophecy is also associated with her brother Frey and with the Danish goddess Nerthus. Njörd is the father of Freya and Frey and in Old Norse the word Njörd is the equivalent of Nerthus. Professor Hilda Ellis Davidson[13] and others suggest that Nerthus and Njörd may have originally been a twin pair of deities and parents of Frey and Freya. The role of the traveling seeress was connected with that of traveling deities. Nerthus visited her people in her sacred wagon drawn by oxen, which none but her dedicated priest might touch. The priest knew the goddess was present and it was time to set off when her wagon became heavy. The reference to the heaviness suggests that at these ceremonies a priestess would embody the goddess. The goddess' arrival was welcomed with great ceremony. Any armed hostilities had to cease and weapons were put away. Frey seems to have been embodied in the person of his priest. The *Flateyjarbok*[14] tells us that King Eric of Sweden led Frey's wagon to a certain place and waited until it became heavy. This was the sign that the god was present. The wagon was then taken into the king's hall and King Eric greeted Frey, drank a horn in his honor and put various questions to him.

Contemporary Heathenism

The revival of Northern European myth and culture was associated in the nineteenth and early-twentieth centuries with a revival of national heritage. Education in Europe was education in the Classics. People knew about Greek and Roman deities but they knew nothing about the standing stones, burial chambers and other religious monuments that littered their own landscape. We do not value what we take for granted. It was only in the nineteenth century, when people began to leave the rural environments in which families had lived for generations in the same houses telling myths and ancient tales around the fireside, that scholars realized they were in danger of losing something important – their own heritage. Often this was associated with loss of language. In Ireland, Irish was being taken over by English, as people moved to cities and needed the new language to get jobs. In Brittany, French was taking over from Breton. In Wales, Welsh was losing out to English. Scholars began visiting remote areas and sat in thatched cottages listening and recording as elderly women and men told them poems, songs, folklore traditions, magical and healing practices, and seasonal rites and customs that had been practiced since long before Christianity.

In Scandinavian countries, interest in the Norse religion began to revive. In the nineteenth century, Danish scholars coined a new term – Asetro, which is now commonly known by the Icelandic version of the word – Ásatrú. Norse religion can also be referred to as Forn Sidr – Ancient Way, Forn sed – Old custom, Nordisk sed – Nordic custom, or Hedensk sed – heathen custom. Icelandic poet Sveinbjorn Beinteinsson (1924–1993) a farmer, poet and singer, was Allsherjargodi, or Head Priest, of the Icelandic Ásatrú organization Asatráarfélagid. In 1972, Sveinbjorn Beinteinsson convinced the Icelandic government to recognize Ásatrú as the traditional religion of Iceland with equal rights to Christianity and it became the first non-Christian religion to be officially recognized in Iceland. Sveinbjorn Beinteinsson was devoted to Icelandic traditional culture and was an expert singer of the sung poetry Rímur, which has no tonal scale but is a free-form wave of sound similar to Middle Eastern vocal chanting. He used Rímur singing to recreate the art of epic singing by using the meter and forms of pre-Christian Scandinavian and English poetry found in the Scandinavian *Völuspá* or *Sybil's Prophecy* and the Anglo-Saxon epic poem *Beowulf*, recently retranslated by Irish poet Seamus Heaney. Sveinbjorn Beinteinsson had strong links to contemporary music and frequently performed with new wave, industrial and punk rock bands. In Iceland, Ásatrú believers can have marriages and other religious rites of passage solemnized by their own community leaders and Sveinbjorn Beinteinsson officiated at the marriage ceremony of rock star Genesis P Orridge.

Today, there are many practitioners of Germanic Tradition, with different emphases and interests. Scandinavians and those attracted to the warrior aspect of Germanic Tradition often call it Ásatrú, which means belief in or loyalty to the High Gods, the Aesir. Others who venerate the Aesir prefer the term 'Odinist'. Others describe their spirituality simply as Heathenism or the Northern Tradition and may be more Goddess-oriented. The focus of many followers of Heathen spirituality has changed in recent years from a patriarchal-oriented worship of the Aesir deities to veneration of the Vanir, the deities of the land, and to working in harmony with the spirits of the land, land wights, for environmental protection. Interest in seidr or prophecy and shamanism has grown and this has attracted more women to the tradition. Freya Aswynn, writer of a beautiful and original book about the runes, is well known in the European community, and Dr Jenny Blain, formerly at Mount Saint Vincent University, Canada, and now at Sheffield Hallam University, England, has conducted research within the heathen community that has encouraged serious study of the Heathen Tradition.

Notes

1   Titchenell, *The Masks of Odin*, page 36.

2   *Lokasenna* or *Loki's Flyting*, see Titchenell, *The Masks of Odin*, page 217.

3   *Völuspá* or *Sybil's Prophecy*, see Titchenell, *The Masks of Odin*, pages 93–4 and Auden and Taylor, *Norse Poems,* page 248.

4   From the *Lodbrok, The Death Song of Ragnor*, quoted in Davidson, *Gods and Myths of Northern Europe*, page 150.

5   Quoted in Davidson, *Gods and Myths of Northern Europe*, page 155.

6   Aswynn, *Leaves of Yggdrasil*, page 268.

7   *Allvismál* or *The Song of Allwise*, verses 14–15, 30–31, see Titchenell, *The Masks of Odin*, pages 225–30 and Auden and Taylor, *Norse Poems,* page 248.

8   *Völuspá*, verse 5, see Titchenell, *The Masks of Odin*, page 46 and Auden and Taylor, *Norse Poems*, page 246.

9   *Völuspá*, verses 3–4, see Titchenell, *The Masks of Odin*, page 46 and Auden and Taylor, *Norse Poems*, page 246.

10   *Völuspá*, verse 5, see Titchenell, *The Masks of Odin*, page 46 and Auden and Taylor, *Norse Poems*, page 246.

11   *Vaftrudismál* or the *Song of Illusion*, verses 43–6, 49–50, Bray trans, *The Elder or Poetic Edda*, pages 55–6; Titchenell, *The Masks of Odin*, page 134–42; Auden and Taylor, *Norse Poems*, page 232, and Hollander, trans, *The Poetic Edda*, pages 42–52. Odin as Gagnrád (Gainful-Counsel) questions the giant Vaftrudnir in a dialogue designed to educate the listener.

12   Tacitus, *Germania 8*, in H Matingly trans, *The Agricola and The Germania*, page 108.

13   Davidson, *Gods and Myths of Northern Europe*, page 106.

14   A page of this beautifully illustrated book can be viewed on the internet, on a page hosted by the University of Washington. The *Flateyjarbok* records the discovery of America in the *Graenlendinga Saga*, or 'Saga of the Greenlanders'.

Traditions of Northeast Europe

Finnish Paganism has roots in shamanism and many concepts are similar to those of Siberian and Arctic peoples. Finland stretches north beyond the Arctic Circle and the free movement of the nomadic Sami or Lapp peoples from Siberia across into Lapland in the north of Finland has ensured a free interchange of ancient religious ideas. The way of life of many of the nomadic peoples remained largely unchanged until recent decades and their rich cultural, religious and spiritual life has still to be fully understood by the West. Little is recorded about the inhabitants of what is now Finland in early times, but people called Fenni,[1] who appear to have been Lapps, are described by the Roman historian Tacitus as living a simple hunter-gatherer existence using flint arrows for weapons and having little in the way of material possessions. These people were pushed north and partly assimilated by the Finns, from about the first century CE onwards. The Finns themselves had come westward out of Asia from an area between the River Volga and the Ural mountains over a period of two to three thousand years. Their descendants are Finno-Ugric peoples – the Finns, Hungarians, Estonians and some inhabitants of adjoining areas of the former Soviet Union.

Finnish mythology was recorded in the early-nineteenth century in two works, the *Kalevala* and the *Kanteletar*. Estonia, just across the water from Finland, has similar spiritual traditions to Finland and Estonian myths were recorded in a similar collection, the *Kalevipoeg*. Although the myths were record- ed much later than the Scandinavian *Eddas* or the Welsh *Mabinogion*, the lateness is relative. Finland was Christianized late and had been Christian for about the same length of time as had Wales when its Celtic legends were first committed to paper. The *Kalevala* was compiled by Elias Löhnrot and has been the main source of Finnish mythology in the English-speaking world. *Kalevala* means the 'abode of Kaleva', an obscure giant ancestor of humankind. The poems of the *Kanteletar* are available in English, but are less well known. The *Kalevala* is oral poetry orated or sung by two poets. The orators would work in pairs, often sitting opposite each other and holding hands, and rocking backwards and forwards as they sang. This had a hypnotic effect on both orators and audience. The structure and rhythm of the *Kalevala* is distinctive, which helped the orators remember the lines. There are a number of repeated or echo lines that enable the singers to make smooth transitions from one to another and to jog one another's memories. The rhythm will be familiar to some because the nineteenth-century poet Longfellow was inspired to use it for his Native American poem *The Song of Hiawatha* (1855).

> By the shining Big Sea Water,
> stood the tent of Hiawatha...

Finland had been a province of Sweden since the twelfth century and had been annexed by Russia at the beginning of the nineteenth century. The *Kalevala* appeared at a time when the Finnish people were beginning to want to assert their independence. One of Elias Löhnrot's aims in compiling the *Kalevala* was to revive the Finnish sense of identity, which had been suppressed by the domination of its neighboring states. He was successful. The *Kalevala* stimulated a revival of the Finnish language, which had been losing out to Swedish, and Kalevala Day on February 28 is now a Finnish national holiday.

Creation

In Finnish myth, the Creatrix of the universe is the goddess Ilmater, Air-Daughter. At first, there is no land, only air and water. For many eons, Ilmater floats a Virgin Goddess above the waters, but she becomes lonely in the empty vastness. She descends onto the surface of the waters beneath her; whereupon the wind whips up foaming waves that make her pregnant. Air-Daughter is now Water-Mother. Ilmater floats pregnant in the waters for seven hundred years, or nine human lifetimes, each age being about seventy-seven years. (Finns were always long-lived.) Still, her child does not come forth. She thrashes about in all directions in her labor pains, until she prays to Ukko, god of the sky, for help. Ukko sends to Ilmater Water Mother a primeval duck, a scaup or possibly a teal. This lands on her knee, which it mistakes for a green hilltop, builds a nest and lays seven eggs. One egg is of iron; the other six are of gold. The myth of creation bursting forth from a primeval egg is an ancient idea and is found in Egypt and in the Mysteries of Orpheus and Mithras. Dion Fortune writes of the Creatrix:

...the Great Goddess is older even
than the gods that made the gods,
for men knew the function of the Mother
long before they understood the part played by the Father;
and they adored the Bird of Space that laid the
    Primordial Egg
long before they worshipped the Sun as the Fecundator.[2]

After a time, three of the eggs in the nest on Ilmater's knee hatch out. The nest begins to irritate her and she jerks her knee. The remaining eggs fall into the water and the shell of the iron egg breaks. Ilmater uses this to create our world. The upper shell forms the heavens and the lower shell the Earth. The yolk becomes the sun and the white the moon. Other parts of the egg become the stars and clouds. After nine years, Ilmater begins the second stage of creation that brings order to Earth. She raises her hand and arranges the headlands. She makes hills, islands, underwater caves, rocks and reefs. The conditions necessary for human survival exist. After another thirty summers comes the third stage. Ilmater gives birth to a son – Väinämöinen, the First Shaman and Immortal Bard. Väinämöinen's long gestation period mean that he is old before his birth and very wise. He completes his mother's work of creation and instructs the young god Sampsa Pellervoinen, Strong-Field, to sow the world.

Finnish cosmology is that of a shamanic culture with an Upperworld, Lowerworld or Underworld, and the world of everyday consciousness, the equivalent of Middle Earth. The Underworld is Tuonola or Manala. Tuonola is on the far side of the Tuoni River, on which swims the Swan of Tuonola. Swans are often symbols of the soul and of the dead in Northern European mythology. Tuonola is the home of the dead and is ruled over by Tuoni, Lord of the Dead. The concept of a World-Tree similar to the Germanic Yggdrasil is found also in Finnish and Estonian myth. Some Finno-Ugric peoples believed that the souls of the unborn congregate in the boughs of the World-Tree and that our destinies are written on its leaves. When a leaf falls, a person dies. In Asia, the Finno-Ugric peoples were tent-living nomads and their image of heaven remained that of a nomadic tent-dwelling people. Four pillars support the sky. In the center is the Pole Star, which is the nail from which the canopy of the heavens hangs.

Deities

Finland is divided into a number of provinces. The eastern region bordering Russia has different deities from those in the west, but they are similar in that they are the deities of a people of the north, reliant partly on agriculture, but mainly on hunting. The first list of Finnish deities was compiled in the mid-sixteenth century and the *Kalevala* tells us of other deities. Some of the better known include Rauni, the goddess of lightning and of winds, but also goddess of the Earth. The rowan tree is sacred to her and is said to ward off lightning. Her husband is Ukko, god of sky and thunder. Hunters would call on him to send a light snowfall when they were hunting bears, so that tracks might be found. Ukko is also called on to help with healing. The forest goddess Mielikki and the god Tapio were important in the wooded landscape of Finland. The word Mielikki comes from the word mieli, mind, and Mielikki is the intelligence or spirit of the forest. Kati-ma Koppana in *The Finnish Gods* describes Mielikki as:

> The golden summer, the forest redolent of resin, a sweet incense-like scent, the forest full of blueberries, wild mushrooms, raspberries growing on the edges and strawberries in the clearings.[3]

She is the essence that stirs the senses, intoxicates and delights. The beautiful Mielikki wears a blue cloak and is called Golden and The Foster-Mother of the Bear. She creates the bear from a ball of wool. Mielikki keeps the keys of the forest storeroom and lets the animals out when hunters invoke her and bring the correct offerings. Stones with hollowed-out centers for offerings of milk or honey are still found in Finland. Tapio is called the Old Man of the Forest, Lord of the Mound, Old Man Hill, Giver of Gifts and the Strong God. Tapio also has power over the hunt. He wears animals around his belt and if hunters invoke him correctly, he will release the animals to them. He will make sure that the hunter's aim is true and gives advice on where to find game. Tapio wears a cloak of moss and a hat of fir twigs or pine needles. He has golden ornaments on his breast. JRR Tolkien was familiar with the *Kalevala,* and Goldberry and Tom Bombadil in *Lord of the Rings* are similar to Mielikki and Tapio. The Sinipiikat or Blue Maidens work with Mielikki, each taking charge of a species of tree. Pihlajatar, for instance, is the Sinipiika and protectress of the rowan. Tapio is said to resemble an old tree and Tolkien's Ents also have some qualities similar to Tapio. As well as having power over animals, Tapio is responsible for the growth of the forest and has many attributes similar to the tree spirits.

Celebrations

Studies of Finno-Ugric peoples who practiced their Pagan religion into this century indicate that religious celebrations were performed by shamans, who could be women or men, or by the people themselves. The major feast of the Finnish seasonal cycle is Ukon Vakat or Ukko's Day held on April 4. Ukko's Day celebrates the end of spring plowing, which takes place much later in Finland than in Western Europe. This was a festive time to relax after the hard work of early spring and before beginning the sowing. The celebrations involved much beer drinking and sex. Some similar rites to those of Mediterranean Paganism are found in connection with the agricultural deities. There are traces in the *Kalevala* of a vegetation god like the Egyptian Osiris. In Finnish myth, Lemminkäinen is cut to pieces by Märkähattu, who throws his body into a river. He is resurrected when his mother finds his remains and pieces them together. She then calls on the bee to bring honey and restore him. Sampsa Pellervoinen is the god who first brought agriculture to the Finns on the instructions of Väinämöinen, the First Shaman. Sampsa's story was sung on Ukko's Day to ensure good crops. At spring, he mates with the Earth to encourage fertility in Nature. Some sources describe Sampsa as arriving for the ceremony in a cart of grain.[4] He is also described as arriving in a boat of grain,[5] which suggests that settlers from further south may have brought knowledge of agriculture and its presiding deity to Finland. At the time of the Christian festival of Palm Sunday, in West Finland there is a festival similar to Halloween. Children dress as witches and visit local houses in the morning. They carry a basket decorated with brightly-colored feathers and containing willow twigs. These are waved about in front of the house and a spell cast over them before being given to the house as a blessing. In return, the children are given sweets.

Contemporary practitioners of Finnish spirituality have developed a cycle of seasonal rites that includes Ukko's Day. These are simple and are frequently conducted outdoors, even in snowy weather. In recent years, there has been a revival of interest in traditional shamanic practices and folk witchcraft, and some merging with Wicca to produce a Finnish synthesis of the religion of Goddess and God, in which Mielikki and Tapio are the principal deities. Finnish settlers took their folk magic practices with them when they emigrated to North America. There are many people of Finnish descent in North America who take an interest in their cultural traditions, and books are now being published in English. Across the water from Finland in Estonia, a Pagan Heritage Protection Club group has been formed at the University of Tartu that performs rituals led by a shaman.

Lithuania and Latvia

The Baltic countries of Lithuania and Latvia lie to the northeast of Europe in a region formerly annexed by the Soviet Union. Their peoples have inhabited the area for about 4,000 years. There are many similarities between Lithuanian and Latvian deities which, like Germanic and Celtic cultures, are of Indo-European origin. The Indo-European origins of the people are evident, particularly in Lithuania where the language contains many words from Sanskrit, the sacred language of India, in almost pure form. The Baltic peoples were farmers and their deities reflect this. Their deities, mythology and celebrations show an earthy zest for life and love of the Earth. People thought of their deities as being like themselves. Theirs was the best of all ways of life so it was good enough for their gods. The gods are thought of as inhabiting farms on sacred hills or celestial mountains, where they work hard cultivating their gardens and fields, and setting an example to human beings. In Baltic Tradition, we can learn much about how Indo-European deities elsewhere would have been venerated.

Deities

Like other Earth Traditions, each aspect of life in Baltic Tradition has its patron deity who could be appealed to for guidance and assistance with activities in its sphere. There were deities for the major features of the cosmos – the Earth, stars, moon, sun, sky, and sea; as well as deities of more immediate concerns – the home, farm, harvest and weather, on whose beneficence people's livelihoods depended, and deities that ruled the mysteries of life – birth, death, fate and chance.

The Baltic religion has strong goddess figures. As in most Indo-European religion, the sun is feminine. In Lithuanian, she is called Saule, Sun. She is depicted as a beautiful woman with golden hair. She has silken clothing and a woolen shawl that is also of gold and wears a golden crown and gold rings. She is a beneficent and protective goddess and cares for orphans. She is invoked to help human beings who are in need, and to heal the sick. She is also a fertility goddess who blesses weddings and is a patroness of women. During the day, she drives a magnificent chariot across the sky. Her course across the sky determines the length of the day. At night, she sinks into the sea. Saule lives with her brother the moon god Menulis, or Meness in Latvian. Menulis has two horses, the Morning and Evening Stars. The sky god is called Dievas in Lithuanian or Dievs in Latvian. The word is similar in origin to the Greek sky god Zeus, the French word for God, Dieu, and the Hindi Devi. When Lithuania became

Christian, this name was adopted for the Christian god. Dievas wears a silvery-colored coat and a gray hat reminiscent of Odin. Like Odin, he visits his people who may encounter him on his travels. He helps with planting crops. Another important god is Perkunas, the Thunder God, who shares many characteristics with the Germanic Thor and Greek Zeus. Like Thor, he is patron of smithcraft, and like Zeus, he dispenses justice.

In Lithuanian mythology, the Earth goddess Zemyna or Zemynele is the Creatrix of the world. In Latvian, she is called Zemes Mate, Earth Mother. Zemyna is the daughter of Saule the Sun and Menulis the Moon, but her parents are divorced and occupy separate kingdoms. Saule can be with her daughter in the day and Menulis can see her in the evening. Zemyna is the giver and the sustainer of life and brings health and prosperity. She is also the receiver of the dead who transforms death into new life. Offerings of beer and suckling pig were made to her and her priestess presided over the harvest feast. In spring, she was honored as the pregnant mother and many rituals to Zemyna accompanied the spring planting. In Baltic Paganism, all of Nature is considered sacred and the Earth is the universal mother. Zemyna the Earth goddess is holy and must not be joked with or spat upon. The earth was often kissed before starting work or going to bed. She was also invoked when swearing oaths and when seeking justice. Gifts are given to her daily as well as at festivals. Her name means 'Earth' and Baltic poetry exalts her productiveness by calling her the bud raiser, flower giver, and blossom bringer. When Lithuania became Catholic, her feast was synthesized with the feast of the Assumption of the Virgin Mary on August 15, a date that would originally have coincided with the rye harvest.

The sea is also a goddess, who is known as Jurate in Lithuanian or Juras Mate in Latvian, the Queen of the Baltic Sea. The Baltic Sea is a major source of amber and many myths in the region associate amber with goddesses. In Lithuanian Tradition, Jurate's palace was made of amber but Perkunas destroyed it in a jealous rage when she fell in love with a human fisherman. Perkunas created a great storm, chained the fisherman to the bottom of the sea, and shattered Jurate's amber palace with lightning.

The Fates in Latvian Tradition are seen as a Triple Goddess, Laima-Dalia-Giltiné. In Lithuanian Tradition, the goddesses have remained separate entities. Laima is goddess of fate and luck. She is depicted either as a woman or a bird. As a woman, she is seen as beautiful and fair. She is clothed in fine clothes and silver brooches and wears flowers in her hair. At weddings, she grants the newlyweds a good life. She also determines the hour of death. Offerings were made to her of woven braids and woolen threads. People made offerings to Laima on rocks called Chairs of Lamia that are thought to bear the impressions of her feet. Dalia determines health and prosperity and the individual's fate. Giltiné is goddess of death and no power on Earth can prevent her coming. She is described as an old woman with a blue face and white hair. As with the Norse goddess Hel, blue is here the color of death. Giltiné travels the world unnoticed by anyone except the dying and dogs, which are psychically sensitive enough to notice her presence.

Festivals

The solstices and equinoxes are important festivals in the Baltic region and there are four other festivals that are important in the agricultural year. Water and fire are considered sacred elements as they are in Celtic and other Indo-European traditions. Both figure in seasonal rituals. The hearth fire has its own deity, the goddess Gabija who, like Vesta in Roman Tradition, was tended by women. It was important that the fire should never go out, so it was carefully dampened down at night using clean, fresh water.

Spring customs were absorbed into Easter, but remained celebrations of the renewal of the Earth and of the vigor of life. Verbas were made, which are similar to the birch twigs used to beat the skin as part of sauna treatment. Verbas are made from juniper, willow and birch twigs interwoven with flowers and colored paper to symbolize the life force. Verbas bestowed purity and were placed on graves and hung around the house. On Spring Equinox morning, everyone tried to rise as early as possible to beat other members of the family awake. This startling alternative to the alarm clock was thought to give good health. The first person awake was rewarded with a brightly-painted egg called a margutis, which symbolizes new life and the cosmic egg from which the snake Gyvate came to grant life and fertility. The Earth was also beaten to awaken the life force from its winter sleep. At Spring Equinox, there were fire ceremonies. The winter hearth was extinguished and a new fire kindled outdoors using a flint. Young people went from house to house playing music and giving out eggs as good luck presents. The Earth goddess Zemyna's twin brother is Zemepatis, the protector of farms and cattle. He is patron of the ritual of Sambariai, which was held at the end of May to mark the end of the spring sowing. Sambariai was a household rather than a community festival. The family and workers of the farm would gather in the fields with food and drink to sing sacred songs called dainos and rounds called sutartinés. Rounds are frequently used in traditional rituals to symbolize the eternal cycle of the life force. Dainos have a similar poetic rhythm to that of the *Kalevala*. Meats were eaten and a special beer brewed for the occasion. A blessing was drunk to wish everyone a good harvest and a libation of beer poured on the ground in honor of Zemepatis:

🥀 Star God, we pray thee,
on grain, fields, flowers, and animals
gracefully and brightly shine.

The festival was concluded with a procession around the fields where the long dainos were sung by one group and then repeated by another. The songs were to bless the fields, to stimulate growth, and to protect the harvest.

Midsummer was celebrated as the feast of Rasa, Dew. The early morning dew of the Solstice was believed to possess exceptional healing powers and to wash naked in this would increase one's beauty. At night, sheets were dragged across the fields so that the dew would be absorbed and could be used for healing. It was a good time to gather healing herbs, particularly St John's Wort, bilberries and yellow blossoming herbs. In Eastern Lithuania, which was influenced by Polish customs, a pole, the kupole, was set up for the festival to represent the World-Tree. The pole was topped with a three-pronged branch, which in some parts of Lithuania represented the three branches of the World-Tree that gave rise to the sun, moon and stars. The pole is similar to a Maypole and many of the Midsummer customs are similar to the May customs of warmer European countries. On Midsummer morning, women made flower crowns and men wore oak crowns. In southwestern parts of Lithuania, the tree was decorated with flower wreaths and ribbons. Unmarried girls stood with their backs to the pole, threw flower crowns over their heads, aiming to catch them on the tree's branches. The number of tries before they succeeded was taken to be the number of years until they would marry. In other parts of the Baltic, the flower crowns of the women were floated on water with the oak leaf crowns of the men. Where two crowns floated together, it was an omen of marriage. At Midsummer, the hearth fire was extinguished and a new fire lit at the aukuras or sacrificial bonfire. Couples jumped over the fire and if they did not break grip, this was thought to ensure a successful relationship. Newly-wed couples would bring the ashes of the sacrificial fire into their homes to ensure harmony in their married life. Straw dolls representing everything old were burned and burning wheels rolled downhill to greet the sun. During the night, there was a vigil to greet the dawn. People walked through the fields to greet the growing crops and then ate a special meal of cheese, eggs and beer laid on a cloth decorated with herbs.

The fall or autumn festival Velines at the end of October/beginning of November was the time for remembering the ancestors and was the equivalent of the Celtic Samhain. It was a time to visit and tend graves and leave food offerings for them. The evening was a feast for the living at which a place might be laid for the dead. The head of the family would fill an offering cup with flour and salt, which were poured on the hearth fire for the dead. A drinking horn was passed round and the dead were toasted. The eldest person present said a welcoming invocation inviting the dead to feast with the living. In Earth Traditions, there is a strong relationship between the living and the dead and they can communicate with one another. The dead can be asked for advice and will endeavor to protect and guide their descendants. In many Earth Traditions, the spirit of the deceased is not a single entity. In Baltic Tradition, when we die our energy essence, Siela, returns to the earth and enters into trees, flowers, animals and other living things that spring from the earth. The soul, Vele, lives with the ancestors and continues to visit the living. Family links are extremely important in Baltic Tradition, as they were in all rural societies. The Veles are honored at the household shrine, which in rural areas would have been in the same families for hundreds of years. In the warmer months, they inhabit trees and fields, where they protect and bless the crops. In the fall/autumn they return home.

Preparations for the traditional Winter Solstice celebrations started on the day when bears were first observed to hibernate. This, rather than the Solstice, was the first day of winter. Winter Solstice is the time when the tides of death and life turn. On the first day of winter, a cherry twig was placed in water, so that the twig would sprout roots in time for the Solstice, to symbolize the hope of new life to come. This custom is also practiced in parts of Germany, where the twig is placed in water on December 4, St Barbara's Day. Two one-day festivals – Kucios and Kaledos – marked Winter Solstice. These have now been absorbed into the Christian calendar as December 24 and 25. At Kucios, a grove of wooden and straw birds with a straw sun was made to decorate the house. Candles were lit and a table prepared for the Veles with bread, salt and Kucia bread, which traditionally consisted of thirteen different foods representing the lunar months of the region's original calendar. These included grain, peas, beans, seeds, nuts, and honey. When a new calendar was introduced with the twelve solar months that we use today, the foods were reduced to twelve. The living relatives sat at another table covered with hay and a tablecloth. The celebration began when the Evening Star appeared in the sky. To prepare for the ceremony, everyone bathed and quarrels were made up. To start the celebration, the oldest person present said a traditional invocation to the Earth Mother and broke the Kucia bread.

> Zemepatis, we thank thee
> for the good bread which Thou hast given us.
> Help us to work the fields while blessing Thee,
> that Zemynele will continue to give us Thy good gifts.[6]

The celebrants then drank beer, poured a libation for the Veles and began the feast. Foods included cranberry jelly, hot beet soup, mushroom dumplings, cabbage and fish. No meat or dairy products could be eaten. At the end of the feast, grains were poured into the hearth and a log representing the old year was burned. Kaledos, the next festival, celebrated the rebirth of Saule Motule, Mother Sun. People carried images of the Sun through the fields and towns and wished everyone prosperity. The Old Man of Kaleda, who is similar to Santa Claus, was about and people dressed in animal skins as goats, bulls, horses and cranes to process through the villages. This practice is the same as the English New Year customs that were condemned at the end of the seventh century by Theodore Archbishop of Canterbury: 'celebrating the New Year by dressing up in the guise of a bull god or stag god and sacrificing to the ancient deities.'[7] Similar customs have continued in carnival celebrations in many countries.

Baltic tradition today

Christianity came late to the Baltic States and their peoples are proud of their traditional religion and customs. Like other countries of Northern Europe, the nineteenth century was an important time of cultural revival. In Lithuania, people began to celebrate the traditional festivities for Summer Solstice led by Wilhelm Storosta, a mystic, playwright and philosopher. Their popularity grew steadily, until Lithuania was invaded by the Soviets, who saw any expression of national culture as a political threat and suppressed folk traditions. Today, traditional gatherings attract thousands of people who believe that participating in the rites of their ancestors is an important part of their cultural heritage. Most Lithuanians do not practice their Earth Tradition as a religion, but see it as an important expression of their cultural identity.

However, there is a strong core of people who are interested in environmental issues and see the revival of the region's pre-Christian Earth Tradition as important for changing human attitudes to the environment. Feminism and the importance of the Goddess have been influential, particularly through the work of Lithuanian feminist archeologist Professor Marija Gimbutas (1921–94) who spent the main part of her career at the University of California, Los Angeles. In Lithuania, the Romuva organization promotes Lithuanian Pagan heritage, and Baltic traditions and culture are practiced far from their homeland. There are millions of people of Baltic origin in the United States and Canada, with active branches of Romuva in Toronto, Chicago, and Boston.

In Latvia, Dievturi or the Followers of Dievs, is a Pagan church founded in the 1920s by Ernest Brastins. Dievturi was suppressed after Latvia was annexed by the Soviets and Ernest Brastins was executed in Astrakhan in the 1940s. Olgerts Auns became a coordinator of Dievturi for many years and a lecturer at a clandestine school of Latvian history. As the Soviet grip weakened, he instituted huge folklore festivals that became a focus for Latvian unrest. Following the collapse of the Soviet Union, Janis Tupesis, a professor at Wisconsin University and a member of Dievturi, returned to Latvia and was elected to the Parliament as a representative of the Peasant Party. He later became the Latvian ombudsman. In 1996, after a great deal of Christian opposition, Dievturi became an officially-recognized religion, with legal powers to baptize and marry its followers.

Notes

1   Tacitus, *The Germania 46*, in *The Agricola and The Germania*, page 141.

2   Fortune, *The Sea Priestess*, page 93.

3   Koppana, *The Finnish Gods*, page 18.

4   *Starlight* magazine, page 24, Helsinki, Time of Berries, 1989.

5   Koppana, *Snakefat and Knotted Threads*, page 37.

6   *Romuva USA 2*, Winter Solstice, 1990.

7   *Liber Poenitentialis* of Theodore Archbishop of Canterbury, quoted in Hutton, *The Pagan Religion of the Ancient British Isles*, page 329.

Native American Traditions[1]

Native North American traditions are as many and even more varied than those of Europe, but like European Earth Traditions there are some common beliefs. Native American and European Traditions share spirituality that comes from living in close relationship to the natural world. The landscape – rocks, trees, rivers, lakes, sky, and stars – are not dead matter but are inhabited by living spirits with whom it is important that humankind lives in harmony. Often there is a vision in Native American sacred histories of a time when humans and animals lived in harmony, but human activity broke the sacred bonds. The sacred history of the Tinde, who are generally known as the Apache, speaks of the time when animals and trees could communicate with one another. This companionship was destroyed when human beings learned to use fire. Trees became resources to exploit and the harmony was broken.

As we have seen with European Traditions, different spiritual outlooks arise from living in different climates and terrain with different food sources. The creation stories of a people dependent mainly on hunting will be different from those of agriculturalists. In the north, the Subarctic region that stretches from Alaska in the west, eastwards to Labrador and Maine, is the homeland of Native American peoples of the Athabascan and Algonkian language groups, whose traditional lifestyle was as fishers and hunters. In the northwest coastal region, the relationship between hunter and hunted is important. Sacred histories describe how a relationship is created whereby animals will sacrifice themselves in order that people may live, but in return people must treat the animals with honor and respect. If people fail to do so, the animal spirit guardians will cease to allow the hunt to be successful. In the Northeast Woodlands, primarily hunting economies, there was an emphasis on the spiritual power within the land. Power, Manitou, was inherent in all of Nature – animals, plants, natural features of the landscape, and people.

❧   Power lay at the center of all concerns. Nothing was more important for life than power. Power meant the ability to live, to grow crops, to woo lovers, to slay animals, to defeat enemies. More esoterically, power meant the ability to heal the sick, to converse with animals, or to visit 'God'. But most fundamentally, power meant the ability of an individual to influence other people and other beings. Power meant successful interaction.[2]

Divine energy was immanent within Nature, and the qualitative difference encouraged by a Christian worldview between humans and animals, whereby humans are persons and animals are not, whereby humans can suffer and have feelings and animals do not, whereby animals are a resource to be used as humans wished, was absent in Native American Traditions. A major stumbling block in trying to convert Native Americans to Christianity was that people could not grasp the peculiar idea that animals did not have souls.

The Southeast Woodlands were home to peoples living from agriculture and building permanent settlements. Their sacred history teaches that the world is an island floating in the primeval waters. The peoples of the Great Plains, which include the Arapaho, Cheyenne, Crow, Dakota and Lakota, depended on hunting rather than agriculture. Trickster figures who mediate between the Divine and human worlds are an important part of Plains Tradition, as is Wakan Tanka, the Great Spirit, or Great Mystery. Myths associated with animals of the hunt, such as White Buffalo Calf Woman, and ceremonies associated with the sacred pipe and the sun are important. In California in the Great Basin region, shamanism was important. In the Southwest, settled pueblo culture emerged, which was dependent on agriculture, but the region is also home to the Navajo sheep herders.

Creation

Native American creation stories are not only a spiritual rationale to explain the cosmos in which people find themselves. They are also oral history. Within the stories are accounts of ecological and historical events. From the Hopi and the Tinde or Apache of the Southwest, for instance, are stories of a time when the world was flooded. Millions of years ago, Arizona was covered by sea and shells are still found there. The stories may be a way that incoming peoples explained regional geology and the incongruous presence of seashells so far inland, or a flood may have been something that occurred in the early history of peoples in the region.

Each Native American people has its own creation history that accounts for the people's existence and that of the world around them. Outsiders often call these stories creation myths, but the use of the word 'myth' can be a sensitive issue. White people have often subtly denigrated Native American history as myth, in contrast to their history that is historical fact. Christian missionaries called Native American stories of spiritual origins myth and taught that their Garden of Eden story was truth. Native Americans often prefer their stories of creation to be called sacred history. All sacred histories of the origins of the cosmos, from European, Native American, Biblical, Islamic, or any other tradition, are symbolic representations of cosmic realities. They represent spiritual and scientific truths in the language of image, symbol, and allegory. Science speaks to the left brain and spiritual tradition to the right. Each has its own valued place in the scheme of things.

In the sacred history of the Hopi pueblo dwellers of the Southwest, people emerged into this world, the surface world, from beneath the surface of the Earth at a particular geographical spot – the spectacular Grand Canyon in northern Arizona. The progression to the surface world was difficult. Below the surface world were three cave worlds. Life began in the lowest of these. Human beings were able to function there but eventually the world became overcrowded and unpleasant. Two enterprising brothers decided that something must be done and broke through to the next level, the second cave world. All was well here for a while, until that too became unpleasant and overcrowded and a new migration had to take place. People broke through the Earth's crust to her surface, but there was no light. People and animals – spider, vulture, swallow, coyote and locust – united to create light, but the new light revealed that this world was not big enough either. There was only a small area that was not covered by water. The two brothers and the vulture created channels to drain the water into rivers and streams, leaving the land to dry out. Order was established and settlement could begin.

Hopi sacred history hints at migrations due to expanding populations and perhaps a time of flood. It also helps people to understand other important human questions about life and death. The history tells us that when the flooded land dried out, tracks were revealed – the tracks of Death. People followed the tracks to the east and caught up with Death, but this exposed them to Death who took his first victim, the beautiful young daughter of a holy man who was murdered by a girl who was jealous of her. The jealous girl was tried and sentenced to death, but the girl was clever and persuaded her accusers to look into a hole in the ground. The hole led back to the cave world, from which they came. The murdered girl was not dead, but walking in a beautiful land of flowers, everlasting summer and fruitfulness. She had no desire to return to the difficult surface world. The sacred history reassures people that however difficult life is on the surface world, there is something to look forward to – a beautiful Otherworld of everlasting life. This is only one of hundreds of examples of Native American sacred histories that explain the cosmology of the world, the arrival of human beings to populate it, and the phenomena that we all must face, such as death.

A different type of creation story comes from the Northwest. The Salish peoples of British Columbia tell us that the Great Spirit made the Earth from the body of an old woman who lies spread out on her back. This Earth Goddess figure is Okanagon, the Mother of Everyone. Her hair creates trees and grasses, her flesh creates soil, wind is her breath, rocks her bones. When she is cold, winter comes, and when she is hot, it is summer. When she moves, there is an earthquake.

Creation myths known as Earth Diver myths are found among many Native American peoples, including the Athabascan-speaking peoples of the Subarctic, peoples of the Great Plains, and among Iroquois peoples of the Northeast. In Iroquoian Tradition, in the beginning there was only sea and sky. Human beings dwelt in the sky world in which grew a sacred tree. The sky chief's wife dreamed that the sacred tree was uprooted, leaving a gaping hole, which she fell down. Animals played a helpful role. Two swans caught her as she fell but could not find anywhere to put her. Different birds and animals dived down to the ocean bed attempting to retrieve soil to make land, but all failed except for the muskrat. The muskrat almost died in the attempt but did manage to retrieve a small amount of soil. A turtle offered to let the muskrat put the soil on its back. This became our world – Turtle Island. Creation stories often reflect property-owning and inheritance practices. Where inheritance is matrilinear and family wealth is passed from mother to daughter, a woman or goddess is usually the Creatrix of the world. Where property is passed down the male line, then the Creator is male. Among Iroquoian peoples, women owned the homes and held ceremonial precedence.

White Buffalo Calf Woman

Powerful supernatural female figures play important roles in Native American spirituality. They are often teachers, bringing to human beings secrets and essential knowledge. Lakota Tradition, for instance, is centered on the seven sacred ceremonies brought to the people by Ptesan-Wi, White Buffalo Calf Woman. Different storytellers tell slightly different versions of her story, but the essential elements are the same. Changing Woman appeared first to two warriors who were hunting buffalo on the sacred Black Hills of Dakota. On sacred ground humans and the spirit world can meet and the unexpected is sure to occur. Out of the north appeared a white buffalo calf, which started walking towards them. White animals are often albinos. They are unusual, unexpected and strange, so are frequently associated with the supernatural. This supernatural animal changed into a beautiful young girl. Some people know instinctively what to do in such circumstances. One warrior treated the maiden with reverence. He knelt and began to pray. The warriors had been away from home for a long time and the sight of the beautiful maiden filled the other warrior with lust. He was foolish enough to stretch out his hand to touch her. The maiden promptly destroyed him. A black cloud descended and stripped his flesh from his bones, leaving only a skeleton. The maiden told the pious warrior to go home to his people to tell them that she would come to them in four days bringing a sacred bundle. On the fourth day, when the warrior had gathered the elders in a circle, White Buffalo Calf Woman descended from a cloud singing a sacred song. She brought a sacred medicine bundle containing symbolic power objects, one of which was a sacred red tobacco pipe, and she spent four days teaching people its meaning. She filled the pipe with red willow bark tobacco and walked around the lodge four times sunwise to represent the sacred hoop, the never-ending circle. She taught them the pipe-filling song and how to offer the pipe to Grandfather Sky, to Grandmother Earth, and then to the four directions of the universe. She told them:

With this Holy Pipe,
you will walk like a living prayer.
With your feet resting upon the earth,
and the pipe stem reaching into the sky,
your body forms a living bridge
between the Sacred Beneath and the Sacred Above.
Wakan Tanka smiles upon us because now we are as one;
earth, sky, all living things –
the two-legged, four-legged, the winged ones,
the trees, and the grasses.
Together with people they are all related, one family.
The pipe holds them together.[3]

White Buffalo Calf Woman also taught the people the seven sacred ceremonies – the Sweat Lodge, the Vision Quest, Ghost Keeping, the Sun Dance, Making Relatives (adoption), the Puberty Ceremony, and Throwing the Ball. White Buffalo Calf Woman departed, but like many sacred figures, she left her people with the promise of return.

❧ Behold this pipe!
Remember it is sacred.
Treat it as such;
for it will take you to the end of days.
Remember, in me there are four ages.
I am leaving,
but I will look back on your people in every age,
and in the end,
I will return.[4]

The sacred pipe still exists and is kept by the Keeper of the Sacred Pipe, a member of the Looking Horse family at the Cheyenne River Reservation in South Dakota. The birth of a white buffalo calf is considered an important omen. Some people consider that we are now in the time of the White Buffalo, following the birth of a white buffalo calf named Miracle on the Wisconsin farm of Dave and Valerie Heider on August 20, 1994. In the year following Miracle's birth, over 65,000 people came to see her.

Changing Woman

Among the Navajo or Diné of the Southwest, one of the most important deities is Estsanatlehi or Changing Woman, who created human beings. Changing Woman represents the ever-changing circle of the seasons. She is birth (spring), fertility (summer), ageing and wisdom (fall/autumn), dying (winter) and is reborn again in the spring. First Man and First Woman planned the birth of Changing Woman. First Man raised his medicine bundle towards the sacred mountain of Gobernador Knob, and from this powerful act, Changing Woman was born. Changing Woman grew quickly, reaching puberty in four days, a number sacred to the Navajo. Her puberty was celebrated by a rite of passage – the first-ever puberty ceremony. Talking God officiated at the ceremony and the Holy People attended. In Navajo Tradition, the natural and supernatural are closely interconnected and for all to be well, people must create harmonious relationships with the spirit world of the Holy People. First Woman dressed Changing Woman in a woven white dress and adorned her with jewels of turquoise, coral, jet and obsidian. She was blessed with pollen collected at dawn and at twilight. She was bathed in dew and instructed to run towards the dawn as far as she could and to return. She did this for four nights. During the four intervening days, she planned the future of the earth. Songs that were sung for Changing Woman are still used in puberty ceremonies today.

> The child of the west – the sounds have returned,
> her turquoise shoes – the sounds have returned,
> her turquoise leggings – the sounds have returned,
> her turquoise clothes – the sounds have returned.
> A perfect turquoise has been placed on her head – the
>   sounds have returned.
> Her turquoise head plume – the sounds have returned,
> now at its tip there are small blue hen birds –
> truly beautiful, it is shining at its tip – the sounds
>   have returned.
> They call as they are playing – their voices are beautiful,
> the sounds have returned.[5]

At Changing Woman's next menstruation, another ceremony was held. This was similar to the first, but it was decreed that no menstruating woman may be present at any ceremonial, a taboo common to many Native American peoples. The order of the ceremony of the Blessing Way, one of the major ceremonies of Navajo Tradition, was established.

After the ceremonies, Changing Woman set off on a trail. She met a stranger who was so dazzling she had to look away. This happened three times before Changing Woman had sex with the mysterious stranger, who was the sun's inner core. She bathed and after nine days, representing the nine months of gestation, she gave birth to twins – Monster Slayer and Born for Water. In four days, the twins grew to adulthood and Changing Woman asked First Man for his sacred medicine bundle. She conducted a ceremony over the mating of the corn, the first marriage, and followed the sun to the west. Here she grew lonely and created the Navajo people from pieces of skin rubbed from different parts of her body. She created four couples – the ancestors of the Navajo nation. She also created teachings for the people. She taught the Blessing Way ceremony to two children of Rock Crystal Talking God who were brought to her by means of a rainbow and a sunbeam. They in turn taught it to the people. When the ceremony had been learned, the two children and the Holy People left the ceremony. The Holy People say that they would never be seen again, but promised that their presence would always be there in the sound of the wind, in the feathers of an eagle, in the growing of the corn, and in the other aspects of Nature dear to the people who dwell on the surface of the earth.

Dreams

Dreams are an important source of knowledge in Native American Traditions. Some peoples have developed elaborate rituals to interpret them. The Mojave of the Southwest and Iroquois of the Northeast believe that dreams can channel power to people from the spirit world. Dreams are useful sources of information containing prophecies and warnings. When we dream, we process information that we have not had time to attend to during the day. We may not even be consciously aware of the impressions that we have received that give rise to dreams. This can be information about our own lives, about other people we have met during the course of the day, or of the atmosphere amongst a group of people. In societies where people live close to Nature, they will notice natural phenomena that are portents of weather to come. We register subliminally all kinds of information about animal activity, plant growth and weather patterns that can help us predict weather patterns.

Amongst the Iroquoian speakers of central New York State and the Ohio Valley, which included the Seneca, Oneida, and Mohawk, dreams were treated as important sources of information. The creation of the Iroquois confederation of nations was foretold by a dream. At the end of the fourteenth century, an Iroquois woman dreamed that her daughter was about to give birth to a son who would bring good tidings of peace and power to his people from the chief of the sky gods. The baby was named De-ka-nah-wi-da. In adult life, he created the league of Iroquois Nations, a model of co-operation between peoples that inspired Thomas Jefferson and Benjamin Franklin when creating the United States as a federal nation. The Life of Chief Ely Samuel Parker (1828–95), a Unionist leader in the Civil War, was also foretold by a dream. His mother dreamed of a broken rainbow that stretched from the home of the Indian agent Erastus Granger in Buffalo to her reservation. She sought help from a Seneca dream interpreter and was told that she would bear a son who would be a peacemaker. He would be a white man as well as an Indian. He would be a wise and respected warrior for the palefaces, but he would never desert his own people. In 1852, the women, the clan mothers, chose Ely Parker as chief. Later he drafted the terms of surrender that ended the Civil War. General Lee described him as 'one real American'. He was the first Native American to hold federal office.

Dreams were an important source of guidance about daily life for the Iroquois nations and helped them to make decisions about fishing, hunting, war, dancing, marriage, and other significant life events. A war party would turn back if one of its members dreamed of failure. Ignoring dreams was dangerous and foolhardy. Dreams were powerful. They could cure physical and psychological disease. Psychological illness was caused by unconscious desires that dreams could reveal. These desires were believed to come from the secret longings of the soul that might sometimes be at odds with conscious intentions. Amongst the Chippewa, dream catchers were used to foster dreams. These webs of cotton on wooden frames are often decorated with beads and feathers. They can trap nightmares while letting good dreams through.

Ceremonies

Rituals and ceremonies are the basis of Native American spiritual practice and are derived from sacred histories. Native American ceremonial life involves rites of passage, and special ceremonies such as the Sun Dance of the Plains peoples and ceremonies of purification involving the sweat lodge. Rites of passage are important in Native American spirituality to mark the transition from one stage to the next in life's journey. Girls celebrate puberty rites at first menses and young boys who are approaching puberty undertake a vision quest. A boy goes alone into the wilderness to fast and meditate in order to receive a guardian spirit who will be close and supportive to him throughout his life's journey and to have a vision that will guide his development and show him his life's path. A successful vision quest bestows spiritual power. Vision quests are also undertaken by men and women at other important life transitions. They are a time to step aside from everyday tasks and be alone with Nature to hear the voice of the spirit world. Vision quests can imbue an individual with spiritual power. Power can also come through participating in the Sun Dance. Sacred objects can bestow power. Among the Plains and Southwestern peoples, circular medicine shields made with the help of a holy person or shaman bring spiritual power.

As well as fulfilling healing and social needs, ceremonies were essential to survival. Hunting ceremonies and agricultural ceremonies for planting and harvesting were part of a rhythm of life that enabled people to live in balance with the food resources around them. Hunting ceremonies encouraged wise use and conservation of animal resources. This is not to say that Native Americans were ecological saints, no human beings are, but the emphasis on the relationship between animals, people and land enabled ways of life to survive for thousands of years. Corn or maize was a particularly important crop and its creation is often attributed to women. The Penobscot, an East-coast Algonkian people, teach that corn first grew from the barren earth when First Mother begged her husband to kill her so that her body might be used to fertilize the Earth. Cherokee Tradition teaches that Selu or Corn, the first woman, gave birth to the first corn by rubbing her stomach and to green beans by rubbing either her breasts or armpits. Selu is commemorated in the Green Corn ceremony that celebrates the first harvested plants of the year, in which young women carrying baskets represent her. In the Southwest, the Zuni and other Pueblo peoples teach that corn was brought by the Six Corn Maidens, and Blue Corn Girl and Yellow Corn Girl are an important part of the Hopi Winter Solstice ceremony.

Purification ceremonies are important before major events and for regular spiritual renewal. Sweat lodges are used from the Arctic to Mexico to cleanse body and spirit. Sweat lodges are similar to the saunas found in Finland and elsewhere in the far north of Europe. Saunas are usually thought of more as leisure or health facilities, but their original purpose was bodily and spiritual purification. Sweat lodges can be small temporary structures to accommodate a few individuals or larger communal structures. In some Pacific Coast areas and amongst the Pueblo peoples of the Southwest, sweat lodges are large communal structures of logs and bark with earth to seal the gaps, built directly over the firepit. Nomadic peoples use bendable branches such as willow, arched to form a hemisphere and covered with blankets or skins. When rocks are used to heat the sweat lodge, near the door or in the center is a depression for the rocks, which are heated outside in a fire and brought in on forked sticks. Amongst many peoples, sweat lodges were used only by men and became in effect men's clubs. Where women used sweat lodges, women and men used the lodges separately.

Navajo ceremonies

As well as ceremonies that mark rites of passage, special ceremonies are held for healing and to prepare people for important tasks. In the Navajo nation, the largest Native American land holding in the United States, the complex ceremonies of the

Navajo people are performed regularly and healing ceremonies are used in conjunction with Western medicine. Holy men or singers conduct ceremonies. They are highly-trained professionals who serve an apprenticeship of up to seven years. The ceremonies are lengthy, involving special symbols and equipment, singing chants, dances, and the construction of sand-paintings for each stage of the ceremony. One ceremony involves 576 songs and 600–1000 different paintings. Most singers therefore specialize in two or three ceremonies.

Seven of the ceremonies are performed regularly, the best-known being the Blessingway, one of the central ceremonies of the Navajo way of life, which is known as the beautiful rainbow. The Blessingway recounts the Navajo creation story, which is similar to that of the Hopi, and is performed on important occasions, such as when a woman is to give birth or when a young man is to go on a quest or journey, attend university, or enter the armed forces. Enemyway is a protection following contact with non-Navajos and serves to exorcize ghosts, violence and ugliness. It derives from ceremonies to protect warriors from the spirits of those they had killed. Chantways focus on healing. Every Chantway ends with at least one song from the Blessingway to seal its intent. When sickness occurs and a Chantway is needed, a diviner enters into trance and identifies the source of the problem and the correct ritual for cure. The ritual itself is performed by a singer. Friends and relatives are gathered for the ceremony. This can be expensive for the immediate kin, who must pay the singer and entertain guests for ceremonies that can last up to nine days. Medicinal plants may be used in the rite as part of the healing process, boosted by the love and support of those attending the ceremony.

The four directions

The circle guarded by the four quarters, the circle-cross, appears in the symbolism of many peoples from Native Americans to Celts. The symbol appears in the pipe ceremony of the Lakota and in the Sun Dance, where a large cottonwood tree is erected at the center of a circle and adorned with six colors representing the four directions plus above and below. The circle and four directions symbolism patterns the sand-paintings of the Navajo, where the colors of the four directions are white for dawn and the east, blue for midday sky and the south, yellow for evening twilight and the west, and black for night and the north. In Navajo cosmology, the Earth is a landmass floating in a vast ocean beneath a dome. The sacred mountains, Blanca Peak in the east, Mount Taylor in the south, the San Francisco Peaks in the West and Hesperus Peak in the north, are the four corner posts of the universe that support the sky, the roof of this world. In the center is Huerfano Mountain representing the round roofed home or hooghan, known as the female hooghan, and Gobernador Knob, to the east of center, represents the conical type of home known as the male hooghan.

The circle and four directions are a symbol of wholeness that represents the totality of creation. When we make this sacred symbol, we are aligning ourselves to wholeness. This wholeness reconciles all those things that normally we cannot accept or understand and we find a new balance. The circle and four directions are therefore associated with healing. In his memoirs, the famous Oglala Lakota holy man and visionary Black Elk described the importance of the circle. The indwelling Divine presence that he calls 'the Power of the World' works in circles. When the Lakota were strong and a happy people, the flowering tree was the living center and the four quarters nourished it. The east brings peace and light, the south warmth, the west rain, and the north the cold and mighty wind. Black Elk points out that everything important in the universe is a circle – Earth, Moon, and stars. The strongest wind whirls in circles, birds build their nests in circles, the seasons are a cycle.

Native American spirituality today

Despite the destructiveness of its encounter with Western culture, Native American spirituality retains its rich diversity. Many Native Americans, especially in the southwest, have retained their original traditions more or less intact. Some Native American families have been Christians for several generations. Others combine both traditional and Christian elements. From the 1970s activist years on, a strong Pan-Indian movement has led to the sharing of ideas, beliefs and ceremonies between different Native American peoples. Sharing is fostered by a regular summer round of pow-wows. Pow-wow derives from an Algonkian word pauau, meaning a gathering of people. At modern pow-wows, Native Americans of different peoples gather for ceremonies, dance competitions, teaching, trading, socializing and giveaway ceremonies to honor those who have helped families or their communities. The Pan-Indian movement has also helped gather support for important issues such as land rights and has raised the profile of these issues with other Americans.

The Native American Church is a Pan-Indian Church that began in Mexico and spread across North America to the Plains. The Church discourages drinking alcohol and uses as its sacrament the sacred substance of the peoples of the Southwest – the peyote cactus, which has been used for spiritual vision for about 10,000 years. Rituals incorporate traditional features such as bone whistles and rattles. They are held in tipis and led by peyote chiefs or roadmen. The Church wishes to keep what it values of Christianity, while incorporating people's native traditions. The modern peyote ritual consists of four parts: praying, singing, eating peyote, and quietly meditating.

Sacred sites are of great importance in Native American spirituality, which is closely bound up with the land. Some sacred places are the sites of creation stories. Others relate to significant historical events in the histories of their people. Others are burial sites, areas where sacred plants or other natural materials are available, or places with ancient structures, carvings or paintings of sacred significance. For many peoples, the continued celebration of sacred rites at these sites is essential to the continuity of their Tradition. Unfortunately, the demands of a materialist society often conflict with those of traditional practice. Many sites are in areas with rich mineral and logging resources. Retaining and regaining control of these sacred sites requires ongoing campaigning by Native peoples and those who share their concerns. Sacred objects and burial remains are also important and many successful campaigns have been directed to return these to their rightful owners.

Native Americans and other Traditions

The great interest aroused by Native American spirituality in recent years among non-Native Americans can be an unwelcome intrusion for many Native Americans, who accuse non-Native Americans of being 'wannabe Indians' who should be finding their own sources of spirituality rather than plundering other peoples'. First whites attempted to destroy their culture; now they want to appropriate it to supply what is missing in their own. Teachers of sacred ceremonies in New Age workshops have been condemned. The work of the Cheyenne teacher Hyemeyohsts (Wolf) Storm and his book *Seven Arrows* and its follow up *Lightningbolt,* and the work of Sun Bear of the Chippewa, who died in 1996, popularized Native American sacred ceremony in diluted forms that could be delivered in weekend workshops. The innovations were helpful in that they show the universality of spiritual practices and symbols and they can be a bridge between people of different ethnicity and traditions. They were less helpful if people mistook them for the original. Hyemeyohsts Storm's publication of *Seven*

Arrows inspired many thousands of people, but it caused great controversy about the rights of Native American authors to represent and interpret tribal religion without tribal authorization. Sun Bear's Bear Tribe Medicine Society and its Medicine Wheel gatherings incorporate elements of Ojibwa and Plains Indian Traditions. Medicine Wheels are created by gathering rocks to create sacred circles in which seven sacred directions are honored. Pipe ceremonies draw the group together, as do drumming and chanting, and sweat lodges are held for purification. The gatherings build a sense of relationship with others, spiritual awakening, and awareness of the Earth and the dangers facing our environment. Teachers such as Sun Bear offer glimpses of their own traditions in order to encourage others to find similar practices within their own cultures. However, things moved on a stage further, when non-Native Americans appointed themselves shamans and transmitters of Native American Traditions and began making a living by doing their own imitations of the Native American New Age offerings – for a fee. Not surprisingly, many Native Americans became incensed at what they saw as exploitation of their culture.

For those of Native American ancestry, a return to the ways of their ancestors can be deeply empowering. For those of us who admire Native American Traditions and see living Earth Traditions that have retained what long-Christianized cultures have lost, there is much to observe and learn, turning then inwards to see how we can find what we have learned within our own Traditions. Native American practices have inspired many people in North America who are seeking to create Earth Traditions that are meaningful in the twenty-first century. At the large summer gatherings that have evolved over the past 30 years in the neo-Pagan community, drumming, dancing and chanting have been incorporated into large ceremonies to bring people together in communal worship. Gatherings often build sweat lodges and the pages of the neo-Pagan press are full of announcements of rites of passage for sons and daughters. Other practices have spread into the general New Age community. Purifying sacred space by burning sage is common and dream catchers abound. For a while gatherings began using sacred chants drawn from the Sun Dance, which caused great offence to holders of real Sun Dance ceremonies, but requests from Native American leaders to stop the practice were respected and a mutual respect between traditions is now fostering positive contacts.

Notes

1   Some Native Americans prefer the term 'Indians'. Others see this term as derogatory and based on Christopher Columbus' mistaken idea that when he sailed west he had discovered India.

2   Dowd *A Spirited Resistance: The North American Indian Struggle for Unity 1745–1815*, page 3.

3   Quoted in Leeming and Page, *The Mythology of Native North America*, page 37.

4   Zimmerman and Molyneaux, *Native North America*, page 104.

5   Based on Page and Page, *Navajo*, pages 152–3.

African Roots

In Africa, the Earth Traditions were discouraged, denigrated and sometimes suppressed during the colonial era, but they have revived since countries gained their independence and they have become part of the main school curriculum. In Africa, practitioners of traditional religions often teach that there is one Divine spirit and that all other deities are aspects of this, but it is unclear whether this was people's original belief, or whether the influence of Islam and Christianity and denigration of polytheism have encouraged people to adopt what is sometimes called modified monotheism. The Afro-Caribbean Traditions of Voudon, Santeria, Shango, Cumina, Kele, Umbanda and Candomblé that evolved in the Caribbean and Meso and South America with the slave trade are sometimes called the African diaspora religions. The victims of the slave trade were mainly from West and Central Africa, the most accessible regions, from which it was easiest for slave traders to transport people. It is their spiritual traditions that have given birth to the Afro-Caribbean Traditions that are practiced today. Afro-Caribbean Traditions venerate deities from different West African peoples, but there are recognizable similarities between the deities of different pantheons. The deity names became slightly different when the first languages of Africans in the New World became French, English, Spanish or Portuguese, but they can be easily traced back to their African counterparts.

The word Voudon or Voodoo means spirit and comes from the Dahomey or Fon people from west of the Yoruba area of southwestern Nigeria, which is now within the borders of Benin and parts of Togo. Voudon is practiced in the French-speaking Caribbean, particularly in Haiti, and in the United States in New Orleans and in cities where there are large concentrations of Haitian immigrants, such as New York, Chicago, and Los Angeles. Around 15 percent of people in New Orleans practice Voudon. One of the most famous New Orleans Voudon practitioners was Marie Laveau (1794–1881), who was known as Queen of Voodoo. She was a free woman of African, Indian, French, and Spanish descent, who lived all her life in New Orleans, remained a devout Catholic who attended mass every day and had fifteen children, one of whom, her daughter Marie Philomene Laveau Glapion, followed in her footsteps to be a formidable Voudon practitioner. People regularly leave offerings at Marie Laveau's tomb and she is honored in the New Orleans Voodoo Museum on the corner of Dumaine and Bourbon where blue candles are burned for her.

France's colonial links with West Africa and her overseas territories in the Caribbean have brought immigrants to Paris and other large French cities who have brought Voudon with them. Voudon practitioners advertise in French newspapers and esoteric magazines. Voudon has suffered from negative media images of zombies, human sacrifice and cannibalism propagated by Hollywood, books and media stories, particularly during the period 1915–34 when the United States government wanted to justify its occupation of Haiti. The stories blur the important distinction between Voudon priests and priestesses and caplatas or bokors who engage in sorcery.

Spanish Catholic slave-owners mocked their slaves' apparent devotion to saints and called their practice Santeria, Way of the Saints, believing it to be Catholic. Today, Santeria is practiced in the Spanish-speaking Caribbean, particularly Cuba. Following the takeover of Cuba by Castro in 1959 and a large outflow of migrants and refugees, Santeria spread to other Spanish-speaking countries such as Mexico, Venezuela, Puerto Rico and the Dominican Republic. Cuban migrants brought Santeria to the United States, settling in Miami, New York, Newark, Savannah, Chicago, Indianapolis and San Francisco. There are also Santeria centers in Washington DC. Practices have evolved to meet modern realities. Santeria practitioners are accomplished herbalists and in the past they would have gathered herbs used in medicines and potions from their gardens and the surrounding area. Today, many rely on botanicas, specialist stores selling herbs and animal parts for use in potions, together with other artifacts and regalia including candles, ceremonial pots, potions, charms, and musical instruments. There are now half a dozen or more Santeria botanicas in Washington DC. Santeria groups vary in the extent to which they are keen to keep their connections with Catholicism or to return to their African roots and rid themselves of the Catholic overlay. Groups that wish to re-Africanize the Tradition often reject the term Santeria as derogatory and prefer to call their religion La Regla Lucumi, or La Regla de Ocha in Spanish, or Orisha Tradition in English, rather than the pejorative term given to it by slave owners. Lucumi or Lukumi is a Cuban term for the Yoruba people.

People with Spanish rather than African ancestry tend to emphasize the Catholic saints and the Virgin of Guadeloupe more than African deities. In Cuba, parish priests in both Catholic and Protestant churches often allow Santeria practitioners to take part in services and encourage people to maintain their links with Christianity as well as practicing their native tradition. Opposing Santeria and the other Afro-Caribbean Traditions can be a lost cause even if churches would prefer to wean their congregations away from them. Where priests condemn their traditions, people usually ignore their statements as the kind of thing priests are expected to say rather than seriously believing they have to give up one tradition for the other. In Puerto Rico, for instance, it is expected that those who wish to become a santero or santera will have first been baptized as Catholic.

Shango is the Orisha Tradition of the Caribbean Islands of Trinidad and Tobago. These were originally Spanish colonies that later passed to the British. Trinidad has a complex cultural heritage and multi-cultural population which has absorbed migrants from Hindu and Muslim India. Unlike the other Afro-Caribbean Traditions, Shango also contains elements of Hinduism and Jewish Kabbalah. Shango (spelled Xango in Portuguese) is also practiced in northern Brazil, in Recife. Shango venerates primarily the Yoruba deity Chango. Shango has spread to Britain and the United States. In London and elsewhere in England, some specialist stores serve the needs of Shango practitioners and other traditions from the English-speaking Caribbean whose descendants have migrated to Britain. In all communities where Afro-Caribbean Traditions are practiced, the help of priests and healers is frequently sought to provide spiritual protection, cure sickness, and deal with other life crises.

Deities

Different Afro-Caribbean Traditions in different localities evolved their own practices and although they draw on deities that have the same origins, over time different emphases and interpretations arose, so no group will be exactly the same as another. All the Afro-Caribbean Traditions are based on West African religions, but they are often practiced under a Catholic veneer. Slaves were forbidden to practice their own religions and were forced to practice Christianity. Unwilling to abandon their own deities, the slaves fused their images and attributes with those of Catholic saints. Partly, this was due to expediency and partly it was an attempt to synthesize and rationalize two different cultures. Christianity was taught to illiterate slaves through pictures. We understand what we do not know by relating it to what we know. When shown a picture of a

Catholic saint, the likelihood that work-weary slaves would grasp the subtle difference between a saint and deity was slim. The peasants of Europe never had. The slaves accepted the saints as the white version of their own gods, fused their characteristics with African deities, and happily paid homage to beings that were at least vaguely familiar and possibly well disposed towards them.

In Voudon, the deities are known as loas, a word that means mystery in Dahomey. They are also known by the French titles of les mystères or les invisibles. The loas live 'en bas de l'eau', at the bottom of the ocean, in a place called Guinée or Guinea, the Guinea Coast, that represents the Africa that the slaves had been forced to leave behind. Les morts, the ancestral dead, live with the loas in Guinea. When the loas comes to visit their worshippers, they come by way of the chemin de l'eau, the water road. In Voudon, there is a supreme deity Odumaré, also known as Grand Mer, who is far removed from everyday life, but the loas are there to deal with everyday issues. Offerings are made to different loas to ensure success in matters of love, happiness, health, family, work and harvest. The serpent god Damballah is father of the loas. He governs the waters of the Earth and in Voudon became associated with St Patrick. Damballah's wife is the rainbow, Aida-Wedo. Like many other traditions, rainbows are viewed as sacred and magical and a bridge between the Divine and human worlds. Damballah and Aida-Wedo are teachers to humankind, showing them how to procreate and how to perform the necessary sacrifices to invoke the gods.

The beautiful water goddess Erzulie is considered a manifestation of Aida-Wedo. Erzulie is goddess of love, and was known as Whydah to the Dahomey people and Oshun to Nigerians. In the New World, she became associated with the Virgin Mary. Erzulie likes to be offered jewelry, mirrors, and honey, which should be tasted before being offered to show that it is not poisoned. She also likes offerings of white chickens. Yamama is the goddess of the sea and a fertility goddess and likes offerings of ducks or turtles. Her power can be found in rocks and shells from the ocean. She is foster mother of the god Chango, who is god of luck, justice, thunder and lightning. Chango's symbol is a lightning bolt and his power is found in meteorites – rocks that have descended to Earth from the heavens. Papa Legba, who is also known as Esu or Elegua, Guardian of the Underworld, when fused with Christian Tradition became St Peter, keeper of the Gates of Heaven. He can be approached to open the door to the other loas and will say if it is appropriate to address them.

Baron Samedi is one of the guedes, spirits of death and sexuality. Baron Samedi takes his name from the French for Saturday – Saturn's day – and his depiction and association with death have elements of the dour Saturn. He is shown wearing dark glasses and in a black tailcoat and tall hat, like an old-fashioned funeral attendant. People possessed by Baron Samedi break normal social boundaries by telling lewd jokes, making obscene gestures, and consuming enormous quantities of food and alcohol. Haiti's former dictator François Duvalier, known as Papa Doc, adopted Baron Samedi's imagery for his public persona and used it to terrify his people into submission by convincing them that he was a powerful Voudon practitioner.

In Santeria, the supreme deity and creator of the universe is Olorun, the 'owner of heaven' and leader of the lesser gods, the orishas. Olorun, like Brahma in Hindu Tradition, is rarely actively worshipped and has neither priesthood nor shrine. The god Obatala (also known as Orishala or Orisa-nla) and his wife Odudua often assist Olorun in his work of creation. Olorun, Obatala and Odudua pre-exist the creation of the world. They live at the beginning when there is only water and chaos. Olorun sent Obatala down from the sky to form land out of the chaos. Obatala descended on a long chain, which could represent the umbilical cord, bringing with him a rooster, some iron and a palm kernel. He put the metal on the earth. On top of this, he placed the rooster, which scratched at the metal and spread it out to create land. Obatala planted palm seed in the new earth and from this grew all types of vegetation. Next, Obatala created human bodies from the earth. Olorun blew into them to give them the breath of life. His followers are not permitted to consume alcohol.

Papa Legba of Voudon is Eleggua or Elegba in Santeria and is identified with either St Anthony or St Peter. Eleggua's role is important because he controls the gateway between this world and the Otherworld and permits the other orishas to go through his gateway to come to earth and possess their human worshippers. Santeria practitioners often keep his image near the doorway or their homes. Eleggua's pivotal role makes him the most important deity in Santeria after Olorun. Spells require his blessing and offerings must be made to him before the other orishas. His colors are red and black, and he is fond of rum and cigars.

Santeria has many goddesses. Oshun is the youngest of the orishas and the happiest. In Santeria, she fused with Our Lady of Charity. Oshun is controler of many of the good things of life – money, sensuality, love, and human pleasure. Not surprisingly, she is a highly popular deity. She loves gold, mirrors, fans, and seashells. Her colors are yellow and white, and pumpkins are sacred to her. She has had relationships with all the male orishas except Obatala and Eleggua. She is the least likely to anger, but once angered, her anger is implacable. Yemaya is the beautiful goddess of the moon, womanhood and pregnancy; daughter of

Obatala and mother of fourteen children. Her colors are blue and white. She gave birth to her children all at once on the top of a mountain, and when her waters broke it caused the great flood. The place where she died became the African city of Ife, an important Yoruba capital and the center of beautiful brass and pottery sculpture that is highly prized by modern art lovers. Yemaya loves sweet things including fruit, particularly watermelon, and pineapples, papayas, apples, grapes, bananas, and pears. She rules the seas and oceans and is the patron of sailors and fishermen.

Chango is one of Yemaya's fourteen children. He is a fire god and spirit of storms, thunder and lightening. Chango's colors are red and white. He is a master dancer and drummer, and carries a mortar in which he mixes his spells. In Santeria, he became associated with St Barbara, who in Catholic iconography is frequently depicted in a red dress and is a protective saint against those acts of God that today are taken care of by insurance policies – fire, accidents, and storms. Chango is one of the most popular deities in his African homeland and in Shango and Santeria. Chango is the archetypal young male warrior hero who is popular with women. He has many goddess lovers, including Oshun. Oggun is a brother of Chango and is often associated with St Peter. Oggun is patron of war and iron. He has some similarities with Thor of the Scandinavians in that he is a patron of ordinary working people. Weapons are sacred to him and he prefers black dogs as his sacrificial animal. His colors are black and green or, in Brazil, dark blue. He also enjoys rum and cigars. His association with iron made him a patron of railways and in contemporary Afro-Caribbean Traditions he has taken on responsibility for airports.

Like other Earth Traditions, the ancestors are also important in Santeria and are known as Ara Orun, or People of Heaven. They give moral guidance and their names are recited at family ceremonies. Another deity important in Santeria, but less so in his African homeland is Babalu-Aye, who is a healing god. In Santeria, he was identified with St Lazarus, the Catholic saint who is the patron of skin diseases.

Leadership

Women have strong leadership roles in all Afro-Caribbean Traditions. There are three levels of participation or initiation. Women leaders in Voudon are known as mambo and men as houngan. The mambos and houngans have complete control over their temples and have the power to initiate people into the tradition.

Mambos and houngans also act as doctors and herbalists. To become a houngan or mambo, people must be perceived by the community as having a vocation, a calling, and must then find a houngan or mambo willing to apprentice and train them. Another important role is played by the hounsi, the 'spouses' of the gods, who are possessed or 'ridden' by the deities. While possessed, they speak as the deities and have the power of the deities. Any advice or counsel that is given is considered to be from the loas, not the individual. The congregation members are the third group. In addition, temples may have important roles for drummers and chorus leaders.

In Santeria, all practitioners can be referred to as santeras, females, or santeros, males, but the term is often reserved for members of the priesthood. Training in the priesthood takes many years and is by oral teaching. It involves learning dance, songs and healing techniques. Traditionally, a santero or santera would undergo a period of isolation before being initiated, but this is less easy to arrange in modern times. Family relationships are important in Santeria. Entering the tradition involves initiation into a spiritual family by the godmother or godfather – the Madrina and the Padrino. Initiation is only a gateway into the tradition. To become a true santera or santero requires lifelong dedication to a particular orisha. The process of acquiring an orisha to venerate is not one-way. The initiate cannot choose the deity; the deity must choose the initiate. Initiation is not open to anyone but only to those who have a vocation, a calling from the gods.

Initiation practices differ among the Afro-Caribbean Traditions and there are also variations within the Traditions themselves. Some practice three different levels of initiation. At the first stage, the initiate receives the ilekes or elekes, necklaces of colored glass beads strung on cotton thread. Each orisha has his or her own necklace of particular colors and numbers of beads. It is usual to start with five necklaces, those of Obatala (white), Chango (red and white), Oshun (yellows, gold, and coral, sometimes with a few green and blue beads), Eleggua (black and red), and Yemaya (blue, crystal and silver). The full traditional consecration ceremony for a necklace is complicated and may be modified in urban settings. The necklace is prepared by a santero or santera who asks the relevant orisha to bless it. It is then stored in a special elixir called omiero. The necklace is then washed in a river and honey and a chicken offered to the deity to ask its blessing. The necklace is then immersed in omiero for another seven days. On the seventh day, the initiate dresses in clean white clothing to receive the necklace. The necklaces protect their wearers from harm and should be worn every day, except when having sex or menstruating.

In Santeria, following initiation, a high priest or high priestess guides the initiate's development. A second stage initiation can be given that is sacred to Eleggua and is the Warriors or Los Guerreros initiation. This follows a ritual consultation or registro with a high priest that reviews the initiate's life and seeks to divine which of the 21 paths of Eleggua is most appropriate for the initiate to follow. Four deities are the warriors – Eleggua, Oggun, Ochosi, and Osun. A special head-shaped talisman of Eleggua is prepared for the rite. The initiate also receives initiatory symbols – an iron cauldron of Oggun and seven miniature tools of Oggun – a rake, spade, hammer, knife, machete, anvil, and pick; as well as the weapon of the hunting god Ochosi – a miniature bow and arrow; and a silver cup with a circle of bells that belongs to Osun. Osun is a mysterious male deity who protects his follows by warning them of danger. A third initiation, the Asiento or making of a saint, bestows entry to the priesthood. It is the longest, most complex and most expensive, involving a number of animal sacrifices.

Rites

In the New World, the descendants of the slaves continued to pass down African Traditions through oral teaching. When people learned to read and write, the teachings were recorded in handwritten books, called in Santeria libertas, which include the outlines of rituals. Afro-Caribbean Traditions have a strong belief in an afterlife but the focus of worship is not to gain merit in the hereafter, but to improve the quality of life in the here and now. Practitioners often value the fact that the traditions are concerned with everyday life and that rituals can be used to ask the favor of the deities to regain health or improve material circumstances. A ritual is a transaction between worshippers and the deity. An implicit part of the contract is that in return for offerings, the deity will grant worshippers their wishes. The deities of Afro-Caribbean Traditions are beneficent beings who provide their worshippers with knowledge and power. Rituals are held in thanksgiving, to avert a run of bad luck, to celebrate the deity's festival day, to ask for help, for dedicatory initiation rites and for rites of passage – birth, marriage and death.

In Voudon, rites take place in a temple called a hounfort, sometimes written oum'phor. The hounfort has a central dwelling room or rooms surrounded by a large area called a peristyle or tonnelle. At the center is a poteau-mitan, a central pole where gods and spirits communicate with their worshippers. The pole is reminiscent of the World-Tree of other cultures. It is painted with designs representing Damballah and Aida-Wedo. The walls and floor of the hounfort are covered with elaborate designs and the walls hung with drapo vodou, flags or banners. Haitian voodoo banners are renowned for their beauty and symbolism. Some hounforts have a special room, a caye-mystère or temple, to welcome the loas. Loas are treated as honored guests who have journeyed far. Each deity has its own altar with candles, pictures and images of the deity, flowers, food and drink, cruches – pots belonging to the dead – and pots-de-tête, containing hair or nail clippings of initiates.

If animals are sacrificed during the rites, this is done by clean butchery – cutting the throat. The intention is to provide a quick clean release for the spirit of the animal and the deities will be displeased if the sacrifice is not performed proficiently. The worshippers may drink some of the blood and the rest of the carcass is usually cooked and eaten. Other important aspects of ritual are feasting before the main ceremony and the making of a vèvè, a symbol of flour or cornmeal to invoke the loas. Drumming and rattling with cleansed and purified instruments, chanting, and dancing by the houngan and/or mambo and the hounsis are other important parts of the ritual.

The first part of rituals is a preparation for the most important part – the deities' descent into the bodies of their mediums. The dancing builds in intensity, until one of the hounsis is possessed by a loa and collapses. The dancer's spirit or ti bon ange has left his or her body and the deity is in control. For those dispossessed from their homelands and disempowered by the horrors of slavery, this direct relationship with the Divine was a blessing that could make bearable the worldly reality of their lives. To their descendants and to others who have been drawn to these traditions today, they offer much valued experience of the Divine.

Santeria rituals are similar. Typically, they begin with drumming and an invocation to the supreme deity Olorun. The Oru or drum rhythm varies according to the orisha who is being invoked. Songs and dances specific to the different orishas are then performed in a predetermined order. Dancing continues until someone is possessed by or 'ridden' by a deity. The mediums dance for a while once possessed and are then taken and dressed in ritual clothing specific to the orisha. They then give advice and prophecy. The number of deities that appear varies according to different traditions, but the pattern of the rites is similar.

Divination

Divination is an important practice in Afro-Caribbean Traditions. If we can see what is coming, we might be able to take timely action to avert danger and encourage good fortune. People seek divination when making life choices or if things are going wrong. There are a number of divination systems. The cowrie shell system, los caracoles or diloggon, is the most commonly used and involves 18 shells, of which 16 are used. The diviner provides a consultation, in Santeria a registro, which involves prayer and then throwing the shells four times onto a straw mat, the estera. The shells are interpreted according the pattern in which they fall and which way up they lie using ancient proverbs that only an expert diviner can understand.

The god Orunmila or Orunla is patron of the most important of all the sacred divination systems, which is known as the Table of Ifa. Divination originally belonged to the god Chango, but he exchanged it with Orunla for the gift of dance. Orunla is associated with St Francis of Assisi. His colors are green and yellow. He likes to be offered coconuts and black hens. Orunla is the personification of wisdom. He is a friend of Eleggua, keeper of the gates between the worlds. He is removed from everyday life and never comes to Earth, speaking only through his divination system. His estrangement from Earth came about because his youngest son treated him disrespectfully and did not bow to him. As a penalty, Orunla departed to heaven. Unable to manage without his wisdom, his children pleaded with him to return. He refused to come back himself, but instead sent 16 palm nuts that could speak in his absence. The palm nuts evolved to become the cowrie shells currently used in divination. A consultation with the Table of Ifa is a serious undertaking that can only be performed by a priest of Orunla, a babalawo. Women cannot perform this divination because it is under the patronage of a male deity. The Table of Ifa itself is a small wooden tray with writing or carvings on it. It is consulted by devout practitioners at all major life transitions – such as marriage, initiation, or the birth of a child. The Table of Ifa and los caracoles can be consulted in an individual consultation in much the same way as someone might visit a clairvoyant or tarot reader.

Ebo

If a divination shows that the person seeking the consultation has been cursed by someone or has otherwise attracted bad luck, a counter-spell, a protective talisman, the making of offerings (ebo) or another remedy will be prescribed. Ebo or offerings are an important aspect of Santeria. A concept found in Afro-Caribbean Traditions is that we must give something to those from whom we wish to receive. If we want the Earth to give us crops, we must make the soil rich and fertile by fertilizing it with manure. If we want deities to help us, we must give them something that we need or that is pleasing to them. An ebo can involve offering fruit, flowers, or candles, or, more controversially, an animal.

Animal sacrifice is an integral part of Santeria and other Afro-Caribbean Traditions. Orishas are believed to need humans to sacrifice to them in order to maintain their power or energy. Sacrifices are offered for good fortune, to avert ill luck, for purification, and for the forgiveness of sins. The emphasis on sacrifice can cause tensions with vegetarian and animal rights groups and with practitioners of other Earth Traditions who place a strong emphasis on the sanctity of all life. Santeria practitioners point out that the animals are killed humanely and are not sacrificed simply for the sake of it. Vegetarians who eschew meat-eating themselves, may have legitimate objections to animal slaughter of any kind and in 1993, Roger Caras, then president of the American Society for the Prevention of Cruelty to Animals, argued that the sacrifice of animals cannot be legitimate in the context of modern America. Meat-eaters might consider that a quick, clean, unexpected, individual death may be preferable to an animal than the fear associated with mass commercial slaughtering. In 1993, the Supreme Court upheld the constitutional right of Afro-Caribbean Traditions in the United States to practice animal sacrifice, but this remains one of Santeria and Voudon's controversial practices and one that allows opponents of Afro-Caribbean Traditions easy ways of stigmatizing them.

The future of Afro-Caribbean Traditions

All Afro-Caribbean Traditions are growing in numbers even though initiation rites are complex and require the payment of fees to the initiators and the purchase of special clothing, candles and other ritual artifacts, and animals for sacrifice. All the traditions are attracting followers from all cultural backgrounds as people are drawn to traditions with ancient roots that create intimate relationships between deity and worshipper and have a practical focus on making life better in the present. While some groups are becoming multi-cultural, other groups are focusing more on their African origins, something that appeals in particular to young African-Americans as a powerful affirmation of cultural identity. The Yoruba renaissance from the 1980s onwards and Afrocentrism have encouraged some practitioners of Afro-Caribbean Traditions in the United States to seek initiation directly from African sources rather than via one of the Afro-Caribbean Traditions. African priests, such as Dr Wande Abimbola,

Dr Afolabi Epega, and Sikiru Salami, have begun initiating Yoruba priests in the United States and have created connections between Afro-Caribbean Traditions in the Old and New Worlds. Yoruba culture and art figure highly in African Studies programs at universities and have introduced many African-Americans to ancestral traditions. Outside North America, supported by the United Nations (UNESCO), Brazil, with its large African population, has taken an active role in cementing links with West African countries and has sponsored the exchange of priests, academics, and museum exhibitions with Nigeria and the People's Republic of Benin. This in turn has paved the way for similar exchanges, involving Haitians, Latinos, Trinidadians, and African Americans. Cuba, with a political agenda of its own, has encouraged the revival of Orisha Tradition in Cuba and the creation of links with African nations. The Cuban government also sponsors workshops, seminars, and tourist events involving drumming and the Lucumi language that is still spoken by Santeria.

Wicca

Wicca is the Earth Tradition of Pagan Witchcraft, also called Wisecraft or, simply, the Craft. Wicca is not just a form of magic using incantations and spells, but a whole system of Earth-centered philosophy and religious belief. Media images often show Wicca as a practice for young women but in reality, it is a tradition for women and men.

The anthropologist Margaret Murray inspired the first phase of the twentieth-century revival of Wicca. In 1921, she published her famous book *The Witch-Cult in Western Europe: A Study in Anthropology*. In this, she analyzed the sixteenth- and seventeenth-century witch persecutions and argued that the inquisitors were persecuting not Satan worshippers or unpopular old women, but an underground Pagan religious movement that worshipped the Horned God. To Margaret Murray, the followers of the Old Religion were those who had secretly kept their true faith throughout centuries of Christian persecution. In remote villages, people met together in small groups, covens, and practiced in secret the rites of their ancestors and the herbal medicine and spellcraft that were the traditional crafts of the village wise woman and cunning man.

Margaret Murray's book was one of a number published in Europe in the nineteenth and early-twentieth centuries, which re-evaluated the witch persecutions. Margaret Murray was not the first person to see in witchcraft the last vestiges of ancient European Paganism; German scholars before her had similar ideas. Karl Ernst Jarcke, a professor of criminal law at the University of Berlin, studied records of a seventeenth-century German trial and concluded that the practices described were a Nature religion, a survival of pre-Christian Pagan beliefs. Historian Franz Josef Mone, Director of Archives at Baden, concluded that the ecstatic practices he found in the accounts of the witch trials were derived from the Greek cults of Hecate and Dionysus through contacts made by Germanic peoples who populated the north coast of the Black Sea. They worshipped a deity that was part horned animal and part human and practiced magic. This Tradition survived into medieval times until its adherents were persecuted as witches. French historian Jules Michelet, in his book *La Sorcière* published in 1862, concluded from medieval accounts of the continuing worship of the Goddess in medieval France that witchcraft was the remnant of Pagan worship. Some of the ideas of these writers are doubtful. Margaret Murray made a leap from deciding that witchcraft contained vestiges of earlier pre-Christian beliefs to arguing that witchcraft had continued as an organized underground religious tradition, surviving hundreds of years of Christian persecution by becoming in effect a secret society.

Regardless of the historical accuracy of their ideas, the religion described by academics such as Murray, Jarcke, Mone, Michelet and others struck a chord with an enormous number of people across Europe. In an era when people felt the traditional rural way of life of Europe was being destroyed by relentless industrialization, there was an immense psychological appeal in the idea that in remote villages people had for centuries practiced a Pagan Earth Tradition that gave power to the people and was secretly practiced by nobles and royals. Interest in witchcraft as the Old Religion developed in the English-speaking world from the 1950s onwards, stimulated by the publication in the late 1940s and early 1950s of the books of Gerald Brousseau Gardner. Through his contacts with the Rosicrucian Theatre in Christchurch on the south coast of England in the 1930s, Gerald Gardner met a group of sophisticated people with a background in ritual magic, who claimed to have contact with traditional British witch groups. Gerald Gardner was initiated into Wicca in 1939. His fellow witches were not keen to publicize their tradition, but Gardner gave out information under the guise of fiction in a novel, *High Magic's Aid*, published in 1949 under his witch name 'Scire' which means 'to know', and later in two classic non-fiction works – *Witchcraft Today* and *The Meaning of Witchcraft*. These were the first accounts of contemporary Wicca. Gerald Gardner's books were followed in the 1950s, 1960s and early 1970s by a spate of publicity, articles and books by and about other leading figures in Wicca, such as Alex and Maxine Sanders, Lady Sheba, Pat and Arnold Crowther, and Doreen Valiente. Wicca, with its emphasis on the Goddess, seemed a movement whose time was ripe.

In the United States, there were many folk traditions of witchcraft that had been brought to the New World by immigrants from all over Europe. Although most immigrants were practicing Christians, folk traditions of healing, divination, and spellcraft were widely practiced and at the root of witch scares such as the Salem witch trials. Dutch and German witchcraft traditions found homes in some states; and later, Italian strega and Slavic witch traditions established themselves in others. As the Wicca movement spread to the United States, many people recognized in British Wiccan practice a similar Tradition to their family folk healing, divination and spellcraft practices, and they began to synthesize the two. New forms of Wicca multiplied and today there are hundreds of different Wiccan Traditions being practiced in the United States and Canada. Wicca also rooted itself in Australia and New Zealand, and soon spread to non-English-speaking Europe. Northern European countries in particular, such as Germany, the Netherlands, Belgium and the Scandinavian countries found that the British tradition was compatible with their own folk magic and pre-Christian beliefs. The spread of Wicca was given further impetus in the 1970s and 1980s by the writings of Janet and Stewart Farrar, Marian Green, Starhawk, and Scott Cunningham. The nineties have seen the next generation – my work and the books of Silver Ravenwolf, Raven Grimassi, Phyllis Currott and others spread Wicca further.

Many Wiccan groups derive from Gerald Gardner's coven. Others spring from Starhawk's work. Some are evolutions of family traditions of witchcraft from different parts of Europe. Some Wiccan groups have sprung up from newcomers who banded together to learn from and teach one another. Some people follow a solitary Wiccan practice, learning from books, their own spiritual experience, and occasional teaching from more experienced practitioners. The internet has also become an enormous resource exchange for Wiccan ideas. Wiccan Traditions have different emphases, but they share similar rituals, deities, symbolism, and philosophy, and are recognizable as derivations of one religion.

Deities

Wicca honors the Divine in the form of the Triple Goddess, whose aspects of Virgin, Mother, and Wise Woman or Crone are associated with the waxing, full and waning phases of the Moon, and in the form of the Horned God. The principal names by which the God is known are Cernunnos or Herne, both of which mean 'Horned One'. Herne is Celtic in origin, but in England after the invasion of Germanic peoples, Herne absorbed some characteristics of the god Odin or Woden. For instance, at Samhain, the Festival of the Dead, Herne is invoked as 'Horned Leader of the Hosts of Air'. This is a reference to Odin as Leader of the Wild Hunt. This synthesis was natural in the British Isles where successive waves of invaders brought with them similar and overlapping deities. The Goddess in Wicca is frequently known by Celtic goddess names, but the most commonly used name is Aradia. This is the Italian version of the name of the Classical goddess Herodias who, some medieval texts tell us, was widely worshipped across southern Europe into medieval times. The name came into English usage via the book *Aradia: The Gospel of the Witches*. This is a collection of the lore and legends of Italian witches, gathered at the end of the nineteenth century by Charles Leland, an American folklorist. A number of other goddess and god names are also used. In Northern Europe, some witches prefer the Northern European goddess and god names of Freya and Frey. In Finland, the forest goddess and god, Mielikki and Tapio, are frequently the presiding deities. Covens may have particular patron deities. Different deities may also be invoked at particular festivals. Thus, in some covens, the festival of Imbolc is sacred to the Irish goddess Bride. As well as the image of the Goddess as the Triple Moon, she is also seen as the Great Earth Mother, the Dark Goddess of the night and the Goddess of the Sun. The God is perceived as primarily dual – a god of summer and a god of winter; but within his summer aspect, we find him honored as the Green Man, the Sun King and the Corn King. In his winter aspect, he is the Hunter, the Shepherd and the Lord of the Underworld. He is also honored at Winter Solstice as the Child of Promise, the reborn Sun. This multiplicity of names and titles does not necessarily imply that Wicca venerates a multiplicity of deities. The various names are often seen as different epithets for the Great Mother Goddess and Father God, who are universal and present in all cultures and at all times.

Initiatory Wicca practices invocation, which has similarities to the trance possession of Santeria and Voudon. The Goddess or God is invited to 'descend into' a chosen individual who then represents the deity for the purposes of the rite and can prophecy, give healing, or manifest other paranormal powers while in an altered state of consciousness. Wicca geared towards family practice tends to invite the Goddess and God to be present in the ritual, without invoking them into a particular individual. Rituals take place in a consecrated circular space, the circle, where the energy of the four quarters is invoked in much the same way as some Native American Traditions.

Teaching and lore

Like many Earth Traditions, Wicca practices magic. Witches believe that the human mind has the power to effect change. As well as honoring its deities, witches also perform spells for healing, or to help people with general life problems. This is seen as an integral part of the work of a witch.

Wicca is largely an oral tradition; although much has now been recorded and published. In addition to what is learned orally, witches keep a book of spells, lore and ritual often called a Black Book or, more recently, a Book of Shadows. Each Wiccan tradition has a core of material that is handed down to its initiates. Traditionally, each witch should copy this by hand from his or her initiator. The Book of Shadows is not a static text. Each witch's book continues to evolve throughout his or her lifetime. Traditionally, witches' books were highly prized and jealously guarded by their owners. This was not only because of their magical content, but because all books were rare and precious. Magical knowledge was prized in much the same way as any trade protected its secrets. Musicians protected their unique interpretations of scores, navigators guarded the measurements and soundings made of their voyages that were essential supplements to sea charts, and cooks of great households jealously guarded their recipe books. Their Black Books were often a means for witches to earn their livelihood. In her book on Finnish magic *Snakefat and Knotted Threads*, Kati-ma Koppana prints excerpts from an interview with Juha Kellokoski, a mid-nineteenth-century Finnish tietäjä, a shaman or cunning man, who was persuaded to part with his Black Book to a folklore researcher. A facsimile of one page is printed in *Snakefat and Knotted Threads*. This is written in red ink on black pages and contains a spell for getting rid of nightmares. In interview, Kellokoski explained that he performed most of his magic by running water – at the rapids where his familiar spirit lived.

Black Books are spell books rather than theological treatises and little has been recorded of the worldview of traditional witches. *Aradia: The Gospel of the Witches* contains a creation myth of Italian witches. The goddess Diana is spoken of as the first principle of this world, 'the first created before all creation; in her were all things; out of herself, the first darkness, she divided herself, into darkness and light was she divided.'[1] We are told that:

> All things were made by Diana,
> the great spirits of the stars,
> men in their time and place,
> the giants which were of old,
> and the dwarfs who dwell in the rocks,
> and once a month worship her with cakes.[2]

There are also other mysterious beings that existed before the creation of the world. They are not part of creation, for Diana is 'the first created'; but female and male beings that exist on another plane. These are described as 'the Mothers, the spirits who were before the first spirit' and 'the Fathers of the Beginning'.

In the Italian tradition, the non-physical world is seen as containing two polarities, male and female. By way of contrast, in the Faery tradition of witchcraft, into which Starhawk was initiated, that which pre-exists creation is seen as female.

> 🌿   Alone, awesome, complete within Herself,
> the Goddess, She whose name cannot be spoken,
> floated in the abyss of the outer darkness,
> before the beginning of all things.
> And as She looked into the curved mirror of black space,
> She saw by her own light her radiant reflection,
> and fell in love with it.
> She drew it forth by the power that was in Her
> and made love to Herself,
> and called her 'Miria, the Wonderful'.
> Their ecstasy burst forth
> in the single song of all that is,
> was, or ever shall be,
> and with the song came motion,
> waves that poured outward and became
> all the spheres and circles of the worlds.
> The Goddess became filled with love,
> swollen with love,
> and She gave birth to a rain of bright spirits
> that filled the worlds and became all things.[3]

Another creation myth is drawn from English witchcraft sources. This describes the creation of the goddess and god, but the first principle is sexless and neutral.

> 🌿   Ere time began, the One who is All
> looked inward on Itself,
> and beheld Itself as though through a reflection in a pool,
> and so came to self-awareness.
> And in that coming to self-awareness,
> the One was made Two,
> subject and object,
> that which looks and that which is looked upon,
> and it divided from itself.

And as the One was made Two,
so the Male and the Female were made separate ...[4]

In other Wiccan creation myths, the cosmic principle is dual. The polarity of light and dark, male and female, are seen as fundamental to the universe as we know it. At the beginning, they are separate and all is stasis. Nothing can come into manifestation until light and dark interact. This is similar to the role played by Fire and Cloud in the Norse Tradition. It also has echoes of the Chinese Tao philosophy; but here light is feminine and dark masculine.

The White Goddess, the pure Light
stood one day in the center of a magic circle,
bathing in her own radiance;
when a shadow appeared.
The Dark Lord came unto her.
He stood outside the boundary of the circle
which barred his way
and begged her to let him in.
But the Goddess feared him;
for he was large and powerful,
his strength much greater than hers.
He would rape her and hurt her;
and seek to subject her to his will.
She was light and he was darkness;
his evil would overcome her good.
She feared him and she would not permit him to enter in.
Then he entreated: 'I seem threatening only because you
    ignore me.'
He sought only to be with her, to love and protect her;
he was her strength; she had need of him,
even as he had need of her love.
Then the Dark Lord who was so full of pride
knelt down before her and wept.
His weakness melted the cold heart
of the Goddess of the Heavens;
She who sails above all,
caring for the plight of no man.
She felt a stab of pain,

a bright darkness in the whiteness of her soul,
She knew pity and love and she let him in
and they were joined as One.
As the power of the Dark Lord flowed within her,
the Goddess of Light knew a bliss
such as she had not known before.
The core of her being expanded
and flowed into the four corners of the universe
and she gave birth to planets and to stars.
The White Goddess became the Mother of All Living.
And it was love that had made her so,
the love of another who suffered for her.[5]

Immanent divinity

In Wicca, the Goddess is within the world as the beauty of Earth, Moon and sea: Wicca has a positive attitude to manifest creation. The Divine is immanent or present within matter, therefore the whole of material creation – the Earth itself and the life forms that inhabit it – are sanctified and holy. This includes the human body: the Divine is present within us.

> *Prayer of Praise to the Goddess*
> Blessed be the Great Mother,
> Without beginning and without ending,
> Blessed be her temple of pure white marble,
> Blessed be the stillness of her holy place.
>
> Blessed be the babe who cries to her,
> Blessed be the deer who lift their heads for her,
> Blessed be the birds who fly the skies for her,
> Blessed be the trees that shake and sigh for her,
> Blessed be the leaf that falls for her and nourishes the soil.
>
> Blessed be the wave that caresses the shore for her,
> Blessed be the sand that succumbs to its embrace,
> Blessed be the shell that is cast up from her,
> Blessed be She, the Mother of Pearl.

Blessed be the stars that shine like jewels for her,
Blessed be the Moon in which we see her face,
Blessed be my spirit that soars the heights for her,
Blessed be my soul that expands in joy for her,
Blessed be my body, the temple of her being.

Vivianne Crowley (1988)

Far from being seen as unclean, the body (and for women this is particularly important) is sacred and holy, a divine gift, the vessel of our divine self.

The positive attitude of Wicca to material creation is carried over into its attitude to religious observance, which is seen as celebration. Witches follow a seasonal cycle of eight festivals. They also honor their deities at the thirteen full moons each year. The moon rites are called 'esbats', a word derived from a French word meaning to frolic. Both sabbats and esbats are joyful occasions. While reverencing their deities is important, witches believe that their deities enjoy mirth and celebration. Witches believe their deities want human beings to dwell on the joy of life and not on humankind's sinfulness and unworthiness. Religion should be joyful, not mournful, and should teach its followers to foster the positive side of human nature, rather than luxuriating in breast-beating self-abasement.

Reincarnation

Wiccan teaching is that after death the spirit is reborn. The Earth Traditions differ from most world religions in their attitudes to life on Earth. In Wicca, Nature is a manifestation of the Divine and life on Earth is a wonderful gift and a source of joy. We should not seek to run away from life in the body, but should celebrate and be thankful for the gift of consciousness that the gods have given us and the ability to experience sensory stimulation and pleasure. To hear great music, to see the beauty of a child's face, or a great painting, or the sunset, to touch another's body, to taste the food that Nature provides for us, to dance, laugh and walk the Earth, and above all to be aware that we do these things, to be aware that 'I am I', are extraordinary gifts that we often take for granted. Our existence is a miracle in itself. We need look for no other. Wiccan teaching about life and death is conveyed in *Legend of the Goddess*,[6] which is a myth enacted at the second stage of Wiccan initiation. The *Legend of the Goddess* has two levels of meaning. On the one hand, it describes an initiatory process and as such is used as part of an initiation rite; but it also describes what happens to the spirit after death. As in many Earth Traditions, teaching about the fate of the spirit after death is conveyed to initiates to sustain them through the rigors of life. The message is found throughout Paganism – that death leads to new life.

The *Legend of the Goddess* has parallels with the story of the Vanir goddess Freya of Germanic Tradition. Female witches often wear a necklace either of amber or of alternating amber and jet beads. Amber has long been seen in European Traditions as a goddess stone because of its organic nature. In traditional witchcraft, amber signifies life and jet is death. The necklace is considered sacred to the Goddess and the alternating amber and jet represents her power over life and death. In Germanic Tradition, Freya wins the magical necklace Brisingamen by descending to the underworld to retrieve it from the four dwarves who made it. In the *Legend of the Goddess*, the Goddess descends into the underworld to learn the secret of death and to ask the God why he allows everything that she loves to age and die. The God tells her that he has no power to prevent the processes of aging and death, but there is a message of hope. Death is merely a staging post and resting place. After death comes rebirth. Everything is reborn on Earth once more, renewed and strong. The Goddess accepts the inevitability of death for material creation, but shows that love can overcome death and that rest leads to rebirth.

The concept of the Goddess as a teacher of hidden wisdom is also found in *The Gospel of the Witches*. Here, in what is the earliest known form of the Great Mother Charge, Aradia explains her role and encourages her followers to worship her at the Full Moon.

When I shall have departed from this world,
whenever ye have need of anything,
once in the month, and when the Moon is full,
ye shall assemble in some deserted place,
or in a forest all together joined,
to adore the potent spirit of your Queen,
my mother, Great Diana.
She who fain would learn all sorcery,
yet has not won its deepest secrets,
then my mother will teach her,
in truth all things as yet unknown ...[7]

The mysteries of God and Goddess are important to witches on many levels. They are teachings about the nature of the Divine, which is also the nature of the cosmos. They also teach us to understand our inner nature and those mysteries that have power over us all – birth, sexuality, marriage, parenthood, and death. Starhawk writes in *The Spiral Dance*:

> Existence is sustained by the on-off pulse, the alternating current of the two forces in perfect balance. Unchecked, the life force is cancer; unbridled, the death force is war and genocide. Together, they hold each other in the harmony that sustains life, in the perfect orbit that can be seen in the changing cycle of the seasons, in the ecological balance of the natural world, and in the progression of human life from birth through fulfilment to decline and death – and then to rebirth.[8]

Wiccan diversity

The twentieth-century Wiccan revival began as coven witchcraft in a secret and initiatory tradition akin to the ancient Pagan mystery traditions. This is still a strong and growing part of Wicca, but Wicca has also branched out in many different forms to suit different needs. Some traditions are for both sexes, some for women and some for gay men. There are forms of Wicca that hold public seasonal celebrations open to all, and many people like to worship in a Wiccan way without the time and intense commitment that coven Wicca can involve. In the United States, there is a strong and thriving Pagan branch of the Unitarian Church that incorporates Wiccan teaching but is geared towards family celebration in which parents and children can take part. Wicca has also moved beyond its European roots. People of African, Native American, Asian, and other cultural traditions have felt drawn to Wiccan philosophy but have wanted to incorporate their own deities. Wicca can seem a long way from Native American Traditions but there are core ideas shared with some Native American Traditions that can be remarkably similar. Coming from another direction, those who have come to Western Paganism from a background in Hindu or Buddhist Traditions have brought with them concepts and practices from Eastern Traditions. These include puja ceremonies to offer veneration to deities and meditation techniques using mantras.

Notes

1 Leland, *Aradia: The Gospel of the Witches*, page 18.
2 Leland, *Aradia: The Gospel of the Witches*, page 121.
3 Starhawk, *The Spiral Dance*, page 17.
4 Crowley, *Wicca: The Old Religion in the New Millennium*, page 228.
5 Crowley, *Wicca: The Old Religion in the New Age*, pages 227–8.
6 Farrar and Farrar, *The Witches' Way*, page 29.
7 Leland, *Aradia: The Gospel of the Witches*, page 6.
8 Starhawk, *The Spiral Dance*, pages 27–8.
9 Carr-Gomm in Jones and Matthews (eds), *Voices from the Circle*, page 63.

Goddess and God

One of the attractions of the Earth Traditions for many people is that they have a much more balanced idea of the Divine than most religions. For Pagans, the Divine is female and male, Goddess and God. Religions that create wholly male deities can never express the fullness of cosmic reality. This is important for women and men. Our societies have been dominated by a patri-archal ethos that was disempowering to both sexes. Societies where people cannot be themselves but only engendered bodies that must live sexually stereo-typed lives do violence to our inner being. No one is a stereotypical male or female. We are whole people. Societies that subordinate one sex to another also do violence to reality and create relations of power and oppression between individuals. Pagan societies were the inventors of democracy – the idea born in ancient Greece thousands of years ago that all were created equal before the gods. Ancient Greece was a patriarchal society and could not give full expression to this idea, but it is an idea that has grown more powerful and now shapes the way we see the world. There is still much social and gender inequality in our societies, but all over the world people are beginning to see the reality – that each individual is a unique child of the gods who should be helped to grow, flourish and to fulfill his or her destiny.

In rediscovering the Goddess, we are returning to the worship of the Great Mother, one of the earliest forms of religious expression. To the child, the moth-er is all-powerful and all-providing. She gives birth to us and nourishes us. To our ancestors, it was natural that the Divine should be female; that Nature, which gives us life, should be Goddess.

She is called by many names by many men;
but to all She is the Great Goddess –
space and Earth and water.
As space She is called Ea,
parent of the gods that made the gods;

She is more old than time,
She is the matrix of matter,
the root substance of all existence,
undifferentiated, pure. ...
Likewise She is called Ge; for
She is the most ancient earth,
the first-formed from the formless ...
She is also the Great Deep whence life arose.
She is all ancient and forgotten things
wherein our roots are cast.[1]

The idea that the Divine is Goddess and God is important for women because it means that religion does not violate a woman's sense of self and self-worth by creating a Divine image that venerates maleness and teaches that femaleness is 'other' and inferior. The anger and abuse that many women have experienced in the traditions of their upbringing can be healed in Goddess-centered religion that is focused on love and acceptance of people of all genders, sexual orientations, and races. The Fellowship of Isis ordains men and women as priests and priestesses of the Goddess, and the Reformed Congregation of the Goddess offers an ordination training program for women. Within the Earth Traditions, women can fulfill the role of priestess to which many spiritual women feel drawn, but which is denied them or given them only on sufferance in monotheistic traditions. Among the Earth Traditions, the role of the Goddess and of women is particularly noticeable in Wicca and in African-based Traditions. However, in the Northern Europe tradition of Ásatrú, which springs from the warrior and seafaring Vikings who around a thousand years ago may have been the first Europeans to ever reach the American continent, the role of the Goddess and of the priestess, the volva or seidkona, is of growing importance. Some Goddess paths are open to women only. The Dianic movement, named in honor of the Goddess Diana, is matriarchal. Many Dianic groups exclude men and see their tradition as a sisterhood. Other Dianic groups work with men, but see the role of men as less important than that of women. There are also groups of women who meet on an informal basis and draw inspiration from a variety of sources for their spirituality. Some are modeled on Wicca, other groups are more shamanic, others have blended aspects of classical Pagan, Native American and other traditions to create an eclectic veneration of the Great Goddess geared to meet contemporary needs.

Feminism gave strong impetus to Goddess spirituality and has inspired many women to question and reject the religious forms that have been familiar since childhood. They have turned away from the image of a patriarchal God to new spiritual pathways. The negative attitude to women displayed in Christianity has derived largely from negative attitudes to sex. When sexuality is repressed, woman is seen as temptress. She is Circe, the mythical Greek sorceress who lures men to her sacred isle and imprisons them by her wiles. She arouses their physical desires and turns them into swine. If sex is sinful then that which arouses sexual desire is sinful. For most men, it is women who arouse desire; therefore women are sinful. It is women who lead men astray, therefore women are evil. Men can best protect themselves from women by segregating them and keeping them apart from mainstream society. Unfortunately, this only exacerbates the problem. In sexually segregated societies, any encounter between men and women who are not relatives has sexual undertones. Interactions between men and women that are not based on sex or power relationships become impossible.

Womanpower

The image of woman as seductress is bound up with another image that arouses fear – the image of woman as witch, as Woman of Power. Many women have turned to Goddess religion to rediscover age-old knowledge about the innate powers of womanhood. This lost knowledge is wisecraft – the powers traditionally associated with what Western society has called the 'witch', but which other societies call 'wise woman' or 'priestess'. Witches believe that human beings have innate powers to cause change through the mind and energy fields of the body. They also believe that the laws of space and time that apply to matter do not apply to consciousness. Consciousness can travel forwards and backwards to glimpse the past and the future and can be aware of what is happening in other places. This awareness often comes first in dreams, but it can be developed through psychic training. Many women who have become more in tune with their psyche and energy flows have discovered that they are able to develop these powers. In earlier societies, people were aware that women's cycles were accompanied by psychic and psychological change. Menstruating women were considered dangerous. Menstruating women have a high level of psychokinetic energy – the energy that causes poltergeist and other paranormal manifestations. At others times of the menstrual cycle, the psyche is more open to the dream world. Through attuning to their inner cycles and seasons, women become aware of their psychic tides and learn to know the times when 'big dreams' will come, dreams which give messages which cut across the boundaries of normal awareness.

It has not been easy for women to exercise womanpowers in recent Western society. The use by women of magical powers was strongly suppressed and condemned by the male Church and women healers and midwives found their role usurped by the male professionalization of the medical profession. However, the image of witch, which is closely aligned to that of shaman, offers women the possibility of harnessing their powers and of using them in positive ways that benefit humankind – to heal and to change that which should be changed. A chant often used in Goddess groups is:

> She changes everything She touches,
> everything She touches changes.[2]

The power of the Goddess is seen as the heritage of every woman, part of her physical being. The American witch and environmental campaigner Starhawk gives a group exercise in her book *The Spiral Dance: A Rebirth of the Ancient Religion of the Great Goddess* that is a Womb Chant.

> Begin with a Group Breath and Power Chant. As you breathe, imagine that you breathe through the womb. See it glow white, like the moon, as you inhale power. See it glow red with blood, with creative fire. Feel the power of the womb to create – not the physical womb only, but the inner womb where ideas and visions are generated. Let your breath become a sound that resonates in the womb.
>
> With each breath – feel its power – feel the woman or man next to you – feel her power – feel how we are linked – how strong we are when we are linked – breathe the power of vision – breathe the womb power of creation – and let your voice carry that power ...[3]

A powerful voice

Women who revere the Goddess have become aware of power in another sense. They are often politically aware. Witches have been at the forefront of some of the most important environmental and social justice campaigns of recent years.

In taking radical political action in defense of ecological issues, many women discovered, perhaps for the first time, a sense of their own collective power, a power to stand against the political establishment. Starhawk describes how she and 600 women were imprisoned after blockading a weapons laboratory. The guards try to remove one of the women.

> The woman dives into our cluster, and we instinctively surround her, gripping her arms and legs and shielding her with our bodies. The guards grab her legs and pull, we resist, holding on. The guards and the women are shouting and in a moment, I know, the nightsticks will descend on kidneys and heads ... And then someone begins to chant.
>
> The chant is wordless, a low hum that swells and grows with open vowels as if we have become the collective voice of some ancient beast that growls and sings...
>
> 'Sit down,' a women whispers. We become a tableau, sitting and clasping the woman as if we are healing her with our voices and our magic. The confrontation has become a laying on of hands.
>
> The guards stand, tall, isolated pillars. They look bewildered ... They do not know what to do.
>
> And so, after a moment, they withdraw. The chant dies away. It is over. For a moment, mystery has bested authority.[4]

Issues of power and control concern all Pagans. Many people attracted to the Pagan Earth Traditions are individualists who reject the control of religion by male priestly hierarchies. Where women have felt themselves oppressed by the structures of patriarchal society, they have been eager not to emulate and reproduce those structures in their own religious movements. Women's traditions are often eclectic and loosely structured. Creativity and spontaneity are strongly encouraged; as is free emotional expression. The emphasis in women's groups is on immanent power, power from within. Starhawk writes:

> In Witchcraft, power is another word for energy, the subtle current of forces that shape reality. A powerful person is one who draws energy into the group. The ability to channel power depends on personal integrity, courage and wholeness. It cannot be assumed, inherited, appointed, or taken for

granted, and it does not confer the right to control another. Power-from-within develops from the ability to control ourselves, to face our own fears and limitations, to keep commitments, and to be honest. The sources of power are unlimited. One person's power does not diminish another's; instead, as each covener comes into her own power, the power of the group grows stronger.[5]

Priestess and witch

The images of woman as priestess and witch are important and empowering to women. Recent societies have taught that women are passive – wombs to bear children, fields that awaits the plough, a body to be impregnated and controled by men and male society. The Goddess images in Western society have also taken on these attributes. The Virgin Mary of Christian religion is 'the handmaid of the Lord' and women's religious role has for centuries been that of follower and subordinate to the male priest and his God. In Christianity, women have been permitted to serve God as nuns, but only recently has women's entry to the priesthood been contemplated. In Pagan Earth Traditions, the image of the Goddess is completely different. It is an image of strength and power. Woman is honored as priestess, Wise Woman and Woman of Power. Women are urged not to be passive creatures at the disposal of men, but women in control of their own destiny, or as *The Pagan Federation Information Pack* puts it:

🌿 Priestesses in their own right, strong and proud, with their own vision.[6]

Pagans believe that religions that portray the Divine solely as male are damaging to women. In her book *Jung and Feminism: Liberating Archetypes*, Demaris Wehr, Professor of Psychology of Religion at Boston University, points out that:

🌿 Symbols have both psychological and political effects, because they create the inner conditions ... that lead people to feel comfortable with or to accept social and political arrangements that correspond to the symbol system.[7]

A dynamic Goddess

By honoring the Pagan Goddess, women internalize those qualities associated with the Goddess – strength, creativity, wisdom, power – and learn to reject social and political philosophies and systems that oppress women. They seek social roles through which they can function as whole human beings; realizing all and not just part of their inner qualities. The Goddess is worshipped as man- ifest in Nature, beyond Nature and within every individual woman. Often ritual incorporates powerful self-affirmation and affirmation by others.

❦ I am Goddess and thou art Goddess.
Within me and without me is She,
eternal yet ever-becoming,
and in all Womanhood we see Her face.

In recent interpretations of mythology, the Goddess is often thought of as the Earth, the passive principle in Nature who is activated by the warm rays of the masculine Sun. However, it is a mistake to believe that across all cultures, the Earth is universally portrayed as feminine and the sky as masculine. In ancient Egyptian religion, which represented one of the most sophisticated flowerings of Paganism, the Earth is Geb, husband and lover of the Sky Goddess Nut, the Queen of Heaven, whose body arches protectively over him. In the Indo-European tradition, the Goddess is active. She is Sun and Fire. To Pagans, the Goddess is Sun and Moon, Earth and Sea, one of the great powers of Nature. Honoring the Goddess inclines us to view the universe in a different way from that of philosophies based on monotheism. Many branches of Western Paganism share a view similar to that of Hindu thought. All manifestation, whether of spiritual consciousness or matter, is Shakti, the Great Mother of All. Shakti is energy and power, but energy and power must take form. This is Shiva – the Great Father of All. This view is the opposite of that found in the Judaic mystical tradition of the Kabbalah where the Great Mother is Binah, Mother of Form, and the Father God is Hokhmah – force; but Kabbalah shares Hinduism's vision of the cosmos being a dynamic balance of female and male energies. In Hindu thought, the female–male polarity of force and form are seen as manifesting everywhere, including within us. Even when there is no universe, these ultimate potentialities still exist, though at rest.

In Western Paganism, the Goddess is not passive but an active and energizing force. She is the Creatrix, the dynamism that activates the universe. She is the power that calls the power of the God to her and, in that movement, the process of creation begins.

> Golden Aphrodite cometh not as the Virgin, the victim,
> but as the Awakener, the Desirous One.
> As outer space She calls,
> and the All-Father commences the courtship.
> She awaketh Him to desire and the worlds are created ...
> How powerful is She, Golden Aphrodite,
> the awakener of manhood![8]

A Sexual Goddess

This Pagan image of the Goddess is far from the desexualized image of the Virgin Mary. The Goddess is fertility and abundance, and the creation of the Earth itself is seen as an act of sexuality between two dynamic forces within the universe. This energizing image of the female is important in Paganism. Women are not acted upon; they act. Paganism offers a spiritual path in which women can honor the feminine aspect of the Divine and play a full role as priestesses and celebrants of the mysteries of the Goddess. Women come to internalize the qualities of the Goddess, rather than to subordinate themselves to a male priesthood serving a male God. The power that is offered is not power over others, but power in the sense of inner energy and strength – power-from-within. In taking on the role of priestess, a woman demonstrates for herself her own inner power and, for other women, she provides a role model of strong womanhood to which they can aspire. When she has experienced this sense of strength, she can move forward. There is a song often sung at Pagan gatherings:

> We are an old people,
> We are a new people,
> We are the same people,
> Stronger than before.
>
> I am a strong woman,
> I am a story woman,
> I am a healer,
> My soul will never die.[9]

For many who are searching for a path through which to express their inner spirituality, the Goddess who is present in Nature, who is all around us, and whose essence is love, has a great attraction. This appeal is not only to women, but also to men. Two thousand years ago, the Roman writer Lucius Apuleius wrote a prayer after his initiation into the mysteries of the Egyptian goddess Isis.

> Holiest of the Holy,
> Perpetual Comfort of Mankind,
> You, whose bountiful grace nourishes the whole world;
> whose heart turns towards all those in sorrow
>   and tribulation
> as a mother's to her children;
> You, who takes no rest by night, no rest by day,
> but are always at hand to succor the distressed,
> by land and sea, dispersing the gales that beat upon them,
> Your hand alone can untie the hopelessly knotted skeins
>   of fate,
> terminate every spell of bad weather,
> and restrain the stars from harmful conjunction.
> The deities above adore You,
> the deities below do homage to You,
> You set the orb of Heaven spinning around the poles,
> You give light to the Sun,
> You govern the universe,
> You trample down the powers of Hell.
> At Your voice,
> the stars move, the seasons recur,
> the spirits of Earth rejoice, the elements obey.
> At Your nod,
> the winds blow, clouds drop wholesome rain upon
>   the earth,
> seeds quicken, buds swell.
> Birds that fly through the air,
> beasts that prowl on the mountain,
> serpents that lurk in the dust,
> all these tremble in a single awe of You ...[10]

The Way of the God

Extremes in religious, political and spiritual thought eventually produce equal and opposite reactions. The dominance of our religious life by a sterile maleness encouraged many people to turn to the worship of the Great Goddess. An imbalance in outer society towards valuing only male activity and the male sex, created feminism and encouraged many men to develop the qualities within them that had previously been stereotyped as feminine. This was of great value to men, because it returned to them a part of themselves that had been suppressed and repressed by Western society. This was male caring, creativity, and joyfulness. However, this is only one side of the lost maleness that Pagan religion has needed to recover. The male is also hunter and warrior. This does not involve random violence or killing for the sake of it, but the use of that strength which protects, nurtures and guards the weak, and prevents the powerful from oppressing the powerless.

In the 1980s, we had New Man. He changed diapers, wept buckets at the movies, and was never angry. He harbored a permanent guilt complex because his organ dangled and hers did not, and he took upon himself the sins of the male world. It was men who had persecuted women, burned them at the stake, unleashed the dogs of war. If his ancestors had done it, then he too had done it. He was guilty by birth. Many men found their inner feminine. They rejected the stereotypical male role that they had been brought up to play and chose other careers and other patterns of life; but there was still something missing. In rejecting the patriarchal God of the monotheisms, there was a danger that the masculine deity would be lost. To play their role in society, men must come to an understanding of how to use their male energy for the greater good. In our contemporary era, both men and women have suffered from false images of what they should be. They have also suffered from false male deities. RJ Stewart writes in *The God in Western Magical Arts* that:

> The God without has, for about 1500 years, been somewhat severely limited to a monosexual and imbalanced image, the 'demon Jehovah', the wrathful father, the creator of pain, suffering, inequality, restriction, elitism, misery, and so forth. This terrible image has been mitigated slightly by that of Jesus, but suffering and pain are also features of this divine son in most orthodox Christian cults or religious branches. The problem of rivalry and pain between father and son, or

older and younger male, seems epitomised in the formal religions, particularly those of near-Eastern origin such as Christianity.[11]

In the Earth Traditions, men have sought and found their Pagan spirituality in mixed-sex groups following traditional Earth-centered spirituality and newer Pagan syntheses. In recent years, there has also been a revival of the male mystery traditions. These include initiatory traditions familiar to the Classical Greco-Roman world, such as those of Orpheus and that of Mithras, whose worship was widespread amongst the soldiers of the Roman Empire. Others have turned to shamanism or to the warrior spirituality of some Germanic and Native American traditions. Some have given their allegiance to Odin All-Father. Others have turned to one of the earliest forms of male deity – the Horned God, whose origins lie in the distant past, when our ancestors were hunter-gatherers living in harmony with their prey, following the seasonal migrations of the animals on which they lived, and taking from them only what they needed. The Horned God is an image of great power that has endured in the human psyche through centuries of repression. Although newer deities have emerged, the Horned God endured. As Pan to the Greeks and Cernunnos of the Celts, he was a dominant force until the Christian era. With the spread of Christianity, the Horned God was suppressed. He was seen as threatening, sexual, and animalistic. His image became associated with that of the Christian devil. In the twentieth century, Wicca brought about a rebirth and rehabilitation of the Horned God. Starhawk writes:

 The image of the Horned God in Witchcraft is radically different from any other image of masculinity in our culture. He is difficult to understand, because He does not fit into any of the expected stereotypes, neither those of the 'macho' male nor the reverse-images of those who deliberately seek effeminacy. He is gentle, tender, and comforting, but He is also the Hunter. He is the Dying God – but His death is always in the service of the life force. He is the power of feeling, and the image of what men could be if they were liberated from the constraints of patriarchal culture.[12]

The Horned God is not cerebral and celibate, but the phallic hunter god of forest and hill. He is Lord of the Animals. His body is that of a man, but his feet are hooves and his antlers or horns reach up to heaven, capturing within them the power of the Sun. He is strong and powerful; but he is also the shepherd, the caring and protecting father. The God is old, but young; he is strong and steadfast, but he is also light, energy, movement, creativity.

> I am as old as time;
> for I sprang forth from the first breath taken;
> yet have I aged not;
> for I am born anew with each gust of wind
> and every gentle breeze.
>
> The leaves dancing on the trees,
> and still water silently mirthful with sudden ripples,
> show that I pass by.
> Fleet of foot with wingèd heels am I,
> the messenger,
> with words you all must hear.
> cascading from my silver tongue.
> I am quicksilver,
> I bring healing with my magic touch,
> I am the wind,
> the very breath of life,
> I am He.

Chris Crowley (1985)

Men and women, God and Goddess

Creativity is an outcome of our establishing an inner dialogue between the masculine and feminine within us all. The psychologist Carl Jung gave a name to this contrasexual other within us. The masculine within woman is named animus and the feminine within man anima. In order to fully understand and fulfill his nature, a man must come into right relation not only with his maleness. He must also achieve understanding of his inner feminine, his anima. Coming from the Hindu traditions, psychologist Arwind Vasavada believes that for men the Goddess plays a role akin to that of the anima in Jungian psychology.

❧ She disturbs man from his state of ease and comfort, rouses his emotions, and all the baser instinctual shadow side of his life, drags him into the open battleground of life so that he may fulfil his destiny, but from which he always fights shy. She appears both as positive and negative mother, compassionate as well as cruel, according to the developmental stage of each individual.[13]

Dion Fortune also describes the role of the Goddess as anima in her novel *The Sea Priestess*. The Goddess is the muse who awakens man's consciousness into creativity.

❧ In the inner She is all-potent.
She is Queen of the kingdoms of sleep.
All the invisible workings are Hers
and She rules all things ere they come to birth.
Even as through Osiris Her mate
the Earth grows green,
so the mind of man conceives through Her power.[14]

What of male deity and women? The role of the Divine masculine is important for women but first we must reclaim the Goddess. For too long in our society, the feminine has been under-valued. Women have been relegated to the bedroom and kitchen, or elevated to the heights of heaven, but we have not been permitted a voice in everyday life, 'the affairs of men'. We have been denied part of ourselves; the part that is strong, decisive, thinking, and constructive. Women have been taught to look for these qualities in husbands, rather than embodying them themselves. The challenge for women is to reclaim these qualities as their own and for this they need to understand the qualities of the Goddess; for in her are these things found. Where women need the God is in coming into relationship with men. Many women have been damaged by maleness and have no image of what a positive male force can be. Pagan deities can provide images of maleness that are strong and gentle, fierce and loving, caring for things beyond an individual man's personal needs and concerns. Women need to see the potential of what maleness can be both for their own benefit and in order to teach this to their sons.

Both God and Goddess are necessary to us if we are to understand the mystery of the Divine and both mysteries are necessary and valuable if we are to understand ourselves and thus play a full role in society. In honoring both female and male, Goddess and God, we bring our visions and ourselves into right harmony. We can be all of ourselves, not denying our maleness or femaleness, but becoming who and what we truly are.

Notes

1   Fortune, *The Sea Priestess*, page 121.

2   Lauren Liebling and Starhawk.

3   Starhawk, *The Spiral Dance*, pages 133–4.

4   Starhawk, *Truth or Dare*, pages 4–5.

5   Starhawk, *The Spiral Dance*, page 37.

6   *The Pagan Federation Information Pack*, page 10.

7   Wehr, *Jung and Feminism*, page 22.

8   Fortune, *The Sea Priestess*, page 158.

9   Will Shepardson and the women of Greenham Common Peace Camp, England.

10 Apuleius, *The Golden Ass*, based on the Graves translation. Language updated.

11 RJ Stewart, 'The God in Western Magical Arts', in John Matthews, ed, *Choirs of the Gods: Revisioning Masculinity*, page 123.

12 Starhawk, *The Spiral Dance*, page 94.

13 Vasavada in Spiegelman and Vasavada, *Hinduism and Jungian Psychology*, page 158.

14 Fortune, *The Sea Priestess*, page 123.

10

Contemporary Rites of Passage

All Earth Traditions put a strong emphasis on rites of passage. Rites of passage are ceremonies that mark important transitions in social status. In traditional communities, they are ways of publicly announcing someone's new status and welcoming him or her into a community of peers. Other than entry into adulthood, the major phases of the life cycle that call for us to change our social roles are marriage, becoming parents, becoming elders in our communities, and the fourth, final and greatest transition of all, transcending the material world through death. An important function of spiritual traditions is to help smooth the way. Rites of passage convey through teachings, myth and symbol how we are to meet the demands of the next phase of life. They prepare us for the adjustments we must make and give us the inner strength and understanding to deal with these challenges. Earth Traditions that have been practiced continuously rather than being interrupted by Christianity, such as many Native American Traditions, have well-formulated rites of passage. People who are reconstructing Earth Traditions in the contemporary world have to think much harder about what rites of passage are important and how they should be carried out. Within the contemporary Pagan community, the important social rites have evolved to be partnership commitment, welcoming new infants to the community, puberty rites, croning and elders' ceremonies, and death rites. Many traditions also have initiation ceremonies that convey a particular status within the religious community and are the equivalent of different stages of ordination in Christian denominations.

Partnerships

Early adulthood leads to relationships and eventually, for most people, to committed relationships. In contemporary Paganism, marriage is often known as handfasting. Divorce was permitted in most Pagan societies. Marriage is a matter of mutual promises and of honor. If people are no longer able to keep those promises, then they must be honest and take honorable steps to dissolve the contract. In Pagan partnerships, the nature of the commitment is a matter for the couple concerned. Attitudes to marriage and the place of sexuality within it are conveyed in this handfasting blessing. The Celebrant takes the couple's rings and places their hands on them.

> Above you are the stars,
> below you are the stones,
> as time does pass – remember:
> like a star should your love be constant,
> like a stone should your love be firm.
> Be close, yet not too close;
> possess one another, yet be understanding;
> have patience each with the other;
> for storms will come but quickly go;
> be free in the giving of affection and warmth;
> make love often and be sensual to one another.
> Have no fear, and let not the ways or words
> of the unenlightened give you care;
> for the Goddess and the God are with you, now
> and always.[1]

Parenting

One of the main requirements of marriage is that children must be cared for and safeguarded. The gift of children is a sacred trust and their welfare is paramount. The fact that children are seen as Goddess-given does not mean that Pagans take the romantic and naive view of some humanistic psychologists that children are born good. Nor do Pagans believe in the Christian concept of original sin – that children are born evil. Children are born with the same balance of positive and negative biological characteristics that beset us all. They have impulses to caring, sharing, and altruism, and impulses to selfishness, cruelty, anger, and hate. The task of parents is to guide their children as best as they can, given their own limitations, towards those actions, thoughts and feelings which are creative, positive and likely to benefit the child and others. In our complex and materialistic world, this is a daunting task.

Since Pagans do not believe in original sin, there is no need for a ceremony after birth to frighten away the devil. However, most Pagans wish to mark the birth of their children with a naming ceremony. This is an occasion for family and friends to come together to share with the parents the joy of welcoming a child to the world. The ritual is often one of protection – to place the child under the care of the family's presiding deities and to ask for their blessing. Ceremonies are simple and often consist of naming, anointing and blessing the child and then a public commitment by the parents to raise and care for him or her.

This rite can be performed by the mother and father or by a priest and priestess. The mother or the priestess anoints the child with olive oil or another non-toxic oil:

> I anoint your feet,
> that have brought thee in our ways.
> I anoint your hands,
> that they may work for what is right and true.
> I anoint your heart,
> that it may beat in strength and love.
> I anoint your lips,
> that they may speak no evil and give forth truth.
> I anoint your brow,
> that your mind shall seek the wisdom of enlightenment.

The mother then addresses the Goddess:

> O lovely and gracious Queen of Living Light,
> You, whose promise is that we will return after death,
> to be with our own people,
> and that we will know, and love, and remember them again,
> bless this child who has returned once more to her/his own.

The priest or the father then takes the child and addresses the God.

> Lord and Hunter, Power of Sleep and Night,
> grant strength and blessing to this child.
> Wrap her/him in thy cloak of thy protection
> and guard her/him through the journey of life.

125

The parents then say:

> I/we take the oath
> to raise, protect and train our daughter/son (name),
> given to us as a trust and sacred gift
> by the Mother and Father of All,
> until s/he is of age
> to take responsibility for her/his own life.
> We will teach the ways of our Mothers and Fathers:
> love, gentleness, good example,
> and firmness when called for we shall give.
> Blessed Be (name) and welcome to the world!

Naming ceremonies may or may not involve committing children to a particular Tradition. In some Earth Traditions, there are ceremonies of religious admission, profession or commitment that take place at birth. In other Traditions, these take place at adolescence and form part of ceremonies that mark the transition to adulthood. Admission or initiation into an Earth Tradition may also take place much later in life. Some paths such as Wicca are more akin to the Classical Pagan mystery religions of Egypt, Greece and Rome that were designed for adult initiates. Many practitioners of Earth Traditions, while exposing their children to the religious beliefs and principles that they hold dear, leave them free to make their own religious choice, accepting that their children's spiritual needs and beliefs may evolve to be different from their own. Others believe that in the complex world in which we live, it is essential that children be given strong religious teachings with which to guide their lives. To deny children this is seen as depriving them of what is an essential part of the responsibility of the parents and their religious community – the transmission of those values, traditions and beliefs that we hold to be best and true. These parents raise their children to follow their religious lead in the same way as the members of other faiths. In North America, many Wiccans with children belong to the Unitarian Church that has a universalist approach that can embrace people of many faiths. Unitarian services can be a meeting ground for many whose religious viewpoints start in different religions.

Adulthood

To enter adulthood, we must have an understanding of our place in the scheme of things. This requires teaching, help and guidance from those who have already entered adult life, to help us understand our religious and cultural traditions and those myths that guide our particular religious path. The aim of such teaching is to awaken in the adolescent a sense of his or her heritage, a heritage that implies responsibility to others and to the world around us. This provides an unbroken sense of historical continuity – a sense of time, place and context in which to live. Ceremonies of initiation into adulthood are also helpful to parents. They mark a transition stage when it is time for parents to let go. They are no longer responsible for their children, who are now responsible for themselves. At this point, teenagers need their own space in which to find out by trial and error the ways of the adult world. In many societies, teenagers lived apart in separate male and female groups, where they had to learn to get on with young people of their own sex to survive. It was the parent's duty to release the adolescent for this, after which their child would return as a member of the adult world, no longer subject to his or her parents, but independent and equal. This formal separation between adolescence and adulthood makes the transition easier for the child and for the parent.

Often today going away to university represents the cutting of the umbilical cord and entry into adult life. In Christian societies, confirmation used to mark a transition into adult life and the age when an adolescent would enter an apprenticeship and start to earn his or her living. Until the mid-twentieth century, it was often the point at which boys started to wear long trousers instead of shorts. For girls, it coincided roughly with first menstruation. Jewish boys have their Bar Mitzvah ceremonies, and in some Jewish traditions, there are now Bat Mitzvah ceremonies for girls. In some Muslim cultures, boys are circumcised around the time of puberty. Parents who practice Earth Traditions often wish to commemorate their children's transition into adolescence with a ceremony that involves family and friends. Many people have turned to Native American Traditions, with their well-thought-out puberty rites, for inspiration. Rites to celebrate a daughter's first menses are usually held by a mother and her female friends and relatives who gather to welcome the girl into womanhood. A period of quietness and meditation, dressing the girl in a white robe and then bathing and changing into a red robe, followed by teaching about what it means to be a woman – its joys and difficulties – and then a celebration, is the pattern of many rites. Boys' rites usually take place with male relatives and family friends.

Camping, spending time in the wilderness and perhaps a period alone for a vision quest, and then teaching about the male role, sexuality, sexual responsibility, and joyful feasting are typical stages. Ideally, rites should create links between young people and older role models who can advise them about the difficult education, career, relationship, lifestyle and morality choices they will have to face. Mentors can advise adolescents much more openly and without the emotional baggage that often accompanies parent–adolescent relationships.

Initiation into Adulthood

One of the functions of our spiritual traditions is to help mark important transitions in the human life cycle. Birth, adulthood, marriage, and death, all require us to take on new roles and responsibilities. Religious ritual shows us how this should be done. Ritual helps us make sense of the major transitions in our lives – from childhood to adolescence, from adolescence to adulthood, and from mid-life to the later years when our physical strength begins to fail us and we become aware of the nearness of death. These transitions are often dealt with by specific rites of passage, but they are also approached in less direct ways. Messages about how we are to fulfil our social roles are also found in the seasonal and other myths of Paganism.

In his book *Iron John: A Book about Men*, poet Robert Bly argues that a return to the initiatory processes that were an integral part of earlier tribal societies is essential to the survival of the Western world. Many of Bly's ideas of tribal society are romanticized, but they are important. Bly argues that his own culture, that of the United States, has undergone an unmistakable decline since the 1950s. He sees initiation as a *third road* between the perils of rampant individualism and ego inflation, encouraged by much of our materialist culture, and the road of depression and failure, the only way out for those who cannot cope with the demands of society.

🌿   We have the grandiose road, taken by junk-bond dealers, high rollers, and the owners of private jets; and we have the depressed road, taken by some long-term alcoholics ... crack addicts, and fatherless men. ... The ancient practice of initiation then – still very much alive in our genetic structure – offers a third way through ...[2]

Others, such as psychologist James Hillman[3], have taken a similar view. Hillman has made an extensive study of myths relating to the initiation of the puer or youth, by the senex, the older wise man. He argues that initiation is a necessary bridge between the world of fantasy and the harsh world of reality – a bridge that can make reality bearable. He sees initiation as softening reality, by filling in its background with layers of mythological perspective. He believes that this makes the hardness of reality meaningful and tolerable, but at the same time truly indestructible. Robert Bly argues that the process of initiation into adulthood is easier for women than for men.

> A girl changes into a woman on her own, with the bodily developments marking the change; old women tell her stories and chants, and do celebrations. But with the boys, no old men, no change.[4]

While this may have been true in tribal society, it is no longer so today. Initiation into the traditional female mysteries has been sadly lacking in contemporary society and has left many women ignorant not only of what it means in spiritual terms to be a woman, but also of their own bodies, their hormonal cycles, and the mysteries of fertility and reproduction. Lack of initiatory experience from older women who have dealt with the demands of today's society also means that many women are confused about their role. Women today are bombarded with media images of the Superwoman, who has it all – beauty, health, husband, children, career, material success, inner fulfilment, fortune, and glory. Against this unrealistic image, even the most successful woman can feel herself a failure. Creating realistic expectations of what we can do, be and achieve requires teaching of women by women. Some women who have created women-only Pagan religious groups perceive their Goddess religion as a sisterhood, in which older women teach younger women the age-old secrets of Wise Craft and of the ways of womanhood.

In tribal society, the role of men was clear – the majority were needed to become hunters and warriors. In society today, where this need has receded and, indeed, where male violence channeled into ends that do not serve society has become a major problem, how are the initiatory processes to be managed and what are we initiating our men into becoming? Robert Bly explores what he believes is happening, or rather, not happening to men in the United States. Bly believes that manhood doesn't happen by itself. What is necessary is the active intervention by older men to welcome younger men into the 'ancient, mythologized, instinctive male world'.[5] In Pagan tribal societies, these matters were managed well and formed an integral part of the education of young men. The adolescent was separated from his parents and often sent out into the wilderness to fend for himself and/or to bring back some symbol or animal that would denote that he had performed an act of courage. This type of initiation is difficult to obtain today and some men who feel the lack have been drawn to Pagan gods as providing an image of wholeness with which to identify. As well as entering the main Earth Traditions, male mystery groups have revived the initiatory rites of tribal society and of ancient male mystery cults such as that of Mithras.

Knowledge is the spiritual goal of many Earth Traditions. This is not knowledge in the sense of facts and data, but an intuitive understanding that may or may not be conscious. In many Earth Traditions, this search for understanding is conveyed through the seasonal myths that tell of a god's quest for knowledge. Chris Crowley, in *Wicca: the Old Religion in the New Age*,[6] explains one version of the journey of the Wiccan God. The God's journey is seen as an evolution from the freedom and natural animalism of youth, through to love, humanity, kingship, parenthood, death, and sacrifice. This comes about through his interaction with the feminine, the Goddess, and through his acceptance of the passage of time and inevitably of change. The seasonal cycle contains a message that speaks to man as well as to God and it is a message that is at the heart of male initiation. Robert Bly argues that only a man can make a man.

> The relevant sentence is the one accepted in New Guinea by men and women of eighty or so tribes: 'A boy cannot change into a man without the active intervention of the older men.'[7]

This may be true in Papua New Guinea, but in Western society it is only partly true. In the European Earth Traditions, initiation is not a one-off event, but a staged process. In the initiatory rites of the Egyptian goddess Isis, the first initiation was that of the Goddess, the second that of the God, and the third that of the Goddess again. This is also the pattern found in the mysteries of Wicca, where the parallels with the life cycle are more explicit. Robert Bly describes the stage of the initiatory process that makes us young adults and embarks us on our life's journey. We are apprenticed to life, but still have to prove ourselves as full adults in society. This initiation must indeed be given by elders of the same sex, as only they can explain to a man what it really means to walk the male path. Similarly, only women can explain to other women what it means to be a woman and bear children and, in today's society, how to balance this with other needs for fulfilment that a woman may have.

In Robert Bly's work, he analyzes the fairy tale Iron John. The story describes a young prince's encounter with a Wildman who takes the boy from his home and then finally sends him into the world to work for his living. He finds work in the palace of a neighboring kingdom. He later proves his courage in war and is rewarded by winning the King's daughter for his wife. From the structure of this tale, Bly argues that every man has at the bottom of his psyche an ancient male covered with hair, whom he calls the Wildman. Bly makes several explicit parallels between the Wildman and the Horned God. He argues that in order to undergo the processes of male initiation, contemporary man has to get in touch with his inner Wildman. Robert Bly's work, although very valuable, has spawned some unfortunate offspring. In the 1990s, movie stars rushed off to men's camps to shout for their long lost daddies and find 'the Wildman within', just as men today sign up for the Promise Keepers. As psychologist John Rowan points out in his book *The Horned God*,[8] this is fine, providing they also get in touch with other aspects of their psyches, but otherwise it is an invitation to 'unconstructed male chauvinism'. The problem with the Iron John story is that no women figure in it other than as ciphers. The young boy in the story learns to live with the Wildman, and this is a valuable lesson, but the story fades out as the young man marries the princess. He has completed one stage of the initiatory process. He has made the transition from adolescence to manhood, but what we do not learn is that there is a further initiatory process – that by the woman of the man. At this stage, we must turn to wise elders of the opposite sex to teach us. This harks back to the Celtic idea of a young man going to a female warrior for the final part of his training in weapons. Coming from Germanic Tradition, Freya Aswynn comments:

> ...it was the wise woman's function to teach magical practices to men, as well as to advise them in ethical matters. In this respect there is a similarity to the older continental tradition where women arbitrated in legal disputes and gave advice in councils of war.[9]

Not all, if any, of these transitions are dealt with well in contemporary secular societies. Initiation into adulthood in particular is a theme that is beginning to concern many people in Western society, because we recognize that we lack the processes to help our young people make a smooth transition between the worlds of childhood and adulthood. Often there is uncertainty about what is required of an adult man or woman. This problem is cumulative, for as each generation fails to pass on the appropriate teaching, so more and more of the inner mysteries of maleness and femaleness are lost to us. We are lacking guidance on the initiatory processes of adulthood at a time when the journey into adulthood is more difficult than it has ever been. In many ways, we have more freedom. We have the choice of what occupation to follow and whether to become parents. These things are no longer decided for us by our families, the village elders, or the state. There may be pressures, both psychological and material, to conform; but we have today much greater freedom than any generation before. We are also lacking in guidance. The extended family has split up, so that there are no longer generations of elders of our own sex to whom we can turn for advice and wisdom. The nuclear family has also broken down. Fathers are frequently absent or non-existent and many men and women have no positive male role models from whom to learn.

The Earth Traditions recognize this lack and many women and men have come to the Pagan mysteries to learn from their myths and initiatory processes a positive pattern of femaleness and maleness. Myths and rites of religion are expressions of the reality of the Divine force and allegories of how it interacts with the world. They are also templates that guide our behavior in society. The image of the Goddess teaches a woman what it means to be female and that of the God teaches a man what it means to be male. Together they teach the nature of both sexes' responsibilities to society and how to reconcile our individual desires and wants to those of our communities. They teach the way of wholeness and how that wholeness embraces all aspects of the life cycle – good and bad, youth and age, pain and pleasure, life and death.

Aging

Many people are reluctant to allow their children to 'fly the nest', because by recognizing that their children are adult, they will be faced with the unwelcome fact of their own ageing process. If their children are young adults, then they must be middle-aged. The early stages of adulthood are welcome. They bring freedom from parental control and the opportunity to explore the world. The later stages are often feared. Many of us fear death. We also fear old age. We fear to let go of our control over the world. The temptation is to hold on to what we have achieved and to refuse to move forward. We can see this in the way in which some people cling on to their children and in the way in which people cling to material achievement and career success. Chris Crowley writes of Wiccan mythology and how this stage of life is reached in the God's journey around the Wheel of the Year.

🦋 This kingship is gained when the God is at his prime, only half way round the circle and at the half way stage of his life. He is at his most materially successful and at his most dominant. It would appear, both in terms of the God's progress, and in most men's, that this in itself produces a dilemma. From the vantage of this material high point, there can appear to be no further upward path. Powers at their prime now can only weaken, albeit very gradually, and the view from the top is to see a continual surging, waves of challenges from younger men, all committed to achieving their destiny and taking his place.

We live in a society that is rapidly changing and in which the wisdom of our elders can seem irrelevant and outdated. Disrespect for older members of society is encouraged by media images of physical perfection, eternal youthfulness and sexual attractiveness. Youth is of great value. It is energetic and idealistic. It rejects outmoded forms and false authority; but it can also be intolerant, selfish, arrogant, and lacking in the worldly wisdom to know how to implement the ideals that it espouses. The vagaries of life, and learning to take responsibility for ourselves and for others, can teach us gentler ways and give us a wisdom that is valuable to pass down the generations. Not all our elders are founts of mystic knowledge – many are not; but society is losing something when there is no honored place of respect for those who have served us well.

In the Earth Traditions, all phases of the life cycle are honored. Many Traditions include special ceremonies for their older members who are passing from a stage of leadership of community affairs to that of advice giver and wise counsellor. The early and middle years are seen as times for establishing ourselves in the world, for developing skills that enable us to earn a living and win status and respect, and for learning to raise others to become well-adjusted adults in society. The third part of life is seen as a time for consolidating the knowledge that we have gained. It is a time to return to study and to learn those things that we need for our onward spiritual journey. Starhawk writes:

In the Craft, old age is a natural and highly valued part of the cycle of life, the time of greatest wisdom and understanding. Disease, of course, causes misery, but it is not something to be inevitably suffered: The practice of the craft was always connected with the healing arts, with herbalism and midwifery. Nor is death fearful: It is simply the dissolution of the physical form that allows the spirit to prepare for a new life.[10]

There are external forces that can help us see the need for this transition. If we are parents, our children grow up and are no longer dependent on us. Free of this, we have time and space to attend once more to our own needs. There may be needs for learning and for spiritual direction that we have had to bury and suppress in order to fulfill our parental role, but these can now come to the fore. We may, as is more customary in the East, turn to the inner quest, the spiritual adventure. In some Eastern societies, individuals who have fulfilled their social 'householder' obligations to society by supporting themselves and their families will withdraw to a monastery to study, learn, contemplate, and to take time for themselves. Many people become interested in the Earth Traditions at this stage, when they are free to pursue their own spiritual development. As we approach late middle age, we need to re-evaluate our role and perhaps change our life direction. Some Earth Traditions have special rites that may be called 'Becoming an Elder' or 'Croning'. These ceremonies recognize aging as a positive transition, when we have an opportunity to lay down some of our responsibilities and to put ourselves first and say, 'I have done my bit. It is now someone else's turn and I will concentrate on developing myself and on growing nearer to the Divine.'

Death

In Earth Traditions, celebrations of the seasonal cycle operate on many levels. On the one hand, they are thanksgivings for the eternally renewing cycle of Nature. There is also another level of meaning: seasonal myths mirror the human life cycle and also the cycle of the cosmos – the cycle of conception, birth, maturation, decay, and destruction. The seasonal cycle tells us that life is continuous, but ever changing.

There are two delusions that create much human suffering: the Delusion of Separateness and the Delusion of Rightness. There is also a third – the Delusion of Stasis. Humans are always trying to stop the passage of time and to cling to that which is outworn and has lost its usefulness; but to cling to stasis is to cling to illusion – for the message of the cosmos is change. Today, many of us are separated from the world of Nature and it is no longer outside the hut door to teach us the lessons of life and death. Separated from Nature, we grow in illusion. We forget the message of change that leads to transmutation. Our problems can assume overwhelming proportions when, in terms of the millennia in which Nature operates, they are small. When our problems seem too great, we can go to a high place in the countryside. There, where the cries of the animals in the fields below fade into the bird song in the skies above, we can see that our individual selves are small in comparison with the greater whole, and so too are the problems and trials that inevitably beset us through our journey in manifestation. We must accept the night and dark things of life. These are part of our legacy in incarnation and it is useless to pretend otherwise; but we can embrace and accept this in the knowledge that after darkness comes light.

❧ My dark eyes look to the night
in the hope of dawn to come.
What do you hope for,
you, who take day as your father and mother,
when day is done?

Vivanne Crowley, 1976

The great darkness that we must all face is our own mortality. The Earth Traditions are not sentimental about Nature. She has many faces – the gentle warmth of a Mediterranean spring, the fierce heat of the Arizona desert sun, the mildness of an English autumn, the cold barrenness of an Arctic night. The Goddess is both beneficent and cruel. She gives but she takes away. The duality within the Goddess represents the true nature of the universe – a continual struggle between life and death, dark and light. In Hindu Traditions, the Goddess represents 'generation and the glories of life with the ever-present process of disintegration and death'.[11] The Goddess has two aspects. One is compassionate, gentle and loving; the other fierce, cruel, violent and dark with destruction.

❧ Yet, even in her fierce aspect, she protects those ... who can
overcome their fears of the terrors of the inevitable process of
continuous change and decay she represents to see her

135

transcendent beauty and the eternal bliss that ultimately she
bestows on her worshippers.[12]

The Goddess is beautiful Virgin and bountiful Mother. In many Pagan Traditions,
the Goddess is also Queen of Night, Lady of the Underworld and the Layer-Out
at death. The magician Dion Fortune wrote in her book *The Sea Priestess*:

🍃 I am the Veiled Isis of the shadows of the sanctuary.
I am She that moveth as a shadow
behind the tides of death and birth.
I am She that cometh forth by night,
and no man seeth my face.
I am older than time and forgotten of the gods.
No man may look upon my face and live;
for in the hour he parteth my veil, he dieth.[13]

This third aspect of the Goddess is darkness. It is an aspect that we need to
accept, but that we often fear and turn from.

🍃 *Dark Mother*
By the Rainbow Bridge across the Abyss,
in the shadow of Yggdrasil tree,
at the Well of the Origin of All-things,
I saw them come to me.

First, the Maiden, pale as death,
a shroud had she for hair;
and then the Mother, babe at breast,
but no milk of kindness there.

And then the Veiled One, blackest Hag,
whose eyes were cold obsidian;
the reeling stars reflected there,
in silent mirrors of oblivion.

Vivianne Crowley, Lammas 1990

Contemporary Pagan ritual often calls upon this darker side of the Goddess. As Morrigan or Hecate, she is the bearer of the sickle that reaps the Corn King. The Goddess represents creation, fertility and the generation of new life; but also the continuous processes of destruction, decay, and death. Both anabolism and catabolism are hers. If we can accept both sides of the Goddess' nature, we need no longer fear the trials of life that none can escape. The death of the body is not the end of existence in any of the Earth Traditions. Life and death are a cyclical process, through which we experience many states of being, both material and spiritual. Death is part of the natural and unending cycle of creation and destruction. Starhawk writes:

> Death is not an end; it is a stage in the cycle that leads on to rebirth. After death, the human soul is said to rest in 'Summerland', the Land of Eternal Youth, where it is refreshed, grows young, and is made ready to be born again. Rebirth is not considered to be condemnation to an endless dreary round of suffering, as in Eastern religions. Instead, it is seen as the great gift of the Goddess, who is manifest in the physical world.[14]

Death is a staging post in the journey of our own individual evolutionary process. It is not the end of life, but a period of peace and rest. Just as the universe goes through cycles and seasons – existence, decay, destruction, lying dormant, and reawakening – so too do the cycles of Nature; and so too do the cycles of woman and man. Death is a time of rejuvenation, renewal and reunion with those who have gone before. At Samhain, the Festival of the Dead, a Wiccan priestess invokes the God as the Dread Lord of Shadows.

> Dread Lord of the Shadows,
> God of life and Giver of life,
> yet is the knowledge of Thee,
> the knowledge of death,
> open wide, we pray Thee,
> the Gates through which we all must pass.
> Let our dear ones, who have gone before,
> return this night to make merry with us,
> and when our time comes, as it must,
> O Thou, the Comforter, the Consoler,

the Giver of Peace and Rest,
we will enter Thy realms gladly and unafraid ...[15]

Earth Traditions teach that the soul continues to live after the death of the body and their myths describe the realms of death. In the Heathen Tradition, when a human being dies, the spirit embarks on a journey to the realm of Hel, Queen of the Dead. Hel is the daughter of the mischief-making god, Loki. She is depicted as half blue. This means that she is half dead, but half alive. Odin, All-father, judges the spirit, but he takes advice from the goddess Urd, the Norn who represents the past. The spirit then goes to its appropriate abode in the Otherworld. This would be a pleasant realm for those whose past deeds merited it and an extremely unpleasant one for those who deeds did not.

The Hindu scriptures of the *Upanishads* tell us:

As a man leaves an old garment and puts on one that is new,
the Spirit leaves his mortal body and then puts on one that
is new.[16]

Many Pagans share with Eastern philosophy a belief in reincarnation. In Wicca, ties between individuals are seen as important and these bonds will draw us to meet again those we love in future lives. The initiate is taught:

We know, that when rested and refreshed among our
dear ones,
we will be reborn again, by Thy grace and the grace of
the Great Mother.
Let it be in the same place and the same time as our
beloved ones,
and may we meet, and know, and remember, and love
them again.[17]

Reincarnation is often thought of as purely an Eastern teaching, but this is not the case. The Roman general and later emperor Julius Caesar comments that the Celts believed that the soul survived the body[18] and that druids taught the transmigration of souls – that after death we would incarnate again. Some in the Heathen Tradition believe that we are born once only. Others believe that individuals bound together by ties of blood and love would be reborn to meet one another again. The volva Freya Aswynn writes:

❦ It is a Northern belief that we are reincarnated into the same
tribe or even the same family. This is connected with the spiritual idea of the evolution of the individual within the framework of a collective unit of which he is a part.[19]

This emphasis on personal ties illustrates a difference between Western and
Eastern attitudes to reincarnation. Eastern philosophy teaches detachment, a
releasing from the bonds of personal love. Western philosophy teaches that we
can learn to love the Divine through first loving one another.

❦ Learn now the secret of the web
that is woven between the light and the darkness;
whose warp is life evolving in time and space,
and whose weft is spun of the lives of men.
Behold we arise with the dawn of time
from the grey and misty sea,
and with the dusk we sink in the western ocean,
and our lives are strung like pearls
on the thread of our spirit;
and never in all our journey go we alone,
for that which is solitary is barren.[20]

Eastern religions tend to have a negative view of material existence. The First
Truth of Buddhism is that 'All life is suffering'. Prince Siddhartha, who was later
known as the Buddha, came to the conclusion that life could only involve suffering and was best avoided when he first managed to venture out into the world
after being secluded by his father in their palace. The myth tells us he had never
had to face the realities of old age, illness or death. When confronted with them,
he despaired of material existence and turned away from life in the body. He left
his gilded palace to live a life of asceticism as a monk. Hindu teaching, from
which Buddhism derived, is also to seek release from material existence. Atman,
the individual's enduring core self, is tied to the wheel of rebirth and can only
find release by identifying itself with the spiritual world of Brahman, the transcendent Divine. Human beings have no choice. They must incarnate until they
gain the wisdom to free themselves from the worldly desires that bind them to
the Earthly plane. These Earthly attachments include both the desire to do good
and negative desires. Release comes from the development of detachment and
selfless love.

To the Earth Traditions, the world is not seen as a negative place from which we must escape but, potentially at least, as a place of great joy and beauty, in which there is the possibility, through Nature, to learn of the mysteries of life, death, and the deities. In Wicca, rebirth is promised by the Goddess and is welcome.

❧ It was I who gave birth to you,
and in the depths of my Earth,
you will find rest and rebirth,
and I will spring you forth anew,
a fresh shoot to greenness.

Vivianne Crowley, Beltane 1982

The European Earth Traditions teach that we can be released from the Wheel of Rebirth, but this is not because material existence is drudgery, but because the soul has gained all the experience it needs from Earthly incarnation and moves on to new experiences in other realms. The point at which we leave the Wheel of Rebirth is illustrated in a Wiccan Autumn Equinox rite. After the Harvest God who represents the spirit of the grain has been cut down at the festival of Lammas, he rises again; but not to rejoin his old life, for that is over. He has attained his godhead and leaves the material world to journey to another place. His place is now in the divine realm, in which we transcend our separateness and enter the unitive reality. We are at one with our Divine source, with one another and with the cosmos itself. When we have learned all that we can on the journey of life, the Wheel of Rebirth ceases to turn. At that final dissolution of our being, we return to the infinite source of all things.

❧ *The Dance of the Elements*
He stepped out of his mortal body,
and bowing once in its direction,
in honor of the Earthly temple of his being,
he began the Dance of the Elements.
He danced upon the waves of sea,
and leapt the clouds across the sky,
he landed on the Earth,
and danced by light of Moon and Sun,
he danced the flashing of the lightning,

and the falling of a flake of snow,
and the journey of a leaf upon the wind,
and the dancing of the rain,
and he did not come back again.
For at the end of the elements' dance,
throwing out his arms to embrace the universe,
and saving until last, the pirouette,
he spun on tiptoe faster,
faster and more fast,
until he was no longer seen.

But do not grieve,
O do not grieve,
for behind the veil of matter,
he shall be dancing still,
weaving between the molecules,
and laughing with the atoms,
and chasing the electrons,
across the cosmos to the stars.

And he shall be in ecstasy,
and he shall be,
he shall,
he all,
all he,
     Ain sof aur,
     Ain sof,
     Ain,
No, he will not come back again.[21]

Notes

1   This speech is adapted from Slater, *A Book of Pagan Rituals*, page 45.

2   Robert Bly, *Iron John: A Book About Men*, pages 35–6.

3   James Hillman, 'Senex and Puer: An Aspect of the Historical and Psychological Present', in Hillman (ed), *Puer Papers*, page 29.

4   Robert Bly, *Iron John: A Book About Men*, pages 86–7.

5   Robert Bly, *Iron John: A Book About Men*, page 15.

6   Chris Crowley, 'The God: Wicca and the Masculine' in V Crowley, *Wicca: The Old Religion in the New Millennium*, pages 199–200.

7   Robert Bly, *Iron John: A Book About Men*, pages 86–7.

8   John Rowan, *The Horned God: Feminism and Men as Wounding and Healing*, page 111, Routledge and Kegan Paul, 1987.

9   Aswynn, *Leaves of Yggdrasil*, pages 194–5.

10 Starhawk, *The Spiral Dance*, pages 27–8.

11 Stutley, *Hinduism*, pages 46–7.

12 Stutley, *Hinduism*, pages 46–7.

13 Fortune, *The Sea Priestess*, page 124.

14 Starhawk, *The Spiral Dance*, pages 27–8.

15 Quoted in Farrar and Farrar, *Eight Sabbats for Witches*, page 133.

16 *Bhagavad Gita, II, 22*, quoted in Lorimer, *Whole in One*.

17 Quoted in Farrar and Farrar, *Eight Sabbats for Witches*, page 133.

18 Hutton, *Pagan Religions of the Ancient British Isles*, page 183.

19 Aswynn, *Leaves of Yggdrasil*, page 78.

20 Adapted from Fortune, *The Sea Priestess*, page 123.

21 Vivianne Crowley for Alex Sanders, Beltane 1988.

11

Honoring the Gods

Why do we worship deities? We do not follow Earth Traditions because we have to. We are not bound to attend religious services because of social or family pressures. We are not afraid that if we fail to honor our deities, they will take vengeance, punish us, or condemn us to burn eternally in Hell. We honor our deities because we love them. Many Earth Traditions also teach us to worship our deities because they enjoy it. Pagans honor their deities because their views of life are different from many of the values of Western society. Material well-being is important, but not the only objective in life. Material things alone will not satisfy our deepest needs. We must also have spiritual sustenance. When we give honor to the source of our life and being, in those moments we draw nearer to the ineffable, the profound mystery of the universe, the life force that sustains us all. To draw nearer to this source is to come like a thirsty person to a pool of cool, clean water. We drink and every organ of our body absorbs the water and draws nourishment from it. So too does our spirit drink, when we return to the great pool of the infinite that is our source. We have a deep inner need to link ourselves with those forces that create and maintain the universe. If we lose this link we are orphans of the universe; separated forever from the Mother and Father of All.

Ritual

Many people, while sharing many of the ideas and ideals of the Earth Traditions, baulk at the word 'ritual'. They feel that ritual is an empty parade and show that is not for them. They may have been exposed to empty religious rituals as children or have seen them only at a distance on television programs or at social occasions such as weddings. Ritual is seen as pompous, boring and authoritarian – a chance for ministers to talk down to their congregations. In the Earth Traditions, ritual is different. It is not something that is done to us, but something that we do. We are the actors not the acted upon.

In earlier societies, ritual functioned to mark the transitions between different life stages. The stages of life – birth, sexual maturation, marriage, giving birth, kingship, war, and death – were marked by rites that gave us patterns of behavior with which to meet their demands. Vestiges of such rites remain in our largely secular societies, but for many people these rituals have become hollow and meaningless. This is unfortunate because rituals are important. They show us the meaning of our lives and how we as individuals fit into a greater whole. Ritual speaks through a symbolic language that allows us to come to an understanding of those processes of life and death that are our lot, and to praise, honor, and thank our deities, who nourish and care for us. Ancient myths and rituals are the cultural treasure store of our ancestors that convey truths about human development. Many would say that they represent metaphysical realities: that they are dramatic representations of the interplay of the gods, the Divine forces of the universe. However, it is not necessary to believe this in order to find value in ritual. Religious rites are not only a way of contacting the Divine outside us, but also a way of understanding our inner psyche and the Divine within. If we neglect our myths and rituals, we lose a sense of the endless cyclical process of the life force that endures in the face of the changing seasons and the brief shooting star of our individual lives.

Our ancestors believed that if the correct rites were not performed at the correct times, then the Sun might fade and die, that summer might not return to the land. Empirical observation shows that this is not so; but if in espousing science we reject the myths which have sustained the human race over the millennia, then we miss the point entirely. Myth is not objectively true, but that which is psychologically true. It is what Carl Jung called 'the bridge to all that is best in humanity.'[1]

Pagan rites

If you say, 'Pagan rites', this brings to the minds of many people lurid pictures of naked orgies by bonfires. Fun though these activities might be, the reality is much more prosaic. People who practice Earth Traditions may perform their rites in ordinary clothes, in special ritual dress, or, going back to Nature, in nothing at all. However, the purpose is the same – to reverence the Divine force that gives birth to us, sustains us and will ultimately receive us when this phase of our existence on Earth is done.

Celebrations may be based on ritual drawn from a particular tradition, or they may be spontaneous and eclectic rites created by the participants solely for that occasion. Whatever the differences in rituals between traditions, the emphasis in all Earth Traditions is on a cycle of activity – the wheel of the year and the wheel of death and rebirth – of which we are all a part. There are rituals to celebrate the important phases of the life cycle, the phases of the year and, in some Earth Traditions, the phases of the moon. Rituals may be as simple as sitting together in silence beneath a tree and meditating for a while, or they may be as complicated as a Latin high mass. They can be similar to a tribal gathering, with drums, fire, and feasting; or they may be formal ceremonies in white robes and with elaborate temple furnishings.

Celebrating at least some seasonal rituals outside in Nature is considered important in most Earth Traditions. Some of our Pagan predecessors had beautiful temples that were the work of cultured civilizations, but in many parts of the world, they had much simpler places of worship. In most of West and North Europe, the idea of worshipping the Divine in temples built by human beings was an alien idea brought by the invading Romans. Their culture was essentially urban, even taking its name from a city. Contemporary Paganism does not reject cities, but we seek to worship, when we can, beneath trees, sky, sun, moon, and stars, by the sound of rushing waters, the ever-flowing sea, wind, and the cry of the birds. Being practical people, Pagans recognize that outdoor worship is not always possible. A visit to a sacred site at dawn is fine at weekends, but not in the middle of the working week. Some of us are fortunate enough to have secluded gardens, but others are not. A cliff top is a pleasant place on a summer's day, but not the most congenial of spiritual venues in a December rainstorm with two screaming two-year-olds. Some rites must take place indoors and those who have sufficient space will often set aside a room within their homes as a temple. Others use a living room or hired hall. Some practitioners decorate their rooms with beautiful altars, hangings, and deity statues. Others have plainer tastes. Some lean towards the beautiful edifices of the temples of Egypt, Greece and Rome; others to the simple forest and natural sites of the Celts, Germans, and Native Americans. Most appreciate both.

Often practitioners of Earth Traditions do not have specially consecrated buildings for worship, so the concept of creating sacred space is important. This involves marking off space to indicate that, for the duration of the rite, this is holy ground. People may emphasize that they are entering sacred space by removing shoes and watches – for the world of the sacred is outside the normal laws of time – or by wearing special robes or being 'skyclad', the term used by witches for ritual nudity.

Sacred space is often thought of as a meeting point 'between the worlds' of the human and the Divine, and human and other created beings such as nature spirits or devas. In many traditions, the blessing of nature spirits on a rite is considered important. Places where two or more elements are present in abundance are considered particularly powerful. Rituals in Earth Traditions often take place in circular sacred space guarded by the powers of the four directions, each of which is associated with one of the four elements – earth, water, air or wind, and sun or fire. The shape of the sacred space we create to commune with our deities is important. It is an indicator of the underlying cosmology and religious beliefs that give rise to it. In Christianity, apart from the innovations of that interesting group the Knights Templar, who had round churches, church space was traditionally rectangular. God sat at one end and humankind at the other, often separated by a barrier or screen which only the chosen male, a priest, could penetrate. When we create circular sacred space, we are saying, 'The Divine is everywhere and is at the center of everyone and everything. All who enter the circle are equal.'

Once sacred space has been created, people call on their deities to be present in the rite. In some Earth Traditions, such as Santeria, Voudon and Wicca, deities are invoked into an individual who enters into a state of union with the Divine force and then speaks as the deity for the duration of the rite. In other traditions, deities are called upon through poetry, prayers, and praise. They may be considered as present in the sacred space and/or within all the ritual participants. In some Earth Traditions, the names given to deities are not considered important. In the Wiccan Tradition, the Goddess is invoked as 'Astarte, Dione, Melusine, Aphrodite, Bride ...' These Goddesses from diverse pantheons are seen as different aspects of the Great Goddess.

At contemporary Pagan seasonal celebrations, the invocation of deities is followed by an enactment or reading of the seasonal myth. This may be solemn or mirthful. Singing and chanting to the deities often follows the seasonal mystery. In Wiccan groups, this may be preceded by spell working, in which case dances and chants to raise energy and power may be used. Ritual feasting often follows. This has always been a feature of Pagan society. Feasts were a means of showing the sacred act of hospitality and were joyful and celebratory. Feasting is not an aftermath to religious ritual, but an integral part of it. To feast with the gods is a sacred act and after such feasts a portion of food and drink will be left out for the deities. This is usually done by pouring a libation to the Earth and by leaving food for the birds and wild animals. The rite will end with a bidding farewell to any Guardians who have been summoned and a thanking of the deities.

Seasonal rites

All the Earth Traditions celebrate a cycle of seasonal festivals. In some cultures, these have been celebrated in an unbroken tradition since before the coming of Christianity. Where indigenous traditions were suppressed, we must recreate our rites, drawing on our own spiritual experiences, and on the wealth of mythology, folklore, fairy tale, and traditional custom that linger in our heritage. The seasonal cycle followed by most Western European practitioners of Earth Traditions is derived from the festivals of Celtic and Germanic mythology. The four Celtic festivals are Imbolc or Oi-melc held on February 1, when the first shooting bulbs appear to herald the coming spring, Beltane or May Eve on April 30, which marks the beginning of summer, Lughnasadh on August 1; and Samhain, Summer's End, or Halloween on October 31. These transitions marked significant points in the agricultural calendar in the mild climate of Ireland and Western Scotland. They related to times for plowing, harvesting, and the winter slaughter of animals. Originally, they would not have been held on fixed dates, but when the people had finished their seasonal tasks. As we moved into the world of calendars and the recording of time, the festival dates gradually became fixed. The other four major festivals in the contemporary Pagan year are Spring and Fall or Autumn Equinox and Summer and Winter Solstice. These were originally Northern European festivals that took place five or six weeks later than their Celtic counterparts. The sowing ritual that occurs at the Spring Equinox in many Western European celebrations is held at Beltane in Norway. Some groups wish to remain exclusively Germanic or Celtic and prefer not to celebrate festivals with other origins; but many contemporary Pagans have combined the two sets of celebrations to produce a year wheel of eight festivals. This is not followed rigidly all over the world. The eight-festival year works well in temperate climates with four seasons, but not necessarily elsewhere. In the southern hemisphere, the pattern of seasons is reversed. Some climates have only three distinct seasons rather than four. In Icelandic tradition, for instance, there appear to have been only three major festivals, which were called blots or sacrifices. These were Thorriblot at Winter Solstice, Siggiblot in spring, which was held before the Icelanders went on their summer sea raids, and a Harvest festival, when any animals surplus to requirements were sacrificed.

African-based traditions have their own seasonal celebrations. Each orisha has his or her feast day and these feasts have been aligned to the Catholic Church calendar so that the orisha's celebration falls on the feast day of a complementary saint. As the saints' days themselves derive from the pre-Christian Pagan calendar of Europe, African Traditions, Wicca, Druidry, Baltic, Finnish and Germanic

Traditions often find their celebrations parallel one another; although there will be differences in emphasis depending on climatic zones. Native American Traditions are based on completely different cycles of celebration deriving from agriculture and/or hunting cycles, depending on the people's origin and traditional livelihood, but Solsite celebrations are often important.

The Wheel of the Year

Each Earth Tradition has its own way of celebrating the cycle of seasonal festivals that is often known in contemporary Paganism as the Wheel of the Year, but as they are based on changes in Nature and the environment, there are many commonalities between traditions. Originally, festivals were celebrations that focused on survival. They marked transition points in the hunting or agricultural food cycle on which people's lives depended. Today, in the era of freezers, central heating, and supermarkets, we are more removed from our biological selves and the importance of the tides of Nature, but the natural cycle is still important to us. Unconsciously, we respond to the season's change and our bodies and psyches program us to different activities at different points of the year. If we learn to recognize these natural rhythms and work with them, they can enhance our lives enormously. We are working with the prevailing trends of the time rather than against them. What are these trends?

Spring is a time of new beginnings. The planet wakes up. Days grow longer, the soil warmer. Birds recognize that this is time to mate and begin courtship dances, mating and nesting. Spring is a time of activity, a time to build. It is also a time when daylight stimulates our pituitary glands, which in turn stimulate our sexuality. The sap in the tree rises, so too do our own sexual urges. Spring is a time of seed sowing and fertility, when day and night, light and dark, are equal and there is a dynamic and creative tension between the polarities of opposites. Spring Equinox rites often celebrate the emergence of the young God in the world and his mating with the Goddess.

Isis of Nature awaiteth the coming of Her Lord the Sun.
She calls Him. She draws Him from the place of the dead,
the Kingdom of Amenti, where all things are forgotten.
And he comes to Her in his boat called Millions of Years,
and the Earth grows green with the springing grain.
For the desire of Osiris answereth unto the call of Isis.[2]

The fertility symbolism of spring is found in the custom of people giving one another Easter eggs. Originally, these were not made of chocolate but were eggs painted red or green – colors associated with the life force and with fertility. The eggs were originally the symbols of the German Goddess Ostara, who in German-based languages gave her name to Easter. Late-spring celebrations, Beltane or May Eve in Celtic Tradition, are held at a time when Nature is abundant. Seeds planted at spring have shooted; trees are hung with blossom. Maypole dancing around a decorated pole was customary in Western Europe. May celebrations were suppressed by the Protestant reformers who were scandalized by the country folk's revels, which involved the young people of the village going a-Maying before dawn in the woods in order to bring back blossoms to decorate the house – or so they said. The nineteenth-century writer Rudyard Kipling captured the spirit of Maying in his *Tree Song*. and this has been adapted and used by many Wiccan groups.

> O do not tell the priest of our Art,
> for he would call it a sin;
> but we shall be down in the woods tonight
> a-conjuring Summer in.
> And we bring you good news by word of mouth
> for woman, cattle and corn;
> for the Sun is coming up from the South,
> with oak and ash and thorn.

Midsummer is a celebration of the Sun, the Lord of Life. Across Northern Europe, bonfires were lit (and are still lit) on hilltops to celebrate the warmth of the Sun. At Midsummer the sun is at the height of its power. In Pagan symbolism, the Sun Child born at the Winter Solstice comes to full maturity with the sun's height; but in the cycles and spirals of creation, that which reaches its peak is already at the point of decline. From Midsummer, the days begin to grower shorter. All around us, it is still summer, but the signs of hidden decline are there. Nature loses its fresh greenness, grasses brown as do wheat and other grain crops. Some contemporary Pagan rituals enact a battle between the Lord of Summer and the Lord of Winter. The Summer King wins but receives a wound, which over the coming months will drain away his strength. This is the symbol of the dying of the year. The wound is also symbolic of the inner wound that scars us all – the knowledge of our own mortality, which is the price of consciousness, our glory and our tragedy. Consciousness brings pain because for the first time we see our Earthly lives as they truly are, as mortal and finite. No one finds this an easy path.

At the end of July and beginning of August, Lughnasadh or Lammas celebrates the grain harvest and, in some Earth Traditions, the sacrifice of the Corn King, whose reaping is necessary to feed the people. The King accepts the inevitability of the ultimate sacrifice and is cut down by the Goddess, who appears as the Goddess of Death, the wielder of the sickle.

> Let us now celebrate the Mystery of Lammas,
> the season of the Summer Queen and Sacrificial King.
> What most we love we must give back again,
> that the Dance of Life may spiral on and on.
> From death comes forth new life, and thus rebirth;
> from joy to grief and sorrow, and back again to mirth.

Vivianne Crowley, Lammas 1982

The way chosen by our ancestors to come to terms with the realities of existence is to celebrate the mysteries of life and death as seen in Nature. It is through observing the cycle of birth, death, and rebirth in Nature that we understand that this too is our own fate – to be born, to die, and to live again. The seasonal celebrations echo the cycles of creation and destruction on the microcosmic and macrocosmic scales. Through participating in these rituals, we come to terms with the processes of ageing and death and understand that they are but part of the life process that is eternal. This is something I wrote at Lammas in 1982, when the daughter of a Pagan friend had just died.

> In the circle, I had for the first time, a sense of the life and death aspect of Lammas. Death seemed truly present. We sang a chant to Hecate and for the spirit of the child, flying free in death. I saw the greatness of the human spirit: how our lives are less than that of a butterfly's in the passing of time; how we have the vision of deities, but are trapped in the bodies of animals; and how great is our triumph and our tragedy.

> The Summer King comes to Our Lady of the Fields,
> and we sing our songs and stories,
> and we do not care that we live or die,
> but only that the Dance of Life goes on.

What we experience through participating in the cycle of the seasonal rituals is transcendence – a reaching beyond the boundaries of time, space, and the material world. Carl Jung wrote in *Archetypes and the Collective Unconscious* that this transcendence was taught in the ancient Pagan mystery traditions.

> ❧ In these mystery-dramas the transcendence of life, as distinct from its momentary concrete manifestations, is usually presented by the fateful transformations – death and rebirth – of a god or godlike hero. The initiate may either be a mere witness of the divine drama or take part in it or be moved by it, or he may see himself identified through the ritual action with the god ... The initiate who ritually enacts the slaying, dismemberment, and scattering of Osiris and afterwards his resurrection in the green wheat, experiences in this the permanence and continuity of life, which outlasts all change of form and phoenix-like, continually rises anew from its own ashes.[3]

The seasonal festivals help to overcome our individual fears, despairs and sorrows at the difficulties of life by showing us that we are part of a greater scheme of things that transcends our individual pain.

> ❧ When all the sorrow of the past
> has melted away like morning dew,
> in the warmth of summer sun,
> then shall we see a brighter dawn,
> when love and hope and beauty are reborn.
>
> *Vivianne Crowley, 1977*

Fall or Autumn Equinox is a time of balance, when the hours of light equal the hours of darkness. We stand poised at the changing of a tide. In spring and summer, the impetus of the life force is outwards towards activity and creation. At fall, the tides turn inwards towards contemplation.

> ❧ We stand at the turning point of summer and winter.
> Summer is the season of action,
> Winter the season of rest, repose and contemplation.
> It is a time for meditation and for study,

a time to seek the deities within and not without.
Renew now the power within us, O Great Ones,
so that as the sun wanes,
our unconscious minds may grow more powerful,
and we may descend into our own underworld,
to explore throughout the winter,
the magic kingdom that we find within.

Vivianne Crowley, Autumn 1984

At the Equinox, the Goddess descends to the Underworld. In some groups, the mysteries of Demeter and Kore are celebrated. The God who was slain at Lammas is now Lord of the Underworld and the Goddess goes to join him. Leaves fall from the trees, birds migrate, the signs of life disappear one by one. Freya Aswynn suggests that in the Germanic Tradition, the theme of descent into the unconscious or Underworld can be celebrated by a ritual symbolizing Odin's initiation on the World-Tree.

Samhain or Halloween is the feast of the dead when the worlds of matter and spirit draw close to one another and the dead may pass to and fro through the veils. It is customary to carve Jack o'Lanterns from pumpkins and to place candles in them to guide the souls of the ancestors to the feast. A meal is left out for the ancestors – usually in the garden. Some Odinist groups celebrate a Festival of the Dead slightly later, on November 11, which commemorates the signing of the peace treaty that ended the First World War. The emphasis is on the links between past and present and the ties of blood and kin.

In the name of the High gods –
Urd, Norn of the Past,
we offer thanks for the blood ties of our house and family.
Verdandi, Norn of the Present, and Skuld, Norn of the Future:
may we not be a failing people and a Springless Autumn ...
Now, to our sons' sons and their sons,
we send our words as messengers,
the way we shall not pass along:
Kinsmen! Unseen, unborn, unknown!
Since we can never see your face and never grasp your hand,
we send our spirits through time and space,
in Odin's name we greet you.[4]

The Winter Solstice or Yule celebrates the birth of the young Sun God. The Goddess is venerated as the Mother. Evergreen boughs or a tree are brought into the house to mark the continuance of life in the cold winter season. Yule is a time of celebration, gift-giving and great rejoicing; for in the cold, dark days of winter, there is the promise of spring to come. In one ceremony, the God is called upon to bring to his people a sign that light will be restored.

🦋   Lord of Darkness, Belovèd of our Lady,
Keeper of the Gates of Life and Death, of Night and Day.
Across the starry heavens, we call to you:
the light is failing in our land;
the trees stand bare and skeletal;
the birds have fled;
and plaintive is the song of those who must remain.
The frozen river stands,
unmoving as though dead;
the days grow shorter,
and the crimson setting Sun
falls too soon beneath the tree tops,
bathing the sky in the color of blood.
Bring us a word, a sign of hope;
speak to your people, our Lord and our God.

The God then responds:

🦋   Behold I answer you:
your hope is reborn.
For in caverns beneath the Earth,
I hear a new born cry;
in the midnight of the year,
my Queen has brought forth our son.

And in the morning at day break,
three signs you will see:
a stag upon the hill,
his antlers glistening in the mists of dawn,
the red breast of a cock robin,
singing on the branch of a holly tree,

153

and all day in the clear blue sky shall hang,
on one side the pale light of the wintery reborn Sun,
and on the other the lingering shadow
of the pale orb of the Moon,
the Goddess' sign,
that her Promised One has come.

I stand for the babe who sleeps in the cradle,
I speak for the King who is to come,
Arthur, Lugh, Balin,
these shall be his names,
and the treasures of the Earth,
to these he shall lay claim.
The Lord of Life is now renewed.
Father of the Child, I come to you,
the light cometh, the Sun returneth,
peace, joy and gentleness descend upon this place,
as we celebrate the Season of the Child.

The Goddess then speaks:

In the deep caverns of the Earth I labored,
and the Sun Child was reborn,
to restore the Earth to fruitfulness,
when winter snows have melted, and he is strong.
Behold the light returneth, the Sun King he is born again!
His father shall furnish him with chariot and horses,
and the Eight Weapons of the Ancients,
I shall give to him as his inheritance.
I shall wrap him in the cloak of the radiance of the Sun,
and arm him with the Shield of Stars,
and the arrows of his enemies shall falter,
and pierce the ground.
The Sword of Truth he shall gird on,
and the Grail of the Wine of Life,
shall inspire his heart and mind.
They will place on his hand the ring of power,
and a crown of gold shall grace his brow.

154

The Spear of Light shall fly the air for him,
and with the war banner of the Morrigan,
he shall drive back the forces of the dark.

Vivianne Crowley, Yule 1984

The appearance of the first bulb shoots is the time of early spring festival, which in Celtic Tradition is Imbolc. Imbolc celebrates the transition of the Goddess from Mother to Virgin. Her child is grown and she is free and independent once more. Winter is a time of rest, of battening down the hatches, and enduring the winter's cold until spring comes again. In the Celtic calendar, Imbolc is the festival of the Goddess and later of the Christian saint Brigid in Irish or Bride in Scots Gaelic. When the ground softens sufficiently for the first shoots to appear, it is time for reawakening. Imbolc is a festival to celebrate the return of warmth to the land and a time to celebrate the birth of the first lambs and ewes beginning to lactate – a welcome event in countryside dependent on lamb and mutton for meat, and sheep milk for dairy products. In a contemporary Imbolc ritual, Brigid or Bride is greeted:

O Gracious Bride,
who walks between the worlds,
bringing light and life to women and men;
come forth once more and walk in our ways.
For where you have walked
will spring forth flowers,
where you have smiled,
the Sun will turn and linger,
where you have sung,
the birds will return.
Gracious Lady, bless our homes,
may there be peace within;
bless our bodies,
may they be well and strong;
bless our hearts,
may they know joy and love;
bless our minds,
may they know the delight of creativity;
bless our spirits,
may they know the ecstasy of the Divine.[5]

Celebrating the seasonal cycle

We can celebrate our seasonal rites with poetic invocations and prayers of praise, but this wordy approach is not essential. We can reverence our deities in silence, by lighting a candle, or planting a tree. The message is that we are free – to worship how and where we will, and to create and recreate our own forms of celebration that can evolve and change over the years. To mark the seasonal rites, we can create our own forms, or we can work with the rites and forms of one of the Earth Traditions; but we do not use these forms simply because we have been taught them, but because they are meaningful.

The seasonal myths are not relics of the past, but expressions of living and eternal truths about humankind and the universe we inhabit. For rituals to be meaningful, they must not become static. They must be a living branch of a tree that is deeply-rooted in the past yet stretches upward to reach present and future. Within each festival are many complex levels of interpretation and meaning and we can choose which to emphasize in different years. As we come anew to each festival of the season's round, those things that are nearest to us at the time, and those things that have touched us throughout the year, come to the forefront and in the symbolism of the seasonal cycle we see messages that we have not seen before. We examine the rite and we may change it slightly, adding or dropping parts depending on their relevance to the group. In explaining this, it sounds as though we consciously decide to invent a new rite, but this is not so. Usually the need for a new emphasis in the rite comes to us through a dream, through writing a poem, or through an intuitive feeling that something is missing and we must meditate to discover what it is. Rites evolve and speak to us in the deepest part of our psyches to express our unity with our deities and our love for our deities.

Notes

1   Jung, *The Collected Works of C.G. Jung, 5*, page 231.
2   Fortune, *The Sea Priestess*, page 123.
3   Jung, *The Collected Works of C.G. Jung, 9, Part 1*, page 117.
4   Stubba, *The Book of Blots*, pages 79–87.
5   Crowley, *Celtic Wisdom*, page 64.

12

Shamanism, Divination and Magic

Many, though not all, of the Earth Traditions practice magic, divination and/or shamanism. Within the Traditions, some practice them purely as paths to spiritual fulfilment; others are also interested in the spiritual powers that the Traditions can foster. Many practitioners of Earth Traditions prefer not to interfere magically in the course of events, but are happy to try to foresee and anticipate the pattern of events by using divination. For those not brought up with these Traditions, the idea of practicing shamanism or magic may seem strange, archaic and outlandish. Even those who accept the possibility of their existence may not believe they have the ability to do them. The Earth Traditions' interest in these practices is not a regression to the wish-fulfilling world of childhood, but part of a contemporary preoccupation that is as much psychological as it is mystical. It is a desire to understand and experience other states of being and other states of consciousness. 'Other states of consciousness' is a puzzling phrase to those who have never experienced them and it is difficult to convey these through words, but they are states whereby we can transcend the boundaries of time and space that normally act as barriers in the material world. We can step beyond the here and now to learn of the past, the future, and events happening in other places and in other realms. We can influence and affect those realms, and through those realms we can influence and affect the world of everyday reality.

The shaman is a voyager into other states of consciousness. Shamanism originated in Siberia and Central Asia and spread from the Russian steppes westwards into Europe and eastwards into North America. Mircea Eliade in *Shamanism: Archaic Techniques of Ecstasy*[1] describes the shaman of the Kazak Kirgiz people of Northern Asia as singer, poet, musician, diviner, priest, doctor, guardian of religious and popular traditions, and preserver of legends. Much of Native American and Inuit religious practice is based on shamanism. Similar practices are also found in South America, the Pacific region and elsewhere.

Shamanism is remarkably widespread. Shamanism has been defined as 'technique of ecstasy'. Much of our contemporary ideas of shamanism have come from the study of those groups and societies in which shamanism is still practiced. The work of the shaman was usually dismissed by early Western travelers, researchers and missionaries as ignorance, superstition and misunderstanding of the laws of cause and effect. This attitude displayed not the ignorance of the practitioners themselves, but the ignorance of those who, steeped in their ideas of the superiority of Western science and religion, were unable to see the value of shamanic practices.

The role of the shaman in society is to enter into an altered state of consciousness in order to act as an intermediary between the spirit world and the everyday world. Shamanism is a path to knowledge; but this is not achieved through the intellectual questioning and rational analysis of the philosopher and scientist, but through inner experience. In the silence of the forest, cave and sacred space, the shaman journeys forth to explore the inner world or Otherworld, the country of the mind. The purpose of the journey is not idle curiosity or self-development, it is to serve the shaman's community. Through their Otherworld explorations, shamans bring back knowledge of the cause of illnesses and problems in their communities, and why the rains have failed or the crops will not grow. Through contact with the spirits of the Otherworld, the shaman can work acts of healing, divination, and magic for the benefit of his or her community. Shamans may also guide others to experience the Otherworld for themselves and so deepen their spiritual lives. The shaman is also a guide who helps those who are dying to leave their bodies and travel safely into the Otherworld.

Accessing the Otherworld

In societies where shamanism is practiced, ordinary reality is seen as a narrow band of experience sandwiched between two other realities, those of the Upper and Lower Worlds. This belief is also found in the European Earth Traditions. To enter the world of spirit, the shaman makes an inner journey. This frequently involves descent into the Underworld, but it may also include ascent into heavenly realms – the Upper World. Together these worlds comprise the Otherworld. The Otherworld is just as real as our everyday realm; although what happens would be thought fantastical and impossible in ordinary reality. The Otherworld is populated by powerful beings, often in animal form, that must be propitiated, persuaded and sometimes fought into co-operating with the shaman's community for its general well being. The shaman is entrusted by his or her community with the task of crossing into the Otherworld to deal with these entities. In making the crossing, the shaman needs protection. This comes in the form of spirit guides or animals that come to the shaman's aid.

The Otherworld is accessed through trance. There are a number of ways of achieving this. In some cultures, hallucinogenic drugs are used. Another method is through rhythmic drumming and/or shaking a rattle. Shaking rice in a sieve is another alternative. Shamans frequently refer to their drum as their 'horse' or 'canoe'. It is the means they use to journey to the Otherworld. This imagery is found in the Finno-Ugric Tradition, where Väinämöinen the First Shaman descends to the Underworld of Tuonola to obtain the three words that he needs to complete his boat.

Trance does not necessarily mean that we have no awareness of our physical surroundings. Trance is a change in our brain state whereby our brain EEG patterns change to those normally associated with sleeping. We are relaxed, we allow dreamlike images to float from the unconscious into the conscious mind – but we are still awake. The shaman remains at a level of consciousness where he or she retains some awareness of this world. This control is essential as the Otherworld journey may need to be directed and its sights and experiences recollected, mused upon and interpreted. It is common for the shaman to be able to report back to witnesses on the progress of the journey while still in the process of undertaking it.

Shamans often enter the Upper World via a pole that reaches to the sky. In Germanic myth, the pole has evolved into Yggdrasil, the World Tree. The pole that leads to an Upper World in the sky is a frequent image in mythology. In the European fairy story *Jack and the Beanstalk*, Jack plants a magic bean that sprouts and produces a tall green plant that grows to reach the sky. Jack climbs up the beanstalk and has a series of adventures. In both African and Native American creation stories, the gods sometimes descended a pole to create our world – Middle Earth. Access to the Lower World can be through an opening – a cave, gully, hollow tree, or through diving into a pond or lake. Some shamans take a more direct approach and create an image of diving directly through the surface of the earth. Whatever the point of entry, it is likely that the shaman will follow a tunnel. This can be easy or arduous depending on the situation the shaman is exploring. The form the tunnel takes – how difficult it is to follow, whether it is almost blocked, and whether by animate or inanimate obstructions – relates closely to the reason why the journey is undertaken. It can, of course, be seen as a metaphor for the journey into the unconscious. Most people undertaking shamanic journeys find that, although their starting point is the same on different occasions, the tunnel can appear different each time. Sometimes it will be more blocked than others. Sometimes it is empty and sometimes it is inhabited with other creatures. These can appear as normal animals – snakes, spiders, etc – or as mythic creatures and monsters of wild imaginings.

Although variations in technique and practice can be found in different cultures, what is interesting is not the variation but the similarity in the belief systems and Otherworld experiences of different peoples at different times and in the widely separated countries where shamanism has been practiced. There is no doubt that the techniques used produce profound changes in consciousness and comprise a psychological reality. Many would say that they also represent a supernatural reality; but the distinction is not important. To those who have explored it, the Otherworld is as real and actual as the ordinary world. People's experiences within it have a commonality that indicates that the Otherworld represents a shared level of consciousness that is present in all humankind. It exists for all who can access it and is more than an individual's private imaginings.

Shamanism in European Traditions

Elements of shamanism are found throughout Europe. In Finnish Tradition, Väinämöinen the First Shaman, son of Ilmater Water-Mother the Creatrix Goddess, helps her to complete her work of creating the world. Shamanism is also found in the Celtic Tradition. Shamans have attributes that are similar to those ascribed to druids. Journeying to the Otherworld to commune with the spirits of the dead in order to gain information or receive teaching was widely practiced by the Celts. In Irish Tradition a would-be bard might sleep on the burial mound of a famous dead bard in order to learn the bardic gift. If he was favored, the dead bard might appear to him in a dream to teach him verse and inspire in him the gift of poetry. In Germanic Tradition, an important function of the seeress or volva was to obtain information from the Otherworld through seidr or prophecy. The *Eddas* describe the volva's costume as a dark blue cloak with a hood set with stones along the hem. There is an inner hood or headdress made from animal skin, gloves made of cat skin with the fur innermost, fur boots, a skin bag to contain power objects and a long rune-staff. Archeological investigations in Scandinavia have found graves with this equipment and with the power objects still intact. These included amber beads, stones, snake bones, squirrel tails, bird claws and seashells. Odin the chief god of the Aesir has many of the characteristics of a shaman. The eight-legged horse is a frequent image in shamanic cultures and one of the ways by which the shaman can penetrate the Otherworld. Odin travels to the Otherworld on such a horse – Sleipnir or Glider – who was fathered by the god Loki on a mare. Sleipnir is therefore part animal and part Divine. We are also told in the *Ynglinga Saga* that when Odin made Otherworld journeys, his body lay as though he were asleep or dead. 'He then became a bird or a beast, a fish or a dragon, and went in an instant to far-off lands.'[2] Odin is a god of knowledge, but like that of all shamans, Odin's knowledge is only achieved at the price of suffering. To obtain wisdom, Odin consults with Mimir's head and drinks each day from Mimir's well, but in order to do so, he must sacrifice part of himself – one of his own eyes.

There are many connections between the European Witchcraft Tradition and shamanism. Rapport with animals was an important mark of both shaman and witch, both of whom had spirit helpers who appeared as power animals and familiars. These are sent out to do the witch or shaman's work. The word witch has a number of derivations, one of the most important of which is 'to know'. Similarly, the Finnish word for shamanic practitioner is tietäjä, one-who-knows. With the coming of Christianity to Europe, many shamanic practices were outlawed, but people continued their ancient practices by painting a Christian gloss on the original. Spells and charms were 'Christianized' by adding names of appropriate angels and saints. Some people continued to use hallucinogenic drugs to enter the ecstatic altered state of consciousness that the Inquisition later labeled 'the Witches' Sabbath'. The knowledge of herbal and natural medicine possessed by shamans became the province of the village wise woman and cunning man. A typical cunning man is described in Lady Wilde's nineteenth-century collection, *Ancient Legends, Mystic Charms, and Superstitions of Ireland*:

Some persons, even at the present day amongst the peasants, have strange gifts and a knowledge of the hidden mysteries, but they can only impart this knowledge when they know that death is on them, and then it must be ... to an unmarried man, or to a childless women, for these are the most susceptible to the mysterious power by which miracles can be worked.

A man now living at Innis-Sark has this strange and mystic gift. He can heal diseases by word, even at a distance, and his glance sees into the very heart, and reads the secret thoughts of men. He never touched beer, spirits, or meat, in all his life, but has lived entirely on bread, fruit, and vegetables. A man who knows him thus describes him – 'Winter and summer his dress is the same, merely a flannel shirt and a coat.'[3]

The cunning man's dress links him to older practices. One of the traditional attributes of shamans, and of Yogis in the East, is control over body temperature and the ability to overcome extremes of heat and cold; even to the extent of sitting naked in snow without freezing. Yogis and shamans, and some Catholic saints, were thought to be able to levitate and fly. Witches were also accredited with these powers. The Inquisition devised ordeals to trap the witch into betraying her supernatural powers to save herself; to float on water for instance when she should have drowned.

Web of Wyrd

The rationale of shamanism and magic is interconnectedness. To any shaman, the concept of oneness is so obvious that it hardly needs to be stated. There is no separateness in Nature. Everything, animate or inanimate, is interconnected. Each separate thing, whether a rock or stone, animal, plant, human or event, is linked. All things are part of a greater whole and in communication with one another. The apparent separateness of things – people, objects, events – is an illusion. If all things are connected, then by examining any part of the Web of Wyrd, we can gain insight into the whole. The rationale of the Web of Wyrd has been related to a more contemporary phenomenon, that of the hologram. Holograms are created because when two coherent rays of light impinge on an object in their path, they produce an interference pattern that can be recorded on film. The film can then be used to create a three-dimensional image of the object. What is interesting is that it is not necessary to have the whole film in order to re-create the object. A tiny fragment will allow the image to be reproduced, although details will be lost as the film area becomes less. From this, it can be argued that each fragment of the universe contains the key to the greater whole. Holograms give us clues as to the true nature of reality: that it is a set of inter-connected worlds woven around one another, intermeshed and interlinking – the Web of Wyrd.

The magical reality is essentially a holistic one – everything is connected. An action in one part of the physical realm can influence events, people, and objects that are separated in time and space. The concept of the Web is important in understanding the concept of time in the shamanic and magical universes. Past, present, and future co-exist. Time is but a measurement of physical change and the realm of Wyrd is beyond the physical. The laws of time do not apply. By achieving a state of consciousness whereby we enter a timeless zone, a deep realm of the unconscious where the personal unconscious merges into the group mind of humankind and that of other aspects of creation, it is possible to discern the future. At the level of the group mind or collective unconscious, we lose our sense of individual separateness and our minds can merge with those of others. To use an analogy, human beings are a bit like rhizomes – each plant appears separate when we look at the surface of the soil, but if we go deeper, we find they are joined at a common root. To use another analogy, we are like different arms of an amoeba. When we look outwards, we cannot see that we are joined as one. It is only when we turn back and look within that we see that we all emerge from and merge into a central core.

At this deeper level of consciousness, the mind operates outside the time/space parameters that hold good for material reality. We enter a world in which meaningful coincidence or synchronicity occurs. Carl Jung used the terms synchronicity to explain those strange coincidences that happen to us on our life's journey and can often totally alter its direction. We have a dream that if we go to a certain shop we will find a certain book in a certain place. The dream is so powerful that we feel obliged to go and look, even though we feel silly in doing so. We find the book and reading it changes our view of the world and the course of our lives. This is synchronicity. Synchronicity and clairvoyant dreaming are spontaneous transmissions from this deeper level of the psyche. Divination is a way of consciously tuning in to seek information. Certain symbol systems such as the tarot, astrology, and the runes can help us access information from the Web because, by the processes of synchronicity, the pattern of symbols in one place reflects the patterning of events in another.

Divination

Most Earth Traditions use divinatory techniques to see into the future and have devised symbol systems to aid in divination. Many European systems use the tarot, a system that was spread across Europe by Romany people, but it is based on imagery drawn from the Western ritual magic tradition. All divination systems work on similar principles in that the diviner must enter a state of light trance during which the diviner's sensitivity and perceptions are heightened and the symbols used help the diviner to give interpretations that go beyond his or her ordinary level of conscious knowledge. In systems such as Santeria and Wicca, where deities are invoked into their initiates, in an altered state of consciousness, the chosen of the gods may give prophecy and perform healing that would be considered beyond his or her everyday powers.

The runes are one of the principal divination methods of Northern Europe. The Roman historian Tacitus,[4] writing in 98 CE, makes one of the earliest references to the throwing of the runes. He describes how Germanic peoples performed divination by cutting off the branch of a nut-bearing tree, slicing it into strips, marking these with signs, and then throwing them onto a white cloth. The community priest or head of the family would select three of the strips for interpretation. In Germanic Traditions, the discovery of the runes is accredited to the god Odin. Odin obtains their secrets through undergoing a shamanic ordeal of being hung from a tree. This aspect of Odin can be equated with the tarot card of the Hanged Man. The story of Odin's ordeal is found in the *Eddas* in the *Hávamál* or *High One's Words*.

> I know I hung on the wind-tossed Tree,
> that Tree that springs from a place unknown,
> nine whole nights, pierced with a spear,
> given to Odin, myself to myself.
> No horn they handed me nor bread;
> I looked downwards and with piercing cry,
> took up the runes,
> and fell to the ground.[5]

The use of runes is also found in the Finnish Tradition. The *Kalevala* describes how Väinämöinen the First Shaman uses slips of alder wood in divination.

> Then the aged Väinämöinen,
> the great primeval shaman,
> hastened to cut alder sticks,
> and arranged the sticks in order,
> and began to shuffle the lots ...[6]

Other sources indicate that the strips of wood would have had signs marked upon them. Kati-ma Koppana in *Snake Fat and Knotted Threads* gives us this spell:

I'll cast my slips of alder wood.
Old Mother Kavé, Nature's own,
Golden Kavé, the Beautiful,
come hither to arrange the runes,
arrange the lots with your own hands,
with your own hands the runes to turn ...[7]

Here the runes are used by one set apart – a shaman. To use any system of divination requires knowledge of the philosophy from which the system springs, its understanding of fate, and the nature of any deities who preside over the divination. Divination should not be engaged in for entertainment. To discern the Web of Wyrd is a sacred act that must be approached with suitable reverence, sincerity and seriousness. The purpose of divination is to help us look into the pattern of Wyrd, so that we can determine the prevailing trends and then work through them to the most positive outcome.

Magic

In the worldview of the Earth Traditions, the future is not fixed. If we can discern the pattern of the Web of Wyrd, through spontaneous clairvoyance, divination or a shamanic journey to the Otherworld, then we can change it. This can involve action on the material plane. It can also involve magic. The Earth Traditions venerate the deities of Nature and help to focus us in the here and now, but they are also concerned with the Otherworld and with magical power. Magic uses techniques such as candle magic, talismans, poppets and cord magic. Generally, the props are not important in themselves. They are ways of focusing the mind on what is to be accomplished. They are used to enter a changed state of consciousness, a trance. Many techniques help induce trance. They work through all the sensory modalities, such as repetitive movement (dancing or swaying), repetitive sound (chants, mantras, litanies, bells, rattles, drumming), lulling the consciousness through fixing the gaze on an object such as a black mirror or candle flame, and the use of incense. Some means of magic, such as crystals and runes, are more than props. Crystals are thought to act as transmitters of energy; so too are runes. The runes are well known as a divinatory system, but their use in magic is less familiar. Specific runes have specific purposes.

🍃 A spell unknown to queens I know,
 or any of humankind:
 'Help' is it named, for help can it give
 in sickness, sadness, and sorrow.[8]

🍃 A fourth I know, if my foes
 have fettered me hand and foot,
 I chant the spell that breaks the chains,
 and they fly from hands and feet.[9]

The right chanting and drawing of the runes is a magical act which activates the forces they represent so that they can be directed according to the chanter's will. In the *Sigridfumál*, the following verse gives instructions on how to deal with a difficult birth. The Disir are female guardian spirits.

🍃 Help runes you should know,
 to help bring forth,
 the woman of her child:
 mark them on your hands,
 take hold of her wrists,
 and invoke the Disirs' aid.[10]

As I do will, so mote it be

In magic, will is an important concept, but one that is often misunderstood. In the English language, we speak of wilfulness to mean that someone is wrong-headed and not acting in accord with the greater good, and willing is equated with striving. The Italian psychologist Roberto Assagioli, founder of the psychosynthesis movement, has provided a better understanding of the nature of will. Assagioli saw will as having seven qualities: energy, mastery, concentration, determination, persistence, initiative and organization. He believed that people should learn to use 'skillful will'. This involves not strain or forcefulness but:

🍃 ...a sense of letting go and yet being fully present. It is cooperating with the benign forces of the world, which is where love and will are fully consistent and almost one.[11]

Magical will is not about effort. It operates more like the muscles of a trained athlete – at ease and without strain. How do we achieve the deep connection to the unconscious that enables us to accomplish these transformations? To our ancestors, magicians were people set apart. They were the scientists of the natural world. Reaching behind the veil of matter, they touched the true and deep nature of things. Their work was holy, for in learning the true nature of reality, they penetrated the innermost secrets of creation. The Renaissance magician and physician Paracelsus explained:

> The natural saints, who are called magi, are given powers over the energies and faculties of nature. For there are holy men in God who serve the beatific life; they are called saints. But there are also holy men who serve the forces of Nature, and they are called Magi ... What others are incapable of doing they can do, because it has been conferred upon them as a special gift.[12]

Many contemporary practitioners of magic see magical ability not as a special gift, but as a skill that many people can develop. However, while theoretically this may be true, the problem remains that it is difficult for those educated in Western intellectualism to let go of their rigid thought structures sufficiently to enter trance states and achieve what Assagioli calls 'letting go yet being fully present'. Many people believe what our ancestors believed – that a four-leaved clover will bring them fortune. For others, belief of any sort is not easy. Magic does not require absolute faith; but we need to be open-minded enough to accept the possibility that it might work. If we are convinced that nothing will happen, then we will not be able to let go sufficiently to do magic.

Magical ethics

It is important not to be romantic about shamanism and the magical universe of our ancestors. The idea of interconnectedness means that in shamanic thought nothing happens by accident. In the shamanic universe, everything happens for a reason and a purpose and everything has a cause. A worldview that excludes the possibility of accident has advantages and disadvantages. Positively, it encourages us to take responsibility for ourselves. If something happens to us, it is for a reason and if we do not like it, we can act to change it. Negatively, it can lead to paranoia. It is a world in which illness is the result of curses or transgressions of supernatural laws. To be cured, we must lift the curse or propitiate the spirit we have offended. Usually this means enlisting and paying for the services of an expert to put things right. It is also important to remember that one of the reasons why witches were persecuted is because people were afraid of what they could do. To some people, the idea that human beings have deep connections with one another is a source of great strength and joy. To others, it is frightening and threatening. As children we often have to fight to assert our individuality and to suddenly find that we are not as separate as we first thought can be alarming and requires us to rethink our notions of reality. This is not always welcome. However, magic is neutral. A car driven by a drunk can maim and kill, but this does not mean that the car itself is evil. What is wrong is its misuse.

Traditional practitioners of magic and shamanism were often amoral in their outlook. They saw their craft as simply that – a skill to be used. It could be used for many purposes, both good and ill, according to what the practitioner and his or her clients desired. In the Earth Traditions today, magic has evolved within a spiritual and ethical framework that limits the use of magic to those ends that are beneficial to individuals and society. In practical terms, this means that the uses to which magic is put are much more circumscribed than they were to our ancestors, whose belief system was often more of the Old Testament 'eye for an eye' variety. Today, the Earth Traditions that practice magic do so if it is really needed; but they do not use magical techniques as a prop to avoid dealing with life's problems in practical ways. Magic is not a crutch; nor is it an excuse for exercising the ego and power drives of the inadequate. It is a powerful technique to be used wisely, sparingly and well. To fail to carry out magic in accordance with ethical principles is foolhardy because we are responsible for our actions and must reap their consequences.

Notes

1   Eliade, *Shamanism*, page 30, quoting J Castagné, 'Magie et exorcisme chez les Kazak-Kirghizes et autres peuples turcs orientaux', page 60, *Revue des études islamiques*, Paris, 1930.

2   *Ynlinga Saga VII*, quoted in Eliade, *Shamanism*, page 381.

3   Lady Wilde, *Ancient Legends, Mystic Charms, and Superstitions of Ireland*, pages 100–1.

4   Tacitus, *Germania 10*, in H Mattingly, trans, *The Agricola and The Germania*, page 109.

5   *Hávamál*, verses 138–9.

6   Quoted in Koppana, *Snakefat and Knotted Threads*, page 76.

7   Koppana, *Snakefat and Knotted Threads*, page 77.

8   *Hávamál*, verse 145.

9   *Hávamál*, verse 148.

10   *Sigridfumál* or *The Song of Sigrid*, see Hollander, trans, *The Poetic Edda*, page 235.

11   Hardy, *A Psychology with a Soul*, page 41.

12   Davies, *The Rebel Angels*, page 153.

13

Ethics

Earth Traditions have a strong emphasis on social ethics. The songs and stories of the Germanic *Eddas* formed part of an oral tradition. These were sung and orated in the communal hall and would be familiar to people from their earliest years. These repeated maxims created a fabric of morality against which people lived their daily lives. They were not taught in a solemn way but conveyed with wit and grace. Many of the teachings of the *Eddas* were designed to smooth the wheels of communal life. A number are gathered together in the *Hávamál* or *High One's Words*.[1] The High One is one of the titles of the god Odin.

> Mead is not good they say for the sons of men;
> the deeper a man drinks, the dimmer his mind.
>
> The herds know their homing time and leave their grazing;
> but a fool does not know how much his belly holds.
>
> Boast not of your cleverness, guard your tongue well;
> the wise and silent arouse no anger in the hall.
> Better friend has no man than good sense.

The teachings were designed to promote community harmony. Harmony is important to all societies, but especially to agricultural peoples. When communities engage in agriculture, the co-operation of a large number of people is essential if the community is to survive. War is counter-productive because it disrupts the cycle of plowing, planting and harvesting, which if not done at their correct time will mean that the community will starve. The disastrous effect of war on agriculture is readily observable in many famine-ridden parts of the world today.

The way of life that causes least harm to others is often the way of balance. This ideal can be found in Celtic teachings where it is seen as the fitness of things. This sense of fitness is found in the teachings of Cormac son of Airt. Cormac was a King of Ireland in about the third century CE. He was a foster-son of King Lugaid mac Con and from an early age displayed such great wisdom that he was considered a receptacle of truth. In the *Tecosca an Righ* or *Instructions of King Cormac mac Airt*,[2] he describes to his grandson Cairbre how he behaved as a young prince.

    I was a listener in the woods,
    I was a gazer at the stars,
    I was blind where secrets were concerned,
    I was silent in a wilderness,
    I was talkative among many,
    I was mild in the mead-hall,
    I was stern in battle,
    I was ready to watch,
    I was gentle in friendship,
    I was a physician to the sick,
    I was weak towards the powerless,
    I was strong towards the powerful,
    I was never hard, lest I be satirized,
    I was not feeble, lest I have my hair stripped off,
    I was not close, lest I should be burdensome,
    I was not arrogant, though I was wise,
    I was not given to promising, though I was strong,
    I was not venturesome, though I was swift,
    I did not deride the old, though I was young,
    I was not boastful, though I was a good fighter,
    I would not speak about anyone in his absence,
    I would not reproach, but I would praise,
    I would not ask, but I would give;
    for it is through those habits
    that the young become old and kingly warriors.[3]

Cairbre then goes on to ask Cormac what is good for him. 'Not hard to tell,' said Cormac. 'If you listen to my teaching.'

    Do not deride any old person, though you are young;
    not a poor man, though you are rich;

nor a naked one, though you are well-clad;
nor a lame one, though you are swift;
nor a blind one; though you are keen-sighted;
nor an invalid, though you are strong;
nor a dull one, though you are clever;
nor a fool, though you are wise.[4]

In another passage, Cormac tells Cairbre how he can best maintain his own self-respect.

If you be too wise, they will expect too much of you;
if you be too foolish, you will be deceived;
if you be too conceited, you will be thought vexatious;
if you be too humble, you will be without honor;
if you be too talkative, you will not be heeded;
if you be too silent, you will not be regarded;
if you be too harsh, you will be broken;
if you be too feeble, you will be crushed.[5]

Other teachings had a deeper meaning that conveyed group dependence and the obligations that each person has to his or her family and society. Great emphasis is placed in any tribal society on contributing to that society, but early human societies did not cast out those whose contribution was less than that of others. Ties of love, obligation, kinship and honor decreed that the weak must be protected and it was the duty of the strong to do so. All had their place and could contribute in their own way.

A lame man can ride;
a handless herd cattle,
a deaf may be a fine warrior;
better be blind than burn on the pyre;
no one needs a corpse.[6]

The questioning attitude and individualism of the 20th and 21st centuries have brought us benefits, but also dangers. Positively, if we can learn to trust our own judgment, we are less likely to succumb to the tyranny of others. On the negative side, we often fail to teach people that society is not there solely to provide for their needs. They are society and must give of their energy and commitment to others. If we fail to teach people that life is a two-way exchange, we produce generations who have no respect for or understanding of the ethics and values that are essential to hold societies together. In the past, a sense of obligation was fostered by people's awareness that, however strong and powerful they might be, wealth, health, and strength were transient. The idea that life was dangerous and uncertain is conveyed in the *Hávamál*.

🌿   Fields and flocks had the rich man's sons;
        now they carry the beggar's staff;
        riches vanish in the wink of an eye,
        the most fickle of friends.[7]

It was also important to help weaker members of society because it was a matter of honor. To fail to provide for the needy was to fail in honor. The attitudes of hospitality and generosity that were encouraged in ancient societies were important for the well-being of the community, as well as for the spiritual evolution of the giver. Attachment to material possessions binds us to the world of the transient. These things are to be experienced and enjoyed, but they are not to be clung to; for in the end all passes, all changes. Wiccan Tradition teaches:

🌿   That in the darkest time,
        there is hope of another day;
        that in time of suffering,
        we shall know release;
        that all beauty is transient,
        and though we honor it while it flowers,
        yet do we give greater honor
        to that which endures and abides:
        Love, Honor, Wisdom, Truth, Courage and Compassion.

Giving is a way of giving of ourselves to others and taking is a way of accepting the generosity of spirit of another. Giving and taking gifts creates a bond of love and friendship. It is also a way of expressing mutual respect. The purpose is to give unconditionally. Society helps us, protects us and gives us its gifts. In return, we must protect and help society.

Religious giving, the making of offerings, was important in ancient Earth Traditions. It represented a subordination of the interests and greed of the individual to the community and to the gods. Religious sacrifices involved offering swords, shields and jewelry. Objects given as religious offerings were considered so sacred that valuable weapons and ornaments could be placed in piles in the countryside or thrown into sacred rivers and wells and left untouched. No one would plunder them. Such a situation is unthinkable today. To the Celts, one of the greatest penalties that could be inflicted on a wrong-doer was to be barred from making offerings with the rest of the community. This made them outcasts from society. The Roman general Julius Caesar wrote that to Germanic peoples an individual, clan or people who were banned from making offerings would be treated as impious wretches to be avoided at all costs. They had no legal rights and could hold no official position. They were believed to be unlucky and contact with them would bring misfortune. Another social sanction was the loss of reputation, which acted as a powerful disincentive against dishonorable acts. In warrior societies such as those of the Celts, Germanic peoples and many Native American societies, maintaining honor and a good reputation amongst one's peer group was essential both for the individual and his or her family. The *Hávamál* teaches:

> Cattle die, kinsmen die;
> you yourself will die;
> but honor never dies,
> for one who has earned a good name.[8]

The bards of Celtic society and their equivalent the Germanic skalds could destroy someone's reputation and were greatly feared. Mean or discreditable acts would be satirized and would echo the communal halls for generations to come. In our enormous communities, where we no longer know our neighbors, such sanctions are irrelevant and Western society in recent years has emphasized an individualism that, taken to extremes, can do much harm. Bonds of friendship were important in traditional societies and implied a definite commitment to help one another. As well as reputation, it was important to have good friends on whom one could depend. The *Hávamál* tells us:

> The fir tree withers in the field,
> without shelter of bark or needles;
> such is the fate of the friendless.
> Why should they live for long?

The way is long to a faithless friend,
though his house be by the road;
but to a good friend there are many shortcuts
though he live far from thee.[9]

The delusion that we can stand alone without the support of others and harm them with impunity leaves us with a 'me first', grabbing and grasping society, in which the strong, under a delusion of separateness, tread down the weak. We are like waves on the ocean of being, the great sea of the collective unconscious of humankind. We see ourselves as separate and individual, but we are part of the greater ocean. One wave alone disappears to be absorbed by the sand and dried by wind and sun. Together we are strong, powerful and eternal.

Truth and trust

Honor implies unselfishness and the protection by the strong of the weak. It also implies integrity. We can only have integrity if we practice truthfulness. In Celtic society, it was considered that if the King displayed truthfulness all would be well in the land. We are told of King Cormac mac Airt:

🥀   It was well with Ireland in the time of that King:
it was not possible to drink the waters of her rivers,
on account of the spawn of her fish;
it was not possible to travel her forests easily,
on account of the amount of their fruit;
it was not easy to travel her plains,
on account of the amount of her honey;
all of which had been granted him from Heaven,
through the truth of his princedom.[10]

To lie, cheat and steal create mistrust and deceit that destroy the fabric of society. The serpent is often thought of as the Wizard of Lies in mythology. In the Germanic Tradition, the serpent Nidhögg gnaws through the roots of the Tree of Life undermining and destroying it. Deception also undermines our inner strength – our will. Starhawk describes the will as similar to what Victorian schoolmasters called character: honesty, self-discipline, commitment, and conviction.

Those who would practice magic must be scrupulously honest in their personal lives. In one sense, magic works on the principle that 'It is so because I say it is so.' A bag of herbs acquires the power to heal because I say it does ... If I habitually lie to my lovers, steal from my boss, pilfer from supermarkets, or simply renege on my promises, I cannot have that conviction.[11]

In Celtic society also, one's word was important. In *The Elements of the Celtic Tradition*, Caitlín Matthews quotes a famous Celtic oath:

 If I break faith with you:
may the skies fall upon me,
may the seas drown me,
may the Earth rise up and swallow me.[12]

Oath giving is a serious matter because at stake is our integrity – that which makes us whole and what we are. In the *Colloquy of the Ancients*, Caoilte mac Ronan is asked by St Patrick what qualities are most valued by the Pagan Irish. St Patrick is told that it is truth in their hearts, strength in their arms and fulfilment in their tongues. These ideals still hold good today. It is a pity that more of our leaders do not practice them.

Society and sexuality

Many religions have negative attitudes to sexuality. This is not true of the Earth Traditions. The body has urges to fulfil its physical functions – to eat, to sleep, to relieve itself of waste, and to mate. These are not good or evil in themselves. They are natural functions necessary to maintain our bodies and our species. In earlier human societies, these urges were fulfilled unselfconsciously in the simplest and easiest way. We ate what was available – human beings are naturally omnivores – and had sex with the nearest available member of the opposite sex. If no member of the opposite sex were available, we would create our own sexual pleasure or would have sex with someone of the same sex. As our thinking function developed, we became more discriminating. We learned to appreciate that some foods are tastier than others. We learned to cook and developed the art of feasting. In some cases, we developed moral codes about our food, which included feeding ourselves in ways that cause least harm to other species – hence vegetarianism. Eating became an aesthetic experience, a social ritual, and a matter of ethical choice. Sexuality also became more complex. It developed into an aesthetic and emotional experience. We learned to discriminate between partners and found that we preferred some to others. We discovered that sex could lead to love and to deep emotional bonding.

Religion and spirituality are often confused with sexual morality. Laws about sexual conduct are not Divinely ordained, but are the creations of society. Early societies living close to Nature had little regulation of sexuality. It was important to ensure that as many women as possible became pregnant. Women could best achieve this by having sex with many different men to optimize their chances. Religious rites often encouraged this. In isolated societies, there might be laws that discouraged in-breeding and marrying one's own kin or clan. There might also be customs that encouraged out-breeding and maximized the gene pool, by encouraging women to have sex with male travelers. As societies become more complex, laws are enacted to regulate sexuality and to limit access to sexual partners. Often these laws are designed to protect property and to ensure that inheritance is passed on to a man's own sons rather than those of someone else. In the West, sexuality has been dominated in recent centuries by the Christian sexual ethos. This endorses monogamy, abstinence from sex except within marriage, and difficult divorce laws that in the past could be negotiated only by the rich and politically favored. Christianity also had a negative attitude to the human body. With the absorption of the idea that matter was evil, the body too was regarded as evil and all forms of sexuality other than for procreation purposes frowned upon. The celibate life was considered the highest good. Admirable though this ethic would have been for conserving the planet by reducing the human population, unfortunately it was combined in many denominations with strictures against contraception.

To contemporary Pagans, there are few taboos about sexuality as such. Sexuality is considered something that can be practiced between consenting adults, providing it does not cause harm to oneself or one's partners. This means that it would be wrong to have sex with someone while one had promised – legally or not – to be in a monogamous relationship with someone else. This would be an act of dishonesty, which would be damaging to all concerned. If we are unable to keep our promises, we must say so and break the contract. To Pagans, sexuality is a positive force, the force of creation that brings everything into being. For unattached adults, there are no barriers to sexual activity with other unattached adults; but we are expected to have regard to the consequences of our actions and to ensure that we do not cause unwanted pregnancy, spread sexual disease, or mislead others as to our level of commitment to the relationship. Sexuality outside of a committed relationship is acceptable providing it follows these ethics. Sexual activity that hurts, coerces or damages others is unacceptable to Pagans. Sexuality between adults and children, or forced sex between adults without both parties' consent, is anathema.

The way of least harm

One of the three Principles of Paganism that many Pagans follow is 'An it harm none, do what you will', which means that actions that do no harm to others are permissible. This ethic is a simple one and many would argue that it cannot apply in all circumstances. 'What about Hitler?' people ask. 'Surely assassinating him would have harmed him, but saved many millions of others.' No formula, whether complex or simple, can cover all situations. The more we try to create codes that cover all eventualities, the more mechanical and unrealistic our ideas of morality become. Simple precepts provide ethical guidance to which we can turn and then make the best judgments we can. The emphasis in contemporary Earth Traditions is not on obeying complex sets of laws, but on teaching people to attune themselves to the Divine center of all things, and to make ethical judgments based on what is true, eternal and abiding. The sense of what is right, true and abiding is conveyed less through direct intellectual teaching than through symbols and myths that speak to the unconscious. These create in the personality a solid and enduring basis of character, a center from which to discriminate between right and wrong.

Much of Pagan ethics is not about striving for impossible perfection that causes only guilt and despair when we fail, but a kinder and gentler ethic. We aspire to live in a way that does not harm those around us, either human beings or others whose environments we affect – the animal, plant, and mineral life of the Great Mother's kingdom. In each action we perform, there will be both positive and negative; something will benefit and something will lose. With each breath we take, our lives are enhanced, but billions of microbes die. In order to live our lives without becoming neurotic, we have to accept that our existence is a threat to the planet and to endeavor to live our lives in the way that causes least damage.

Love and kinship for Nature

Earth Traditions encourage us to live in harmony with our environment. One of the Three Principles of the Pagan Federation is:

❧   Love and kinship with Nature: rather than the more custom-
     ary attitude of aggression and domination over Nature ...[13]

Western civilization has lost sight of the need to live in harmony with the planet. Living in harmony with Nature means finding a balance between our needs and those of the animal and plant kingdoms. The Earth Traditions believe it is important to live in harmony with our environment and not to cause unnecessary suffering. Conservation of our plant environment is also important. A traditional witchcraft custom was that we should explain to any plant we pluck or tree we fell why we are taking its life. Holding conversations with plants and trees may seem odd, but the idea of stopping to think about what we are doing to the plant and tree life we use makes sense. A related tradition is that of offering a gift in return for what we take. If we take fruit from a tree, we should offer something in return. If we cut down a tree, we should plant one or two more. We are much less likely to destroy wantonly if we stop to consider why we need to take something and what we are going to give in return.

Many of those who practice contemporary Earth Traditions believe that meat eating and the killing and suffering it entails should be avoided. In becoming vegetarians, they are following in the footsteps of many ancient Pagan Traditions. The Greek Neoplatonists were vegetarians and the priests and priestesses of the Egyptian goddess Isis were permitted to eat eggs and lentils but not fish or meat. To many practitioners of Earth Traditions, a Nature-centered religion is incompatible with taking life unnecessarily. Others argue that practicing an Earth Tradition is part of a return to a more natural way of life. They would argue that human beings are hunters and natural omnivores, eating fruit and flesh, fish and fowl. Many people raise their own animals for food and believe that to give an animal a good natural life and then to kill it cleanly and painlessly is ethical. They would argue further that it makes no sense to eat plants and not to eat animals. Killing a plant deprives it of life in just the same way as killing an animal. Others, while not complete vegetarians, believe that we should eat down the protein chain, consuming those things that will experience least harm and suffering.

Whatever our beliefs about meat-eating, there is a general agreement that certain aspects of meat production are not compatible with Earth Traditions, which emphasize kinship between humans and other species. They endeavor to avoid factory-farmed meat and eggs. Others believe that excessive meat consumption by Westerners encourages intensive farming methods that have a bad effect on developing countries by forcing them to grow foodstuffs for Western livestock rather than for themselves. In this way, Western greed distorts the world economy to the detriment of the economically less powerful.

The respect for Nature and importance of living in balance with our environment that is evident in many Native American teachings is similar to that found in European Traditions. Baltic Traditions, for instance, teach the sacredness of Nature, respect for ancestors, and promote the search for harmony. Harmony in Lithuanian is Darna. The aim of existence is to seek Darna within us, within our home and within our communities. The essence of Darna is preserved in this old Lithuanian prayer.

> That I may love and respect my mother, my father and
>   old people;
> that I may protect their graves from rending
>   and destruction;
> that, for their rest, I may plant in cemeteries
> oaks, junipers, wormwoods and silverweed.
> Those who do not love and respect their bearers
> will find hardship in their old age, or will not grow old
>   at all.
>
> That my hands may never become stained by human blood.
> That the blood of animals, fish or birds may not taint
>   my hands,
> by my killing them satiated and not hungry.
> Those who today kill animals with delight
> will tomorrow drink human blood.
> The more hunters live in Lithuania,
> the further fortune and a happy life escape us.
>
> That I may love and respect bread.
> If a crumb should accidentally fall,
> I will lift it, kiss it and apologise.
> If we all respect bread,
> there will be no starvation or hardship.

That I may never hurt anyone;
that I may always give the correct change;
that I may not mistakenly steal even the smallest coin.
The gods always punish offences.

That I may not denigrate foreign beliefs
and may not poke fun at my own faith.

That I may not fell a single tree without holy need;
that I may not step on a blooming field;
that I may always plant trees.
The gods look with grace
upon those who plant trees along roads,
in homesteads, at holy places,
at crossroads, and by houses.
If you wed, plant a wedding tree.
If a child is born, plant a tree.
If someone beloved dies,
plant a tree for their soul.
At all festivals,
during all important events,
visit trees.
Prayers will attain holiness through trees of thanks.
So may it be![14]

Good and evil

Many Earth Traditions believe in a universe in which order and chaos are in a perpetual struggle. These two forces are not good and evil but anabolism and catabolism, creation and destruction. Both forces are necessary for the existence of the universe. The universe is neutral and has its own purposes, which may or may not be perceived as good in human terms. The image of deities as dynamic forces or powers that move the universe is important. In many Traditions, there are 'everyday' deities who are concerned with ordinary human affairs and 'cosmic deities' or High Gods, who act as universal tides beyond the concept of good and evil in the sense understood by human beings. Human beings take the anthropocentric and egocentric view that those things that benefit us are good and that which opposes us is evil; but on a cosmic scale good and evil are seen differently. The deities represent forces that are neither light nor dark. They are the power of the natural world, the force of life itself, which seeks ever to renew and express itself. We are not a chosen species, but one of many experiments that the life force conducts. In time, we will be surpassed. This does not mean that the Divine will allow evil to grow unchecked. The life force seeks equilibrium, a balancing of the forces of order and chaos. There is a struggle between the two inherent tendencies – existence and non-existence, creation and destruction. It is a struggle that may have an ultimate resolution; but this will be within a time-frame way beyond the comprehension of human beings, who as a species are but a blip in the on-going history of the universe. Nor is that resolution an ulti-mate triumph of good over evil, but rather a stilling and a calm, a dissolution into nonbeing that is beyond both these poles of activity, until the universe wakes and creates again.

Most practitioners of Earth Traditions do not see their deities as good guys opposed by the universe's baddies. The Divine is neither good nor evil, but a force that permeates the universe. It emerges into action out of eternal tranquil-ity and contemplation and returns to stillness once more when each phase of creation is done. There is good and evil, but it is within human beings, not the cosmos. This idea is found in the Greek myth of Pandora's box. All the troubles of the world are kept securely in a chest and Pandora is instructed never to open it. However, her human curiosity and intelligence, which are both humanity's blessing and its curse, prompt her to open the forbidden box and evil is unleashed into the world. Evil arises when there is the possibility of choice and action. Human beings have the option of performing acts that serve the greater good or acts that create misery and destruction. These choices, which face us daily, are subject to our conflicting emotions – love, hate, pity, cruelty, greed, selfishness, and altruism – all the realities of the human heart.

Fate and free will

Ethical choice implies free will; for how can we choose between right and wrong unless we are free to make that choice? Earth Traditions believe in free will, but also in the concept of fate, wyrd or destiny – hence the popularity of divination as a way of seeing into the pattern of fate. How can these things be reconciled? Different Traditions vary in their ideas on the changeability of fate. Some people take a fatalistic Hindu approach:

❧ ...that we all are guided by fate, the Unknown. It takes us through the tortuous journey of our life to our Individuation – to Wholeness. We may refuse this guidance at our own cost. Truly, we cannot even refuse it for long. It is more powerful than our will.[15]

Those who practice Western Earth Traditions tend to be less fatalistic than their brothers and sisters in the East. They believe that we are not bound by fate, though we are guided by it, but we have free will and moral choice. The Germanic Tradition teaches that the Web of Wyrd creates situations and demands that we must meet – this is our destiny or wyrd – but the way we meet our destiny depends on us. We can choose the way of honor and right, or we can choose the way of dishonor and wrong. We can choose the way that benefits others, or that which harms and injures them. Having seen into the pattern of the Web of Wyrd, the possibilities are to succumb, to fight or to change our destiny. Our circumstances and upbringing may influence us for good or ill in these choices, but the responsibility for the decisions we make and the consequences of our actions are ours. In some Earth Traditions, but not all, the concept of reincarnation may mean that we have a legacy from past actions, both good and bad, that will help determine our future. This karma is the accumulated consequences of our own past actions. We are not being punished for them, but we will continue to be confronted by them until we learn more adaptive ways of behaving.

The concepts of original sin and karma are ways in which human beings have attempted to make sense of the fact that life is not fair: that bad things do happen to good people. If we follow an Earth Tradition we are not obliged to reconcile ourselves to this problem by demanding some philosophical construct that will make sense of the unfairness and illustrate that it's all right really: people do deserve what they get and get what they deserve. The universe is much more arbitrary than that. Human beings are not the center of the universe. We are but small cogs in its machinery. The universe is not run for our benefit to ensure that we make a profit on our karmic balance sheet. Bad things do happen to good people and we have to put up with them, make the best of them, learn from our experiences, and triumph over them.

Guilt and sin

Evil exists not in the form of an external tempter or demon, but in the actions of human beings. The Divine itself is neither good nor evil. In the words of Mahatma Gandhi, 'The only devils in the world are those running around in our hearts. That is where the battle should be fought.' Sometimes we are successful in fighting this battle and sometimes we are not. When we fail, the knowledge of our own wrongdoing creates guilt and a feeling of sinfulness. Paradoxically, we may become most aware of our deficiencies if we decide to try to follow a spiritual path and to live our lives in a better way. The more we draw nearer the Divine and the source of all being, the more we become aware of ourselves. Often Earth Traditions teach that one of the purposes of life is to learn to see ourselves as we truly are. This involves a spiritual quest and, if we go on a spiritual quest, we cannot expect the way to be easy. The hero in fairy tales must face monsters and dangers before he achieves his destiny. If we set out on a path seeking spiritual knowledge, our gods will grant us what we seek; but the initial results may not be entirely welcome. Enlightenment brings insight and revelation. In the clear light of insight, we perceive our own deficiencies and failings. This often produces feelings of guilt, inferiority and worthlessness. Freya Aswynn writes:

> Anyone who evolves along a spiritual path, whatever that path may be, will develop a set of personal ethical values by which he or she chooses to live. However, human nature being what it is, we do not always live up to our self-imposed standards and consequently experience a sense of failure. This sense of failure smashes a dent in our self-esteem and restricts us in our creativity. All this is necessary, however, and is unavoidable if we are to learn from our mistakes ... Nidhögg gnaws at the roots of Yggdrasil in an attempt to destroy the Tree. We can interpret this myth psychologically. Nidhögg can be viewed as the shadow in the unconscious, gnawing at or undermining the sense of self symbolized by Yggdrasil.[16]

Many religions deliberately capitalize on and even encourage feelings of guilt and inferiority. The Earth Traditions teach that each individual is unique, worthy and holy. Our individuality is to be respected. Each of us is needed in the world and has a role to play. Marian Green, a practitioner of natural magic, writes:

You are unique, your life is valuable, and you can learn to shape Creation to bring health, to bring joy and to bring fulfilment, if you follow the path of your spirit, as it wanders through the tangle of life's lessons. Within you are the seeds of greatness, and only you can release them, nurture them that they may flower and fruit for the benefit of the whole universe.[17]

Feelings of inferiority lead to doubt and anxiety that make us believe that our wishes and hopes are without value and inhibit us from living at our full capacity and achieving the maximum we can within the range of our abilities. The paralyzing effect of doubt is conveyed by the *Eddas*.

Doubt is the river that flows between
the ground of the deities and the giants;
it shall flow free and open forever;
no ice may form on Ifing.[18]

In order to make our spiritual quest we must overcome these barriers. Doubt and anxiety sap our courage and our will and are purposeless emotions. The *Hávamál* or *High One's Words* of the *Eddas* contain some homely advice.

A fool lies awake at nights
worrying about this and that;
weary is he when morning breaks,
and all is still as before.[19]

Different spiritual paths have evolved different ways of dealing with guilt. Catholicism has the confessional. The believer is taught that the priest has the power to forgive his or her sins and can lift the burden of guilt. Some branches of Protestantism teach that, providing one believes in the right version of God (ie their version), one is 'saved'. It doesn't matter what one does or how repulsive one's conduct, one has an assured seat in heaven. These attitudes do not accord with the belief of the Earth Traditions that we are responsible for our actions. Breast-beating when we have done something wrong and lapsing into shame will not help matters. When things go wrong we have to live with the knowledge of our wrongdoing. We cannot be forgiven or saved by anyone else. The Earth Traditions believe in the concept of balance. If we have committed wrong actions, we must seek out opportunities to redress the balance and to give something back in return for what we have taken. Once we have admitted our mistakes to ourselves and done whatever is possible to put them right, we must put them behind us and begin again. Ritual can be helpful here, for it is a way of marking a transition between one state and another. We can create our sacred space, perform actions of cleansing and purification and then emerge again to start life anew. All the Earth Traditions have purification ceremonies that allow us to let go of the past and look to the future. Native American Traditions use the sweat lodge. Starhawk has devised a witchcraft ceremony for dealing with guilt and regrets which she calls the Indrinking Spell. We can perform the ceremony by creating sacred space in whatever way is familiar to us. Deities can also be invoked in the customary manner. We sit facing north, the point of the Sun's nadir, and light a candle. There should be a large bowl of earth at the center of our sacred space, together with a cup of water and something to drink – wine, beer, mead or milk. We take the cup filled with clear water. Then we are told to:

> Visualize all the negative things that you are feeling about yourself, the mistakes you have made, the things you have done wrong. Talk to yourself and admit you feel bad. Tell yourself, out loud, exactly what you have done wrong, and why. Let your emotion build energy, and project it all into the cup. Breathe on the water.

We next visualize the Goddess as a forgiving Mother and imagine her hands covering ours. She is saying:

> I am the Mother of all things,
> My love is poured out upon the Earth.
> I drink you in with perfect love,
> Be cleansed. Be healed.
> Be whole. Be changed.

We pour the water into the bowl of earth and fill the cup with the wine, beer, mead or milk and visualize ourselves as we would like to be – free of guilt and sorrow, changed so that we will not repeat the same errors. We charge the cup with strength and the power to be the person we want to be. We then visualize the Goddess once more, her hands covering ours, and she says:

186

Mine the Cup and Mine the Wine of Life.
Drink deep!

We then drink the charged liquid and feel ourselves filled with strength. We know that we have changed, that we are, from that very moment, a new person, not bound by the patterns and errors of the past. The ritual is then closed and the negatively charged earth is scattered to the four winds. The rite can be performed alone or in a group.[20]

Within us is our own darkness, that which psychologist Carl Jung called the shadow. Within the greater mind of humanity is a greater darkness, the collective shadow, the negativity of humankind. One of the most important functions of our spiritual traditions is to help us resolve this most formidable of problems, which has beset humankind since its rise into consciousness. In order to come into the light we must pass through the places of darkness; we must confront those aspects of ourselves which lie deep and hidden and integrate them into our lives in their true place where those qualities which we have sought to repress may become of value to us. We must transmute anger into energy and complacency into true serenity born of knowledge, not the complacency of ignorance. This is essential not only for ourselves but also for society. If we succeed, we shall fulfil the destiny of humankind. If we fail, we shall perish utterly, a forgotten experiment in the laboratory of time.

We picked some flowers and they were fair,
but as we watched they withered there;
the petals fell from our trembling hands;
blood red stains on silver sand.

We tried to fly but only fell,
down the dark to the Gates of Hell,
and the twinkling stars went twinkling on,
and did not notice we had gone.[21]

Notes

1   *Hávamál*, or *The High One's Words*, see Titchenell, *The Masks of Odin*, pages 110–30; Auden and Taylor, *Norse Poems*, pages 147–67, and Hollander, trans, *The Poetic Edda*, pages 14–41.

2   Meyer, trans, *The Instructions of King Cormac mac Airt*.

3   Based on Meyer, trans, *The Instructions of King Cormac mac Airt*, page 17.

4   Based on Meyer, trans, *The Instructions of King Cormac mac Airt*, page 21.

5   Based on Meyer, trans, *The Instructions of King Cormac mac Airt*, page 45.

6   *Hávamál*, verse 71.

7   *Hávamál*, verse 78.

8   *Hávamál*, verse 76.

9   *Hávamál*, verses 50 and 36.

10   Quoted in Ross, *Everyday Life of the Pagan Celts*, page 150.

11   Starhawk, *The Spiral Dance*, page 111.

12   Matthews, *The Elements of the Celtic Tradition*, page 13.

13   *Pagan Federation Information Pack*, page 4.

14   Old Lithuanian prayer based on the translation of Jonas Trikunas in *Romuva USA, 8*, Sambariai 1992.

15   Vasavada in *Hinduism and Jungian Psychology*, page 14.

16   Aswynn, *Leaves of Yggdrasil*, pages 44–5.

17   Green, *The Path Through the Labyrinth*, page 4.

18   *Vaftrudnismál*, verse 16.

19   *Hávamál*, verse 23.

20   Starhawk, *The Spiral Dance*, pages 116–17.

21   From Crowley, *Illusions*, Autumn Equinox 1970.

14

Mysticism: The Self
and the Grail

The goals of Earth Traditions, and indeed of all religion, are many. There is worship – the honoring of deities, the forces that give rise to and maintain our universe. There is ethical teaching. There is also the inner message of religion, which is found most often in its esoteric traditions and has often been the goal of the few rather than the many. This is the goal of mysticism – achievement of an inner union with the Divine. While many religions promise this after death, mysticism teaches spiritual practices through which this unity may be achieved on Earth.

The seasonal cycle has an underlying message that speaks to us even more powerfully because it is not overt. This message is that the force of life is eternal, ever renewing and ever becoming and, like all things in Nature, we too have our cycles and seasons. We learn that beneath the fabric of the Goddess' cloak of Nature, there is a spirit that is enduring. It is both changing and changeless. This paradox is not easy for the Western mind to understand. Our educational system teaches us to think in rational categories in which something must be this or that. It cannot simultaneously be both. These truths of the spirit are better understood in the East, where the spiritual seeker is taught to step beyond the traps of the conscious analytical mind. In Zen Buddhism, these truths are taught through koans, paradoxical statements that are designed to confuse our thought processes and teach us their limitations. In the Earth Traditions, they are taught through myth and allegory. Myth and allegory lead us beyond the boundaries of the ego and the conscious mind, to travel in the uncharted country of the spirit and to discover our true nature – who and what we really are.

Shared human goals

Religions based on the inner revelations of one prophet and his interpreters must inevitably ossify and crumble. Their teachings are carved, sometimes literally, on

189

tablets of stone and, once their originators have passed away, they become over the centuries outer forms and teachings whose original spiritual essence has been lost. We are taught from without, through the conscious and rational mind, what can only be truly realized from within. Spiritual teachings degenerate into a series of dos and don'ts. If we believe the teachings of one set of prophets and follow their prescripts, then we shall be enlightened or saved. This type of teaching is false. We cannot find salvation or enlightenment from without. We can only find them from within; from experiencing for ourselves unity with the source of all being. If we experience this, then our ethical behavior will be altered dramatically, not because we have been told that this is how a good person behaves, but because we have learned that we are part of a whole which is Divine and we are infused with love for our fellow creatures. In loving those with whom we share our planet, then we love the Divine source which is our ultimate home. The Earth Traditions represent a return to mysticism, but unlike Eastern systems, it is a mysticism that is suited to the West. Most Eastern systems teach austerity and a turning away from the material world. The Earth Traditions are also non-materialistic, in the sense that wealth and power are not seen as the main aims of existence, but the created universe is not Maya, illusion, but the work of the gods – the Divine made manifest in Nature. In the worship of the Divine both immanent in Nature and transcendent beyond it, we find our true religion.

The goal of the spiritual quest has been expressed in many different ways throughout the ages, but the mysticism of all religions leads to the same end – unity with the Divine. This fact that mystical Oneness can be achieved through many different spiritual paths and by different means illustrates the absurdity of religions that teach that there is only one right way – theirs. Achieving religious understanding is rather like climbing a series of mountains. Each human generation reaches a peak and believes that, 'This is it! We have found the Ultimate Truth.' Then we see that another mountain peak, still higher, beckons and we must begin our journey again. The old truth is only partial. There is ever more to discover; more to be revealed. Then, at the end of our Quest, we discover that that which we sought we carried with us all the time. No outer journey was necessary, but there is a paradox. If we had not made the journey, we would never have gained the wisdom to know that we already knew what we sought. Such are the strange spirals in the inner journey of the heart.

Although the routes may differ, there are commonalities in the spiritual quest that can be distilled from the wisdom of all faiths. The ultimate experience is often called being in touch with the center or the true self. Jean Hardy, in her book on psychosynthesis, *A Psychology with a Soul*,[1] writes that this is achieved by being constantly aware of the strength within oneself, and of spirit at work in the world. She distinguishes six important attitudes:

> being able to see the transcendent and the immanent qualities in
> other people, in animals, in all creation;
> recognizing that a spiritually aware person is on a journey towards
> becoming aware of what he or she can be;
> being able to live and share with other people in a more humble
> and accepting way;
> being able to work well and give to the world from a centered place;
> being committed to the causes one sees as important; and
> being aware of the creative forces which have occurred throughout
> human history and upon which we can all draw.

The realization of unity and centeredness in something greater than us is important not just for our personal spiritual attainment, but also for society. The achievement of inner unity within individuals is essential if society is to progress. Many religions and political creeds have endeavored to create a Utopia, a perfect society. However, they tried to do so by changing the structure of society. Society is the creation of those who live in it. If society is deficient, it is because we are deficient. In order to create social harmony, we must first find harmony within ourselves. Otherwise our vision of what constitutes social harmony will be false and distorted by the flaws within our own personalities.

Much of what has been taught in religions has taken us away from the Divine source. Many religions preach love, but in its name torture and kill others because their views of reality do not accord with theirs. True love comes from inner harmony and the learning of wisdom. To achieve wisdom, we must have the humility to see that our views of reality are limited. If we follow our spiritual path with these truths in mind, then it can be a force for creativity that will help and benefit the world around us. If we follow our path in order to gain power over others, to impose on others our view of right and wrong, or to oppress and maim the spiritual strivings of others, then whatever name we give our religion, it is a religion of tyranny and evil.

The Earth and Her peoples have need of those whose understanding of the needs of humankind is greatest. The spiritual quest can be a selfish pursuit if it is engaged in solely for the benefit of the individual concerned. That is not its purpose. Our minds are far-reaching. They range like spacecraft across the uncharted starry skies of consciousness, seeking to reach the gods and to know their purposes. Those whose inspiration has helped them to reach heaven's heights and to see the universe as it truly is, theirs is the task of helping human beings evolve on the next step of our journey. The objective of the mystical quest in the Earth Traditions is not to flee Earth but to serve our planet and its people.

Practitioners of Earth Traditions do not, in the main, feel the need to create intellectual definitions of their religious understanding. Words such as pantheist, panentheist and polytheist are not widely used. Categorization of our belief systems is not important. We recognize that all such intellectual exercises are ultimately futile. Rational explanations, and the dogmatic theological creeds to which they give rise, were a stage in humanity's evolution, but they are ultimately illusionary. All religious dogma is an attempt to codify what is beyond the word-based conscious mind. We can only understand it by entering into unity with it. Contact with and exploration of the worlds of inward reality have always been the goals of mysticism. It is a goal with a clearly-defined end – that of becoming at-one with Goddess or God, of finding the Divine self which is present within us all and of uniting our external personality with this Divine center. The mysticism of all religion seeks to help us integrate the disparate parts of our psyche and to find a point of centeredness and peace. We seek the integration of the personality into a coherent and well-functioning whole, which can then find union with the gods – the divine source of all being. 'Stop knowing and become' is at the heart of religious thought; as is the teaching that we are not separate and alone but that each one of us is valuable, unique and part of the interpenetrating, intercommunicating reality that is the Divine All.

Isis-Nuit

You sit enthroned within the caverns of my mind,
but Thy throne is empty.
No image will I fashion to grace its seat.
All images are limitation;
and Thou, my belovèd, art infinite beyond all vision.

In realms beyond my imagining,
lies indwelling your eternal spirit,
dreaming to birth the universe
and nurturing the galaxies.

Hail to Thee, Great Mother,
whose robe is the universe,
whose sequins are the stars!

In the cold places of the night,
I dream of Thy Great Halls:

three columns of black marble,
by the pool of the sleeping lotus,
white petals on dark water.

Where breath turns to mist,
and infinity turns to meaning;
beyond the sound of harp strings,
where the voice no longer echoes,
and silence rings with sound;
where vision can only struggle and fail,
to encapsulate Thy being;
I hear Thee calling and I come –
across the Abyss, below which is Nothingness,
only the empty sighing of the wind;
across the shaking rope-bridge,
which spans the endless chasm.

I walk to Thee in trepidation;
yet seek no other destination;
I do not fear to cross the walk-way,
I do not fear to cross the chasm;
I come with a heart free of longing or desire;
I come to the place of the column
of blue-white-light-fire.

No words now come, or thought, or feeling;
in the reality of Thy presence,
All is as Nothing.
My being fades,
the blue-white consumes,

I-We are One,
           are One,
                    are One.

Vivianne Crowley, 1990

Spiritual practice

How is this unity achieved? Meditation can be an important route. Another way is through participation in ritual with others. By following the seasonal cycle and experiencing and meditating on its symbolism and hidden truths, we come to recognize the enduring nature of the life force and that it is part of us and we of it. This is not just an intellectual understanding. The processes of ritual have a profound effect on the human psyche and bring about deep changes in consciousness, whereby we achieve inner stillness. The ritual processes of the Earth Traditions bring us to this state through exposure to symbols, the enactment of myth, the use of meditation and visualization and, sometimes, shamanic techniques and trance states where people experience unity with their gods.

The journey

Initiation rites are another means of spiritual transformation. These use ritual as a form of spiritual purification and realization. Alchemy is a related mystical system, which is concerned not so much with finding material gold, as with finding the true gold of the spirit. The series of purifications and mental disciplines necessary to produce gold bring about a change in the consciousness of the practitioner. The original purpose of the quest becomes irrelevant. It is the journeying that is important. The word journeying appears often in mysticism. The language of mysticism is frequently expressed in terms of a Sacred Quest – a spiritual journey to retrieve a treasure from a giant, a monster or even from death itself. Often there is imagery associated with a descent, a descent into the unconscious. It is portrayed in myth and legend as a heroic journey into the Underworld.

In Wicca, the Goddess descends into the Underworld not to seek a treasure, but to find the answer to a question; to ask the Lord of Death, 'Why dost thou cause all things that I love and take delight in to fade and die?' She discovers the answer to this age-old question that troubles humankind and in return receives a treasure – the Necklace of Rebirth. In the Germanic myth of Freya's descent to the Underworld to win the necklace Brisingamen, which shines like fire, she must spend a night with each of the four dwarves who forged it. Similarly, in the Welsh *Mabinogion*, King Arthur has to enter the Underworld, Annwn, to retrieve the Cauldron of Rebirth. Later stories in the Arthurian cycle describe the quest by King Arthur's knights for the mystical treasure of the Holy Grail. The Grail is a Christian symbol, but it is based on much older Celtic legends of the Cauldron of Rebirth and Plenty that contains all blessedness. The Quest is also often expressed in terms of a journey to the four quarters of the world.

> We came then,
> the last Children of Cerridwen,
> Daughters of Light and Darkness,
> and Sons of Death.
> We sought your presence on the wild hills of the North,
> but in the loneliness,
> we found you not.
> We sought your presence in the light of the East,
> but in the mists of dawn,
> we discerned you not.
> We sought your presence beneath the Sun of the South,
> but where shadows shrink,
> we could not see your face.
> We sought your presence where the wind sleeps in the
> West,
> but in the silence,
> we could not hear your voice ...[2]

After journeying in all the four directions, we find what we seek at the center, at the point from which we started. The symbolism of the quest captures the imagination still. JRR Tolkien's *Lord of the Rings* was enormously successful because it spoke to people of a sacred quest in mythological terms. Many contemporary computer games such as Dungeons and Dragons are also based on this theme.

Many people at some point in their lives choose to make a physical journey that is really a voyage to discover who they truly are. When we break away from adolescence into adulthood, or as we make the transition from parenthood to being free adults again when our children leave home to fend for themselves, can be good times to make the inner or the outer journey. The treasure that is sought in these quests is rebirth; not rebirth of the body, but rebirth of the personality as the true self – ourselves as we can be when the fears, weaknesses and imperfections of the outer personality are cast aside.

The self within

What is the true self that we seek? To describe the self is difficult. It is an inner experience and as such is beyond words. The language of poetry can sometimes convey it or an image. Here is a description from the Indian sacred texts the *Upanishads*.

> As an eagle weary after soaring in the sky,
> folds its wings and flies down to rest in its nest,
> so does the shining self enter the state of dreamless sleep,
> where one is freed from all desires.
> The self is free from desire,
> free from evil,
> free from fear.
>
> As a man in the arms of his beloved
> is not aware of what is without and what is within,
> so a person in union with the self
> is not aware of what is without and what is within;
> for in that unitive state,
> all desires find their perfect fulfillment.
> There is no other desire that needs to be fulfilled,
> and one goes beyond sorrow.[3]

The realization of the self is an experience that is well documented in mystical literature. It is often accompanied by a sense of bliss and dissolution. The boundaries of the personality are found to be false barriers and we discover that within us is a greatness that is beyond our imagining. It is both 'me' and 'not-me', I and Other. Indian psychotherapist Arwind Vasavada describes it in this way:

> ...the self is pure awareness, light and illumination, the fulfilment of one's destiny. It is not the state of unconsciousness of a stone or matter ... It is not a metaphysical concept or a

hypothesis of science, but a matter of experience, supported
by all the mystics and prophets of the world ... the end and
aim of the journey of life.[4]

As well as the language of myth, Pagans use the contemporary language of
humanistic, transpersonal and depth psychology to explain humanity's quest to
come to terms with its deeper needs and its spiritual destiny. Many psychologists
and those following spiritual paths now recognize that the outer spiritual quest
for God is in part an inner spiritual journey. This is not to denigrate the spiritual
quest, or by a process of reductionism to turn it into mere psychology, but to recognize that 'if that which thou seekest thou findest not within thee, thou wilt
never find it without thee.'[5] The Divine is present within us as well as in the
world outside and beyond. Jean Hardy, in her book *A Psychology with a Soul:
Psychosynthesis in Evolutionary Context* explains:

> In transpersonal psychotherapy terms, the search for spiritu-
> al meaning is also the search for the self, the 'God within',
> which is linked to the soul of the world.[6]

In entering into contact with universality, paradoxically we do not lose our individuality, but we become more aware of our uniqueness, while at the same time
recognizing that we are facets of a greater whole.

Individuation

The discovery, or recovery, of the self, for it is always there, is what Carl Jung
described as the process of individuation. This is the process of becoming who
and what we really are. In a sense, it is the aim of all mystical and initiatory
processes, in whatever religious symbolism they are dressed. The old outer form
is taken from us so that we can find what is beneath. As we go deeper into ourselves through our spiritual training, we come to the core of our personality, the
bedrock, where the individual verges on the collective and where we meet with
the greater whole, the group mind of humankind. Carl Jung wrote that as we
gain in self-knowledge and awareness, and act accordingly, so the layers of the
personality are stripped away.

In this way there arises a consciousness that is no longer imprisoned in the petty, oversensitive, personal world of the ego, but participates freely in the wider world of objective interests. The widened consciousness is no longer that touchy, egotistical bundle of personal wishes, fears, hopes, and ambitions which always has to be compensated or corrected by unconscious counter-tendencies; instead it is a function of relationship to the world of objects bringing the individual into absolute, binding, and indissoluble communion with the world at large.[7]

Individuation is becoming what we were meant to be from the beginning. This process involves letting go the false images of ourselves that have been built up by our environment and by the projected visions of parents, teachers, friends, and lovers. This is often symbolized in initiation rites by the removal or change of clothing. On this symbolic level, the process is simple, but inwardly painful. It involves the destruction and letting go of the ego and all that we thought was us, but was not. This is difficult. The human mind seeks refuge always in the security of the known. It fears the unknown and change.

There is much emphasis in initiatory traditions on clear-seeing, the original meaning of the word clairvoyance. In the East, it is the task of the guru to help remove the veil of ignorance from the disciple so that he or she may see him- or herself and the world as they really are. It is in clarity and in developing a true understanding of the nature of reality that we can return to the Godhead from which we came. Clarity is hampered by the confines of doctrine, because all religious teachings are only human beings' imperfect attempts to understand the Divine reality. All doctrines are transcended as we come nearer our goal.

In Eastern spiritual thought, transcendence is achieved by disidentification from attachments to mind and body. Our sensory and intellectual processes are seen as traps that attempt to classify the world for us. However, they can only classify the world according to the limits of their mechanisms. In the end, they are biologically based and constrained by their structure, just like any engine or mechanical device. They can only take us so far down the road of understanding. True understanding comes from inner experience that is beyond the classifications invented by the mind and senses. In order to find the self, the wiser and deeper part of ourselves, we must make a spiritual journey. This is the process of spiritual initiation. The initiation ceremonies that make us an adult member of society, or that initiate us into a particular spiritual tradition, are entry points to this process, but they are not the process itself. The process is life-long – hence the sight of the Grail often ends in death; for after we have achieved total Oneness with the ultimate reality, then we have reached our spiritual home. No more journeying forth is necessary.

The imagery of initiation is strongly bound up with that of death and rebirth. The old personality dies and a new one is reborn. The initiate is both the same and different. As in reincarnation, something remains from the old, but life begins anew. The close association between the world of dream, individuation, and death emerges strongly in Dion Fortune's work.

> There are two deaths by which men die, the greater and
>   the lesser.
> The death of the body, and the death of the initiation.
> And of these two, the death of the body is the lesser.
> The man who looks upon the face of Isis dies;
> for the Goddess takes him.[8]
>
> In death men go to Her across the shadowy river,
> for She is the keeper of their souls until the dawn.
> But there is also a death in life,
> and this likewise leadeth on to rebirth.[9]

The ultimate end of the initiatory process is found at the end of many lifetimes, but we need not be in a rush to reach our goal. Journeying hopefully is worthwhile and enjoyable in itself. It is also necessary that the more spiritually advanced members of our society do not take it into their heads to dissolve into Nirvana too soon. In the religions of the Piscean Age, the focus was on the salvation of the individual. In the 21st century, the lives of the whole human species and of the planet on which we live are threatened by environmental catastrophe. The issue is not our individual needs, but the needs of the world as a whole. We seek the Grail in order to become it – that we may become vessels so that others too may drink from that source.

The Grail
> I was a walker of the ways,
> and a wanderer of the waste,
> I was a mariner upon the deep,
> I was a seeker of the most High,

then I came by night to the dark mountainside
and slept and dreamt.

And now I am light in the eyes of the prophet,
I am a sapphire sparkling in the Sun,
I rest upon the breast of the Great Mother,
I am the belovèd of the mountain's heart.

I am a well in the desert,
I contain both light and water,
they may draw from me which they will.
The light of Sun and Moon,
and the rains of heaven replenish me,
I am the Grail.

Vivianne Crowley, April 1988

Notes

1	Hardy, *A Psychology with a Soul*, pages 60–61.
2	From Crowley, *The Children of Cerridwen*, Autumn 1984.
3	Easwaran, trans, *The Upanishads, Brihadarankaya Upanishad*, chapter iv, verse 21, page 45.
4	Vasavada in *Hinduism and Jungian Psychology*, page 157.
5	From 'The Great Mother Charge', quoted in Crowley, *Wicca: The Old Religion in the New Millennium*, page 191.
6	Hardy, *A Psychology with a Soul*, page 61.
7	Jung, *The Collected Works of C.G. Jung, 7*, page 275.
8	Fortune, *The Sea Priestess*, page 124.
9	Fortune, *The Sea Priestess*, page 125.

Practicing Earth-Centered Traditions

Few people are brought up in families that practice Earth Traditions, so beginning to practice a tradition is a matter of returning to an ancestral tradition that we might know only superficially, or learning a tradition from the beginning. If you have read and learned about the Earth Traditions and feel called to a spiritual practice that honors Earth as well as Heaven, body as well as spirit, female as well as male, how do you go about it? If we want to become Christians, we can attend a local church service and then decide if we want to become more involved. If we want to practice an Earth Tradition, the path can be harder and lonelier. We can begin by joining a group that will teach us everything we need to know, but this may not be possible. Most of the Earth Traditions are practiced in some localities but not others. We may find ourselves far away from anyone else who shares our idea. If we do not have immediate access to people who can teach us their tradition, we can start to learn on our own. These are some possible stages in developing an Earth-centered spirituality.

- Reading about the Earth Traditions.
- Deciding, 'Yes, this is for me.'
- Developing contact with Nature.
- Incorporating the myth cycles into our lives by celebrating seasonal festivals.
- Deepening our sense of inner peace and drawing nearer the Divine through ritual, meditation or prayer.
- Deciding whether we want to practice a particular Earth Tradition.
- Deciding whether we wish to meet others who practice Earth-based spirituality.

Deities and mythology

If we want to learn about the Earth Traditions – their deities and their sacred history – there are now many books available. In the Resources section at the end of this book are some suggestions for introductory reading. You can get books from bookstores (any bookstore can order any book for you) or you can buy online through internet booksellers. You can also borrow from libraries. Reading further will give you an idea of whether the Earth Traditions are right for you. From reading this book and/or from studying further, you may decide that the Earth Traditions make sense and resonate with your own beliefs. It may be that you have already developed your own spiritual philosophy and have realized for the first time that this can be described as an Earth-centered Paganism. To become a Pagan, no formal ceremony of admission is necessary – we become Pagans by deciding that we are; although particular traditions may have their own ceremonies of admission. If you want to become a member of a particular tradition, you may need to contact an organization that is a member of the tradition and seek formal admission through initiation.

Contact with Nature

The words Pagan and Heathen mean 'country dweller'. The Earth Traditions are religions that honor the Divine made manifest in Nature. Contact with Nature is essential if our spirituality is to be a deeply rooted and permanent part of our lives. Many people feel a deep mystical bond with the Earth and the environment around them. These bonds are found in farming families, who for generations have tilled the same soil, lived in the same homes, and have been linked to the same community. This bond is also found in hunting societies in which every part of the terrain is known to people. They read their environment as others read a book and each trail, track, and mark can be interpreted. These communities were attuned to the land in the most natural of ways – by working it and living its seasonal cycle of growth, fruition, decay, rest, and rebirth. In contemporary times, commitment to the land is important for all of us. Not all practitioners of Earth Traditions can uproot themselves from their cities and set up organic farms in idyllic countryside; although some do. Those of us who no longer till the soil must create this communion in another way. Creating gardens, taking part in tree-planting campaigns, and visiting sacred sites and natural places full of elemental energy, provide time and space for us to meditate on the forces of Nature and renew our commitment to love, protect, and nurture her. We can take time each seasonal festival to spend time outside. This can be in woods or forest; on seashore, moor or mountain, anywhere where we can experience the natural world. If this is not possible, it need not prevent us from experiencing Nature. We can observe the growth processes of the seasonal cycle by choosing a tree in the local park and visiting it each festival. Those brought up in an urban environment can re-learn the sensitivity to Nature that our ancestors took for granted. If we start out in simple ways to contact the Divine within Nature, we will find that it will begin to reach out to contact us.

Spiritual practice

As we become more aware of Nature, we will begin to notice much more than before about the changes that occur in the world around us with the season's change. These seasonal changes mark changes in Nature. They also mark changes within us. Our bodies and psyches respond to the lengthening and shortening of days, to sunshine and cold, to times when Nature seems full of activity and times that seem to be for sleep and rest. The natural changes we see around us and our reaction to them evoke symbolism and imagery that respond to different phases of the human life cycle. If we meditate on these, we will find that we have the basis for prayers, invocations, magical hopes and wishes that are appropriate to the season. In this way, we can begin to create simple seasonal ceremonies to honor our chosen deities in a way appropriate to the season. There are many books that can help us create rites and ceremonies to venerate our deities and some of these are also listed in the Resources section.

We can celebrate seasonal festivals in many ways. We can create complex ceremonies or simply commune with Nature at the appropriate times. Once we have established a link with our deities, we need to strengthen our understanding of them. We must study their mythologies and decide how we will address ourselves to them. We must not only take the written liturgy of others, but must create our own rites and prayers so that our spirituality is a living and ever-growing treasure store within us. This is not easy. Many of us who start out on the spiritual path are building a spiritual life from scratch, often with nothing but our own intuition and contact with the Divine to guide us. On this lonely road, many of us can feel lost at first; inspired to go forward on the spiritual quest, but unsure how to begin. To go forward, we must have confidence in ourselves and that the way is there if we seek it. To develop our spirituality, we must reopen the gateways between the worlds. All spiritual training is based on establishing clear channels of communication with the Otherworld. Only regular communion with it can achieve this. All of us are bad at regularity and this is doubly hard if we are practicing our spiritual tradition alone. We may have families, jobs, educational courses, all competing for our time and attention. How can we fit in another demand? If our spirituality is to be strong, it must be a part of our everyday life. If we wish to practice our spiritual tradition, it is important that we take a small amount of time each day to be in conscious contact with the Divine. This does not mean that we have to perform elaborate ceremonies, nor does it mean that unconscious links are not present as we go about our everyday lives; but our spiritual life is like a young plant. It must be carefully nurtured, especially at the beginning, if it is to flourish in a hostile climate.

As with other spiritual paths, many of those practicing Earth Traditions advocate daily meditation as a way to draw nearer to the Divine. An important concept is being centered. This means being tranquil and still, listening to the inner voice, the voice of the Divine self within us, which is in communion with the Divine without. Centeredness is a form of prayer; for prayer is not asking for things from our deities, it is being with our deities. We may wish to ask for their help or guidance, but that is not the main object of the exercise. To take time each day to center ourselves and commune with the Divine spirit that permeates the universe is like paying a visit to a friend. Often words are unnecessary. Merely to be in the presence of a wise friend refreshes us, makes us clear in our thought, and more certain of our purposes. Meditation can be helpful in developing an ethical sensitivity. Most of us have ethics that we aspire to follow, but often our behavior, thoughts, dreams, and feelings, deviate far from the ideals of harmony, love, and honor that we are seeking to embody. To develop an ethical sense, we must be ruthlessly honest with ourselves about our behavior and motives. We must also have enough self-acceptance to forgive ourselves when we fail to meet our ideals and the courage to try again. Taking time to examine the events of the day and our role in them can help us change ourselves to be what we would like to be. A spiritual diary is helpful. In this time of reflection, we consider how we have gone about the day's activities and whether our actions have been centered – proceeding from that center within us which recognizes what is in accordance with the greater good – or whether they have arisen from envy, jealousy or fear of others. Following a spiritual path is done a step at a time. We seek to refine the way we live our lives so it grows ever closer to our ideal. This does not mean that we can attain it all at once, or even in one lifetime, but little by little we evolve and grow to express the wholeness within us that comes from living in harmony with the Divine.

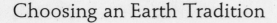

Choosing an Earth Tradition

In this book, I have described a number of different Earth Traditions. Those I have described are only a fraction of the world's rich cultural heritage. In some countries, there is one tradition that can be identified as the true spiritual tradition of the land, and this makes a choice of tradition easy. In English-speaking countries, the situation is much less clear. The British Isles, for instance, have been the destination of immigrant peoples over thousands of years. Its inhabitants are a mixture of Europeans of different heritage, Africans and Asians. In earlier centuries, the pioneering spirit of the Vikings and the wanderlust of the Celts took them to many lands, whose people and environment were different from their own. In North America, Australia, and New Zealand, migration created transplanted European peoples, who in turn were followed by waves of Africans and Asians. We will need to take time to meditate on the different pantheons and deities to discover which seem to speak to us most strongly. It is not just a matter of us choosing them. They must choose us. Some of us may be drawn to the deities whose places of origin and myths originated in our own landscape; sometimes we will be drawn to the deities of our own racial heritage; sometimes other deities will speak to us. Many people all over the world worship the Egyptian deities, particularly the goddess Isis, whose archetype is so strong in the collective unconscious that it appears spontaneously to many people in vision and dream.

Your personal ethics will be important in choosing a tradition. If you are a vegetarian, however attracted you are to African-based Traditions, their emphasis on offering live animals to the gods is likely to be a barrier to your participation. If you have ethical doubts about the use of magic, Traditional Wicca is unlikely to suit you, but particularly in North America you may be able to find a Goddess-oriented Wiccan-based group that is purely religious and does not practice magic. If you prefer a multicultural multiracial environment, then a Tradition that is strongly linked to a particular ethnic group may not be appealing. If, on the other hand, you are seeking to reconnect with your ethnicity in order to forge a sense of identity, then reconnecting with the tradition of your ancestors can help you reawaken your cultural and spiritual heritage. Valuing and cherishing our heritage is important to everyone, but it is important not to be blind to the dangers of ethnically-based religious Traditions. Ethnic spirituality can slip into racism. This has been a problem in the past with some Germanic Traditions. There are now groups practicing various forms of Germanic Tradition all over Europe and North America. A minority of Ásatrú groups describe themselves as 'folkish' from the German word 'volkisch' and emphasize loyalty to one's family and own ethnic group as supreme virtues. 'Volkisch' teaching can be that all races are equal, but that people should seek their spirituality with their own gods and leave other people to theirs. While this can seem superficially logical, it is a slippery slope from separate but different to separate but unequal and taken to extremes it leads to doctrines of racial supremacy and the classification of people based on spurious racial genetics. Given that all homo sapiens are descended from a small number of African ancestors, this would be amusing were it not dangerous. Heathen groups that do not follow these doctrines usually make a point of stating that they are open to people of all colors and sexual orientations who feel that the Aesir or Vanir have called them.

For some people, a Tradition such as Wicca, in which the many gods and goddesses of the world are seen as different manifestations of the Divine rather than as separate beings with a cultural identity, will be more appropriate than an ethnically-derived Tradition. For others, a synthesis of different traditions, drawing on the richness of all our cultural heritages, seems most natural in the contemporary world. Many followers of the different Earth Traditions now celebrate together and are moving ever nearer each other to produce what may be a religion of the future – a multi-faceted contemporary Paganism that is the Western equivalent of the many Indian spiritual Traditions that are now collectively called Hinduism. We tend to forget that Hinduism has only been considered a single religious path since the nineteenth century. Before then, the many rich traditions that make up the tapestry of Indian spiritual practice were not considered a single religion. Many streams of thought enrich contemporary Paganism. The different Earth Traditions are rivers that have as their source one stream – human love for and aspiration to understand the cosmos around us and our place in it. The rivers separate out, flow through different landscapes, and take on different colors according to the soil through which they pass; but in the end, all return to the one sea.

Meeting others

We can venerate our gods on our own, either from necessity or from choice. Some people prefer to follow their spiritual path alone and attend no communal gatherings. They commune with Nature in her woods and fields and follow the ways of their ancestors. In some Earth Traditions, meeting others may not be necessary, but personal contact with others on a particular path can be very helpful. Earth Traditions are based on oral teaching and not all aspects of the tradition can be conveyed by the printed word. For instance, creating rites and ceremonies when we have never seen any can be difficult unless we are particularly gifted in this direction. Many people decide that they would like to meet and talk with others who share their ideas, but find this difficult. They may have tried to talk with friends or family about their beliefs and found rejection, puzzlement or ridicule. At this point, they may write to a Pagan organization asking if they are the only Pagans in the world, they feel so isolated.

Practitioners of Earth Traditions conduct religious rituals because they are considered pleasing to the Divine; but worshipping with others also has a social purpose. Group rituals represent a shared enactment of religious myths. Joining with others to recognize common spiritual beliefs creates a sense of community between Pagans and a knowledge that we are not alone. This can give us the strength to stand up for our beliefs and to pioneer them in a society that can at times be hostile and fail to understand other spiritual traditions. If we decide to meet others, how easy this will be will depend on where we live. If we have access to a large city, then we are likely to be able to find groups that welcome newcomers. If we live in less densely populated areas, contact will be a matter of chance. However, there are larger festival gatherings in many countries that are run by national contact organizations, so once a year we may be able to meet with others, even if much of the time we have to practice our spirituality alone. A good starting point is to join one of the larger organizations and to get to know more about the Earth Traditions by reading the organization's literature and attending its meetings. There are also groups that can assist newcomers by providing postal tuition, workshops, conferences, etc.

Joining groups

If we wish to follow a particular Earth Tradition, we may wish to contact an appropriate group or organization and study for admission. The big advantage of learning and celebrating with others is that it overcomes the laziness and inertia factor. As we all know, studying alone is hard when we have to parent our children, hold down jobs, study for qualifications and carry out the myriad other tasks we are trying to perform in the world. The advantage of learning together is that we know we have to do our share when other people are relying on us and so it gives us that extra incentive to persevere.

Finding a group may not be easy. The Earth Traditions are not missionary religions and do not proselytize. Most people believe that anyone who sincerely seeks contact with their path will be drawn to the right source. Earth-based spirituality is therefore a path for the persistent. However, groups do exist and we may be lucky enough to find that there is a suitable group on the doorstep. If this is not the case, we can study through books, and some Earth Traditions offer home study courses to assist those who do not have access to a local group. Some suggestions are found in the resources guide. If you decide to seek admission to a particular Tradition, this may involve a period of training and instruction and passing through a formal induction or initiation ceremony. Whether this is open to you may depend upon your age. Some Earth Traditions believe that undertaking a particular religious path is more in the nature of answering a vocation, a response to a call from the gods. This is not something we are able to do until we reach adulthood.

Having made contact with a group, how do you decide if it is right for you? There are two major criteria – respect and liking. Respect does not mean a one-sided respect for the group and its leaders, if it has them. Respect means mutual respect. Are the people in the group interested in you as an individual and prepared to listen to your views? Do the people in the group seem emotionally stable? Beware of those who claim mystical powers, but whose personal lives are a mess. Mystical vision alone may be of use to a hermit in a cave, but it is not sufficient to guide a spiritual group whose members must live in the real world. Beware also of those who promise to endow you with the secrets of the universe, great magical powers, and an easy route to making money and anything else you want. Charlatans can be found in all spiritual Traditions and even the most idealistic Tradition will attract those who want to exploit it for their own ends. Some people become clergy and spiritual teachers in order to prop up their own inadequacies, seek power over others, and sexually and/or financially exploit them. Use the qualities that the gods have given you – common sense and discrimination – before involving yourself extensively in any spiritual or religious group. These personality issues may seem far removed from the primary purpose of joining a group, which is to meet with others to celebrate the mysteries of the deities and possibly, but not necessarily, to obtain knowledge and training from those who are more experienced on the path. However, groups can stand or fall on the personalities, adequacies or inadequacies of their members and leaders.

Liking is the second criteria for choosing to join a group. It is possible to celebrate the festivals with a group whose members you respect, but who are not people whom you would normally choose as close friends. Often groups are mixed in terms of age, education, occupation, and interests. This can be a great source of strength as different members bring different knowledge and life experience to the group. Do not be put off if you find that, when you meet your local group, the members seem on the surface to be very different from you. Find out what lies beneath the surface appearance and you may find that what you have in common transcends outer differences. Celebrating together in an atmosphere of mutual trust can lead to a deep friendship and liking between people of different ages, social groups, sexualities, and ethnicities, whose paths would never normally cross.

Creating your own group

If you are not able to find a suitable group in your area, you could set up your own. In forming a group, the advice of others can be invaluable. This can be obtained from one of the national organizations representing a particular Tradition, or from one of the umbrella organizations that represent Pagans in general. If you go down the road of creating your own group, there are a number of practical problems. Space is one. A new group may be able to meet in your home and in the summer months your group may be able to meet and celebrate outside. If the group gets bigger, you may need to rent a room.

The next issue is people. At first, your group is likely to be small. You may have a group of friends who share your interests. You may find that everyone is interested in a particular path – be it shamanism, Goddess worship, Celtic mysteries, or whatever. This simplifies things. However, you may find that one of you is a budding Odinist, another is a Goddess-oriented woman not entirely sure about doing ritual with men and others would really have liked to join a Wiccan coven, but there isn't one available. Some of you want to do ritual with your clothes on, others want to go back to Nature and throw their clothes to the winds, others fancy a nice black hooded robe that your Goddess-oriented friend thinks looks Satanic. Some parents want to bring their children to every meeting and some members are distinctly child-unfriendly. How can you tackle these problems? Apart from giving up in despair at the first hurdle, the obvious answer is that there are no easy solutions, but only a difficult one – compromise. If you are setting up an eclectic Pagan group and you are yourself a novice, then you cannot impose your own views and ethos on the group. What has to emerge is a consensus, which is inevitably a compromise, but which will enable you to get your group off the ground and working. This is by no means easy. The psychological literature is full of texts about the complexities of small group dynamics.

Making compromises is one of the disadvantages of group working and why many people decide that groups are not for them. They have distinct views that they feel are right and do not wish to compromise them. Such views must be respected. Even those working in the same Tradition will not agree entirely on their interpretation of that Tradition. On the positive side, one of the beauties of working in a group is learning to interact with others in a meaningful way on deep spiritual issues. We may be the world's greatest druids, witches or shamans, but if we cannot relate to other human beings, then what use are we in the world?

What is necessary in a group is not complete conformity of ideas, but commitment. In order to build a group that works on a spiritual level, it is necessary that people meet together on a regular basis. Most groups wish to celebrate the seasonal festivals. Some groups may also wish to celebrate the full Moons. It is good to celebrate these on the exact day, but in practice, unless members live near one another, it can be easier to choose a particular day of the week for meetings and to stick to that. People can then plan their other commitments to fit. Most practitioners feel comfortable about celebrating festivals and full Moons on the nearest possible date. It is also important that people pick a pattern of meeting that is practical. Many groups start out enthusiastically meeting every week and then quickly run out of steam. It is better to choose a slightly less ambitious schedule that people can keep. Some groups may be able to meet weekly. Others may have work and/or family commitments that make that impractical. A pattern of fortnightly or monthly meetings often works well and is sufficiently frequent for members to get to know each other and build up a group mind.

What can a group do when it meets? Not all meetings need be serious and reverential occasions. Other meetings can be for socializing, reading, discussion, meditation, pathworking or, if the group practices magic, to develop particular magical or divinatory techniques. While there may be no experienced ritualists in the group everyone will have a little bit of knowledge about something and everyone's areas of knowledge are likely to be slightly different. This is a basis for developing self-teaching and a pooling and sharing of knowledge and expertise. Different people can take turns to lead on a particular topic and other people can read up on it and bring their particular piece of research to the discussion. In this way, everyone can contribute and people learn from one other. It is possible, for instance, for a group to teach itself about the Celtic Tradition by two members reading up on the Irish and Welsh deities and between them giving a talk on Celtic mythology. Another member could learn the runes and demonstrate a method of divination. Others could devise a rite in honor of some of the deities of a particular pantheon. The rite might be rather ragged the first time it is worked, but as people become more familiar with the format and revise the rite to run more smoothly, its power and energy will grow.

Group visualization and pathworking exercises are another important activity. To conduct meaningful ritual that is not just a theatrical display by the main participants, it is necessary for everyone to be participating in the ritual on an inner level, not just through external words and actions. Even if people want to work from the perspective of different Traditions, it can be a good idea for the group to develop its own way of opening and closing rites which can then be adapted to different pantheons and Traditions. Having a familiar opening and closing gives the group a sense of focus and identity. It is a way of saying, 'This is us and this is our space. This is what we are here to do.'

In a new group, a natural leader or leaders may emerge whom the other group members are happy to allow to take on the organizing role. However, in an eclectic group where no one has the mandate of leadership, this can be a tricky problem. What the group will need if it is to survive is not so much a leader as people who are prepared to take responsibility for some aspect of the group's activities and someone with good enough people skills to persuade the others to volunteer for those responsibilities. At the outset, it is a good idea to have an administration meeting and to decide what the group needs to do to organize itself. Do people need to contribute money on a regular basis to hire a room, invite occasional speakers and pay their travel expenses, buy candles and incense? Can the group organize itself in another way with people bringing and supplying different items in turns? It is important that some people do not find their generosity taken for granted by the other members or resentments will build up that can destroy what could have been a successful group. If the group always meets in Sarah's house, are members taking it for granted that she will clean up the ritual space for them, clear up afterwards, and supply all the candles, incense and maybe even food and drink? If so, the group will be short-lived. Groups need to assess realistically the inputs that are needed in terms of time, effort, and cash, and to make sure that the burden is evenly spread. All these problems can be solved, providing the group makes sure that it gives time and space to administrative meetings as well as its rites, celebrations and learning. A regular meeting is needed to discuss: How we are doing? Are we satisfied with what we've done so far? What do we want to do next? Is everyone contributing as they should? How do we decide if a new person should join the group? All these domestic issues are mundane in themselves, but the skill with which we learn to deal with them will determine whether we have a creative group which teaches us not only mystical and spiritual knowledge, but also how to relate better with other people – something which will stand us in good stead in the outer world as well as the inner.

Coming out

Regardless of whether or not we join a group, a decision which every practitioner of an Earth Tradition must make is how public to be about our spiritual path. Identifying yourself as a practitioner of a 'different' spiritual path will arouse people's interest. They will want to ask you questions about your beliefs. Some people are happy to deal with this; others prefer to keep their beliefs to themselves. However, the more people who are prepared to be open, the more people will come to know and understand the Earth Traditions and to see their beliefs as part of the normal spectrum of spiritual belief in our multicultural societies.

Telling people about our religious beliefs when they ask us is different from preaching to them. Whenever we discover some truth that works for us, it is tempting to try to convince others of its rightness. This can be counter-productive. There is nothing worse than the born-again bore and it is insulting and arrogant to ridicule the beliefs of others while flaunting the superiority of our own. How open you wish to be about your beliefs depends of course on your working environment. If you work in the music business, somewhat exotic interests may be as obligatory as keeping a pet snake. If you are a banker, being seen as weird or eccentric may be translated into unreliable and be the death of your career. Much also depends on where we live. In large multicultural cities, unusual spiritual beliefs arouse no interest at all. In small conservative communities, coming out as a member of a minority religious group may lead to being socially ostracized or worse.

Another factor in how public we want to be about our spirituality is the brand we adopt. For Wicca, Santeria and Voudon, the problems can be greater than for people practicing other Earth Traditions, but for those who live in conservative areas, even practicing something as seemingly innocuous as druidry can lead to being branded a 'weirdo'. In the case of Wicca, the word witchcraft can be confused with Satanism. Publicity about contemporary witchcraft has done much to dispel misconceptions and to educate the public that it is a Pagan religion and not an anti-social cult; but the 'W' word undoubtedly causes difficulties and sensationalism rather than serious publicity. Many Wiccans prefer not to use the word witch, because it creates too much misunderstanding. For some people the words wise woman, cunning man, shaman, priest, or priestess seem more accurate descriptions of their spiritual practice. Others believe, more robustly, that it is time to rehabilitate the word witchcraft and to educate people about its true meaning. Fortunately, interfaith dialog between Christians, Wiccans and others is growing and Christian-Pagan conferences have enabled people from the two faiths to share views and to come to mutual respect. In the United States, the Unitarian Church has an active Pagan branch. As Paganism has become more widespread, Christian ministers also find themselves meeting Pagans performing their ministry in settings such as hospitals, prisons, and student counselling. From these working relationships, mutual friendship and respect have developed. Dialog between Christianity and the Earth Traditions does not mean that followers of all religions are going to come to the same view; but it does mean that we can learn from each other and that the insights that we have gained from our respective systems can enrich each other's spiritual lives.

Children and the Earth Traditions

How open we are about our spirituality will also depend on whether we have children. In recent years, certain campaigners have sought for their own perverse ends to brand Pagans as child molesters and devil worshippers. This is a problem both for Pagan parents and for those who work in the caring professions. Generally, people are more frightened by things they do not know and understand. Parents who practice an Earth Tradition find that talking to their children's teachers about their beliefs often raises fewer problems than little Rachel going to school on Monday morning and telling her teacher that her parents, 'Took me dancing round the cauldron with the witches on Saturday'. However, children's views must be paramount. Many children go through a stage when they do not want their parents to be unconventional, odd, or different from other children's parents, and for a child to be labeled as 'different' in a school can lead to bullying and difficulty in finding friends.

Finding a suitable group will also be influenced by whether we wish our children to worship with us. Many women are attracted to Wicca and while some groups welcome children, others see Wicca as a mystery Tradition that is suitable for adults only. Children's participation will alter the type of activities groups can perform. Group activity is unlikely to appeal to children if it involves intensive meditation sessions that are beyond children's attention spans, or complex ritual that can only be performed by adults. Similarly, adults will become bored if ritual and other activity has always to be geared to children's needs. Ideally, most parents are likely to need some family-oriented gatherings and some child-free occasions when they can practice more intensively and further their spiritual development rather than having to focus on meeting children's needs. The Unitarian Church has been found to be a welcoming home for many Pagan parents who can take children to services that are child-friendly and continue to practice adult-oriented Wicca elsewhere. Apart from local gatherings, large Wiccan festival camps can be wonderful experiences for children, in which they can mix with other children and have vast amounts of safe space to run around in. Festivals often include children's programs involving storytelling, theater, creative activity, outdoor skills, and special rituals in which they can take part. Druid gatherings are often family-oriented and the Order of Bards, Ovates and Druids in particular has an active festival program in Europe, North America and Australia that is family oriented.

Commitment and spirituality

The Earth Traditions are not for the faint-hearted, but for those who are prepared to take responsibility for themselves and for their own spiritual development and learning. This can be daunting and we will make many mistakes and fail often, but this does not matter if we have the courage to go onward in pursuit of our goal. There is only one thing we need and that is commitment. WH Murray, the leader of the Scottish Himalayan expedition, wrote:

> Until one is committed, there is always a hesitancy,
> the chance to draw back, always ineffectiveness.
> Concerning all acts of initiative and creation –
> there is one elementary truth, the ignorance of which
> kills countless ideas and splendid plans:
> that the moment one definitely commits oneself,
> then Providence moves too.
> All sorts of things occur to help one
> that would never otherwise have occurred.
> A whole stream of events issue from the decision,
> raising in one's favour all manner of unforeseen incidents

and meetings and material assistance,
which no man could have dreamed would have come
    his way.[1]

I have learned deep respect for one of Goethe's couplets:

❧   Whatever you can do, or dream you can, begin it:
     boldness has genius, power and magic in it; begin it now.

The message of the Earth Traditions

The message of the Earth Traditions is one of love and reverence for our planet, its inhabitants, and the cosmos of which it is a part. It is wonder at the extraordinary gift that we all take for granted – the gift of consciousness, the awareness that allows us to cry out to the universe, 'I am.' When we look out into the starry skies at night, we know that we are not alone. Out there in the vastness of space are other sentient beings looking out at the stars, just as we are – but biological life is rare in the universe and beings like humans who have conscious awareness are even rarer. Let us remember then the wondrous miracle of existence and rejoice in the Divine force that has brought us into being, each one of us a unique and individual spark of the Divine whole.

❧   Let the Elder Faiths be reborn in the hearts of their people;
     so that we who worship Goddess and God
     made manifest in the beauties of Nature,
     within the souls of women and men,
     within the ever-encircling stars,
     and beyond all these things –
     in the Hidden House of the Spirit;
     that we may rekindle the eternal flame of truth so
       long extinguished;
     that we may rejoice with chant and song, with poem
       and story,
     and dance once more the Spiral Dance of Life and Death.
     All belief comes from within,
     and all truth is sought and found,
     in the Cup of the heart,

and the Temple of the spirit;
in the deep places of the forest,
where sunlight patterns the leaf-strewn floor,
and there is only the song of the birds,
to break the silence of the soul;
there shall we find our gods;
beneath tree and leaf and waving bough,
beneath sky and cloud and in wind and rain,
reborn of the ever-returning Sun
like a Phoenix from the Flame.

Vivianne Crowley, 1994

Notes

1   WH Murray (1951) *The Scottish Himalayan Expedition.*

Resources

There is a wealth of excellent literature on the Earth Traditions. Just some of the many books on offer are listed in the Bibliography. You can also find many more in local bookstores and through on-line bookstores. There is also a vast amount of information on the web. Use a search engine to find out information on the particular Tradition that interests you. There are e-mail discussion groups for most Traditions and these can be found through links provided on the websites listed here. Listed below are some magazines and organizations that can help you find out more about Pagan Earth Traditions. The listings are by no means exhaustive. The magazines and organizations listed are those that have been running for some time and have relatively stable addresses. All have different orientations and can evolve and change with time. Listing does not necessarily imply recommendation. You must judge for yourself. Costs of magazines and membership fees for organizations have not been given as these will necessarily change, but they will be able to send you up to date details. If there is no relevant organization listed for your own country, then write to one of the main bodies in the USA or UK. These should be able to help you with international contacts. If you run a group or organization that is not affiliated to the organizations listed here, you may wish to contact them to foster networking and contacts.

All these organizations and magazines are run on tight budgets. You are unlikely to receive a reply unless you send postage. In your own country, send a self-addressed stamped envelope (SASE). To overseas addresses, send two International Reply Coupons. These can be bought in large post offices and can be exchanged for stamps all over the world. Do not send checks in your own currency to addresses overseas. The cost of cashing them is usually greater than the value of the check. Remember to write your address on your letter and not just on the envelope.

Asterisked organizations are larger networking organizations that have websites and are good starting points for learning about Earth Traditions.

Contemporary Paganism

Aquarian Tabernacle Church, PO Box 73, Index, Washington 98256–0409, USA; www.aquatabch.org. A Pagan-Wiccan church active in interfaith work.

*Australian Pagan Alliance, PO Box 823, Bathurst, NSW 2795, Australia; www.geocities.com/Athens/Thebes/4320. A Pagan network for Wiccans and others.

*Church of All Worlds, PO Box 488, Laytonville, CA 95454, USA; www.caw.org. A Pagan organization that owns land, raises ecological awareness through its subsidiary organization, *Forever Forests*, and publishes the magazine *Green Egg*.

*Circle, PO Box 219, Mount Horeb, WI 53572, USA; www.circlesanctuary.org. Organizes Pagan events, fosters contacts and networking, and publishes the quarterly journal *Circle Network News*.

*Covenant of Unitarian Universalist Pagans Inc. (CUUPS), 8190A Beechmont Ave, PMB 335, Cincinnati, OH 45255–3154, USA; www.cuups.org; email: CUUPS@uua.org. An Independent Affiliate of the Unitarian Universalist Association of Congregations (UUA) committed to furthering Pagan and Earth-centered thea/ology within the UUA. There is an on-line journal at: http://www.connectionsjournal.com.

Dragon, www.gn.apc.org/dragon; adrian@gn.apc.org. A network combining eco-magic with practical conservation and campaigning.

EarthSpirit, PO Box 365-N, Medford, MA 02155, USA; www.earthspirit.com. A non-profit organization providing services to a nationwide network of Pagans and other followers of Earth-centered religions.

Invisible College, BCM-SCL QUEST, London WC1N 3XX, UK. Run by Marian Green, a magician in the Western Ways, who provides courses in natural magic and produces *Quest* magazine.

*Nordic Pagan Federation, (Nordisk Paganistforbund), Postboks 1814, Nordnes, 5816 Bergen, Norway; www.bgnett.no/pagan. Provides information on Wicca in Scandinavian countries.

*Pagan Federation/Fédération Païenne Canada (PFPC), PO Box 8312, Station I, Ottawa, Ontario, K1G 3H8, Canada; www.pfpc.ca. A Canadian organization for Wiccans and other Pagans.

*Pagan Federation International, PO Box 473, Zeist, NL 3700 AL, The Netherlands; www.paganfederation.org. The international division of the Pagan Federation. Its website has links to Pagan Federation groups worldwide.

*Pagan Federation, BM Box 7097, London WC1N 3XX, UK; www.paganfed. demon.co.uk. The main Pagan body in Europe. There is a magazine *Pagan*

Dawn which lists groups, courses, conferences, contact networks, social meetings, etc, in Britain and other parts of Europe, covering many Earth Traditions including Wicca.

Steinkreis Pagan Network ev, c/o Uta Sprenger, Puntheide 21, D-33619 Bielefeld, Germany; www.derSteinkreis.de. A network for German Wiccan and Pagan groups which has links to Pagan Federation International.

Pagan books

Adler, M (1997 ed.) *Drawing Down the Moon: Witches, Druids, Goddess-Worshippers and Other Pagans in America Today.* New York: Arkana. Overview of Pagan groups in the United States and useful section of contact addresses by Pagan journalist Margot Adler.

Albanese, CL (1990) *Nature Religion in America: From the Algonkian Indians to the New Age.* Chicago and London: University of Chicago Press. Academic book helpful for understanding the background to contemporary Paganism in the United States and packed with interesting information about nature religion among Native Americans and other Americans.

Crowley, V (1996) *Principles of Paganism,* London: Thorsons. A useful introduction to contemporary Paganism.

Hutton, RB (1991) *The Pagan Religions of the Ancient British Isles: Their Nature and Legacy.* Oxford: Basil Blackwell. Excellent background material on the Pagan Traditions of Britain by British academic Professor Ronald Hutton.

Hutton, RB (1999) *The Triumph of the Moon.* Oxford: Oxford University Press. The first real history of contemporary Wicca and essential background reading for those with a serious interest in the Tradition.

Jones, P and Pennick, N (1995) *A History of Pagan Europe.* Routledge: London. Prudence Jones, President of the Pagan Federation, and writer Nigel Pennick provide an important insight into the continuation of Paganism in Europe during the Christian period.

Goddess spirituality

Fellowship of Isis, Clonegal Castle, Clonegal, Enniscorthy, Ireland; www.fellowshipofisis.com. A worldwide Goddess organization. Some of its members run Iseums, Goddess groups that meet regularly. There is provision for training in the Goddess priesthood.

Reformed Congregation of the Goddess. A Goddess religion incorporated in many US states and recognized as tax-exempt by the IRS. Its Thealogical Institute offers a Cella Training Program for those drawn to the Goddess priesthood.

SageWoman, PO Box 641, Point Arena, CA 95468, USA; www.sagewoman.com. A quarterly magazine of Women's Spirituality, celebrating the Goddess in every woman.

Goddess books

Budapest, Z (1990) *The Holy Book of Women's Mysteries*. New York: Harper and Row. A useful book for women starting on a Goddess path.

McCrickard, J (1991) *Eclipse of the Sun: An Investigation into Sun and Moon Myths*. Glastonbury: Gothic Image. Janet McCrickard gives the background to many of the goddesses that are venerated in the Earth Traditions today.

Patai, R (1990 ed) *The Hebrew Goddess*. Detroit: Wayne State University Press. Dr Raphael Patai is an academic whose book on Hebrew goddesses is a revelation for those unaware of the long Hebrew Tradition of Goddess worship that co-existed with the worship of Yahweh for hundreds of years.

Raphael, M (1999) *Introducing Thealogy: Discourse on the Goddess*. Sheffield: Sheffield Academic Press. Dr Melissa Raphael's excellent account of contemporary Goddess spirituality is an important book for women of all spiritual Traditions.

Roberts, WH (1998) *Celebrating Her: Feminist Ritualizing comes of Age*. Cleveland: Pilgrim Press. Don't be put off by the subtitle if you do not consider yourself a feminist. This is not feminist rhetoric but a serious, thoughtful, and thought-provoking book about creating Goddess ritual. It is Wiccan-based but can be used by women of all faiths. As well as providing ideas for seasonal rituals, it offers insight into issues of leadership, child-rearing, interfaith celebration, and other important aspects of practicing Goddess spirituality in contemporary life.

Starhawk, (1979 ed) *The Spiral Dance: A Rebirth of the Ancient Religion of the Great Goddess*. San Francisco: Harper. Starhawk's book is a classic work on Goddess witchcraft as practiced in the American feminist Tradition.

Witt, RE (1971) *Isis in the Graeco-Roman World*. London: Thames and Hudson. This is a classic work about the worship of Isis. While it is mainly historical, describing the widespread worship of Isis and its challenge to the supremacy of Christianity in the Roman Empire, it shows a veneration of the Goddess that has inspired many men to explore Goddess spirituality.

Wicca

Cauldron magazine, available from Mike Howard, Caemorgan Cottage, Caemorgan Road, Cardigan, Dyfed, SA43 1QU, Wales, UK. An informative journal of the Old Religion and one of the oldest Craft magazines. It is based in a conservative rural area. Please do not write *Cauldron* on the envelope.

*Children of Artemis, BM Artemis, London WC1N 3XX, UK; www.witchcraft.org. Can help people in Britain wanting to contact Wiccan groups. There is a magazine and the web site hosts a discussion group.

*Covenant of the Goddess, Membership Officer, PO Box 1226, Berkeley, CA 94701, USA; www.cog.org; email: mailto: info@cog.org. A network of Goddess and Wiccan groups that has a newsletter and an annual festival MerryMeet.

Elad and Adair BranDubh, PO Box 876, Station B, Ottawa, Ontario, K1P 5P9, Canada; email: imawitch@cyberus.ca. Advice on contacting initiatory Wicca in Canada.

Gaia Group, c/o PO Box 911, Boulder, CO 80306-0911, USA. An initiatory Earth Religion with Wiccan roots, dedicated to the care and protection of Mother Earth through magickal and practical means.

Greencraft België vzw, Greencraft België vzw, p/a Boekweithofstraat 26, 9120 Haasdonk, Belgium; www.greencraft.webplace.cx. A foundation representing a number of Alexandrian covens in Belgium, The Netherlands and the state of Texas that provide training in Wicca. Greencraft also provides distance training.

Museum of Witchcraft, The Harbour, Boscastle, Cornwall, PL35 0AE, UK; Tel: 01840 250111; www.museumofwitchcraft.com. A 'must' to visit for anyone interested in witchcraft. It is open from April to Samhain and houses the world's largest collection of witchcraft artifacts and regalia.

North Star, BM North Star, London WC1N 3XX, UK; www.geocities. com/Athens/Oracle/8173/northstar.html. A network of initiatory Traditions of British witchcraft which assists UK-based individuals make contact with local groups.

Quicksilver Coven, PO Box 32, Stn 'B', Ottawa, Ontario K1P 6C3, Canada; www.ncf.ca/~cq081/qs. Information on British Traditional Wicca in Canada and the United States.

*Reclaiming, PO Box 14404, San Francisco, CA 94114, USA; www.webcom. com/cauldron/. A Center for Feminist Spirituality and a collective of women and men working to unify spirituality and politics. It offers workshops, summer programs, public rituals, and a newsletter. Inspired by work of Starhawk.

Red Garters International, PO Box 162046, MH Sacramento, CA 95816, USA; http://www.angelfire.com/ca/redgarters. The official newsletter of the New Wiccan Church, dedicated to the promulgation of British Traditional Wicca. There are branches in other states and the Church will deal with enquiries for admission.

*Sacred Well Congregation of Texas, PO Box 58, Converse, Texas 78109, USA; www.sacredwell.org/indexa.htm. An international, universalist, independent Wiccan Church with many branches that can provide information and training. Offers assistance to Pagans in the US military.

Salem Witch Museum, Washington Square, Salem, Massachusetts 01970, USA; www.salemwitchmuseum.com. A memorial to the witches of Salem killed in the witch persecutions of 1692. The whole of this part of Salem has become a tourist area dedicated to witchcraft, with a host of occult stores to supply every witchcraft need. A mix of serious and tourist witchcraft that is worth a visit if in the region.

Silver Bayou Traditional Wicca; email: mel@tpao.org. Teaching circle that holds annual Wicca Intensive immersion seminar for beginners in Houston, Texas. Also provides referrals for Gardnerian and Alexandrian training.

Wicca in Scotland: Write to Charis and Jim, PO Box 932, Edinburgh, EH17 7PW, Scotland, UK.

*Wicca Study Group, BM Deosil, London WC1N 3XX, UK; www.witchcraft.org/vivianne.htm. email: BMDEOSIL@aol.com. Established in 1988 by Vivianne and Chris Crowley to provide workshops, an evening course, and a home study course for people seeking the Wiccan path.

Wiccan Church of Canada, 109 Vaughan Road, Toronto, M6C 2L9, Canada; www.wcc.on.ca. A network of Wiccan groups in the Odyssian Tradition. It offers training, information, ritual celebrations and a magazine.

Wiccan Rede, PO Box 473, Zeist, NL 3700 AL, The Netherlands; www.silvercircle.org. An English/Dutch Wiccan magazine which can assist with contacts in the Netherlands.

Wiccan books

Berger, H (1999) *A Community of Witches: Contemporary Neo-Paganism and Witchcraft in the United States*. Columbia: University of South California Press. Fascinating insight into the lives of contemporary witches by an academic.

Beth, R (1990) *Hedgewitch*. London, Hale. Beautiful and poetic insight into the British witch Tradition by witch Rae Beth, written in the form of letters to newcomers.

Crowley, V (1996) *Wicca: The Old Religion in the New Millennium*. London: Thorsons. In-depth insights into coven practice in British Traditional witchcraft.

Crowley, V (2001) *Thorsons Way of Wicca*. London: Thorsons. An introduction to Wiccan practice for those starting out on the path.

Guiley, RE (1999 ed.) *Encyclopedia of Witches and Witchcraft*. New York: Checkmark Books. This is Rosemary Guiley's second edition of this comprehensive work that covers everything you might want to know about the development of Wicca, leading figures in its development, and key practices.

Orion, L (1995) *Never Again the Burning Times: Paganism Revived*. Prospect Heights, Ill: Waveland Press. Loretta Orion's PhD thesis on witchcraft in America provides a helpful insight for those interested in this path.

Druidry and Celtic Tradition

Ar nDraiocht Fein (ADF), PO Box 15259, Ann Arbor, MI 48106–5259, USA; http://www.adf.org. A Druid Fellowship offering a journal and training on the Druid path.

*Order of Bards, Ovates and Druids, PO Box 1333, Lewes, BN7 3ZG, UK; www.druidry.org. The largest Druid order with many groups worldwide. Training in Druidry covering healing, divination, mythology, history, and folklore through correspondence course, workshops and retreats.

Celtic books

Bradley, I (1999) *Celtic Christianity: Making Myths and Chasing Dreams*. Edinburgh: Edinburgh University Press. An academic insight into the development of Celtic Christianity that shows the beauty of this Tradition.

Carmichael, A trans. (1972) *Carmina Gaedelica*. Edinburgh: Scottish Academic Press. Alexander Carmichael's collection of Celtic prayers and rites from nineteenth-century west of Scotland shows the strong links Celtic Christianity maintained with its Pagan roots. The material has been incorporated into many contemporary Pagan prayers and rituals, including Wiccan sabbat rituals.

Crowley, V (1998) *Celtic Wisdom: Seasonal Festivals and Rituals*. New York: Sterling. Ways of celebrating the seasonal cycle drawing on Celtic myth and tailored to contemporary life.

Low, M (1996) *Celtic Christianity and Nature: Early Irish and Hebridean Tradition*. Belfast: Blackfast Press. A beautiful and thoughtful book on Celtic spirituality by academic Mary Low.

Restall-Orr, E (1998) *Principles of Druidry.* London: Thorsons. Emma Restall-Orr is a leading British druid priestess and her book is essential reading for those wishing to explore the druid path.

Heathenism

American Vinland Association, PMB 2154, 537 Jones St. #2154, San Francisco, CA 94102–2007, USA; www.freyasfolk.org. A membership organization with extensive information about the practice of Heathenism in the United States and elsewhere. Their website is a treasure trove of useful information, including Prudence Priest's article on the use of amber, and has links to other Heathen organizations and to academic and other sites hosting Germanic texts including the *Eddas,* sagas, poetry, prose, fairytales, folk tales and mythology. Also has useful information for those thinking of joining Ásatrú groups and links to a wide range of groups in North America and elsewhere.

Ásatrúarfélagid (The Icelandic Ásatrú Assocation), PO Box 1423, 121 Reykjavik, Iceland; www.islandia.is/~asatru. The representative body of the Ásatrú religion in Iceland.

Aswynn, Freya, BM Aswynn, London WC1N 3XX, UK; www.aswynn.co.uk. A volva who can provide rune readings. She is currently acting President of the Ring of Troth Europe, see below.

Midgard's Web, c/o Twigshof, 51 Toorack Road, Harrow Weald, Middlesex, HA3 5HR, UK; www.astradyne.co.uk/midgard. A network for people inspired by pre-Christian Traditions and religious lore originating in Scandinavia, Germany and the Anglo-Saxon countries.

Odinshof, BCM Tercel, London WC1N 3XX, UK. Provides clergy training, contact with groups and a correspondence course. Also runs a land guardian scheme to preserve land for conservation and worship.

Ring of Troth Europe, BM Troth, London WC1N 3XX, UK; www.aswynn.co.uk. Acting president, Freya Aswynn, promotes all aspects of Ásatrú, Vanatru and Runelore. Program includes ritual training, clergy training, rune training, public meetings, interfaith dialog, and monthly newsletter *The Heathen Path*. Full membership is available for practitioners and associate membership for practitioners of other Traditions who are interested in Germanic Tradition.

Troth, c/o Diana L Paxson, Box 472, Berkeley, CA 94701, USA; www.thetroth.org/. A membership organization offering a clergy training program, annual gathering, magazine and publications.

Wyrd's Well Press, 1A Station Road, Hathersage, Hope Valley, Derbyshire, S32 1DD, UK; http://home.freeuk.net/wyrdswell. Publishes the work of Dr Jenny Blain, an academic and seidr practitioner, and can provide information on networking in the UK, and on occasional training courses and rune readings.

Heathen books

Aswynn, F (1998) *Northern Mysteries and Magick: Runes, Gods, and Feminine Powers* St Paul's, Minn: Llewellyn. Written by volva and rune-mistress Freya Aswynn this is an updated version of her book *Leaves of Yggrdasil* and an excellent introduction to Northern European spirituality and magic. There is also a CD of runic chanting, which conveys the power and beauty of the runes.

Aswynn, F (2000) *Principles of Runes.* London: Thorsons. Excellent introduction to runes.

Blain, J (2000) *Understanding Wyrd: the Norns and the Tree.* Hathersage: Wyrd's Well Press. Insightful guide to this aspect of the tradition.

Blain, J (2000) *Wights and Ancestors: Heathenism in a living landscape.* Hathersage: Wyrd's Well Press. Insightful guide to this aspect of the tradition.

Davidson, HR Ellis (1964) *Gods and Myths of Northern Europe.* Harmondsworth: Pelican. Hilda Ellis Davidson is a British academic who has made an extensive study of Germanic and Celtic Pagan Traditions. All her books are excellent background reading for people drawn to these Traditions.

Davidson, HR Ellis (1988) *Myths and Symbols in Pagan Europe, Early Scandinavian and Celtic Religions.* Manchester: Manchester University Press. Shows the beauty of these European Traditions.

Davidson, HR Ellis (1993) *The Lost Beliefs of Northern Europe.* London and New York: Routledge. A treasure trove of myth and folk tradition.

Titchenell, EB (1985) *The Masks of Odin: Wisdom of the Ancient Norse.* Pasadena, Ca: Theosophical University Press. Elsa-Brita Titchenell's book is a beautiful exposition of the Scandinavian Tradition.

African Traditions

There are no central networking bodies, but there are many local groups. Some are incorporated as churches. Two churches are listed here as starting points. Many churches have websites on the net with links to other groups.

African resources, www.africana.com. Useful information on cultural, religious and
   topical issues.
Church of the Lukumi Babalu Aye, PO Box 2627, Hialeah, Florida 33012, USA;
   www.church-of-the-lukumi.org. Works in the Afro-Cuban Lukumi/Ayoba religious lineages. It offers baptism, marriage and funeral services.
Palo and Lukumi Organization, PO Box 1053, Lancaster, CA 93584, USA;
   www.palo.org/contact.html.
Voodoo Spiritual Temple, 828 N. Rampart Street, New Orleans, LA 70116, USA;
   ww.gnofn.org/~voodoo.

Books on African Traditions

Awolalu, JO and Dopamu PA (1979) *West African Traditional Religion.* Ibadan,
   Nigeria: Onibondje Press & Book Industries. This is a classic work that has
   introduced many people to African religions.
Brown, KM (1992) *Mama Lola.* Berkeley: University of California Press. Karen
   McCarthy Brown draws on a decade-long friendship with Vodou priestess
   Mama Lola and describes the lives of five generations of Vodou healers. The
   book conveys what it is to live as a Vodou priestess.
Deren, M (1985) *Divine Horsemen: The Living Gods of Haiti.* London: McPherson &
   Co. Classic 1953 study of Haitian voudoun religion. There is also a video:
   Divine Horsemen – The Living Gods of Haiti VHS. Maya Deren was a pioneering
   Swedish filmmaker who gives a profound insight into the spirituality and mys-
   ticism of Voudon Tradition.
Fernández Olmos, M and Paravisini-Gebert, L eds. (1999) *Sacred Possessions: Voudou,
   Santeria, Obeah and the Caribbean.* New Brunswick, New Jersey and London:
   Rutgers University Press. An excellent academic book on these traditions.
Gleason, J (1987) *Oya: In Praise of the Goddess.* Boston: Shambhala. Judith Gleason
   is a priestess of the Yoruba goddess Oya. This is an excellent introduction to
   the veneration of an African goddess.
Hurston, ZN (1990) *Tell My Horse: Voodoo and Life in Haiti and Jamaica.* New York:
   Harper and Row. Zora Neale Hurston's book is an excellent introduction to the
   traditions as practiced in the Caribbean.
Some, MP (1995) *Of Water and the Spirit.* New York and London: Arkana. Dr
   Malidoma Patrice Some, whose name means 'He-who-makes-friends-with-
   the-stranger', was born in African Francophone Upper Volta (now Burkina),
   West Africa, and received an education by a Jesuit priest in a seminary. He
   returned to his people, the Dagara, at the age of 19, having almost forgotten his
   own language, was initiated and became a shaman. He has since become a

spiritual teacher of African Tradition to Westerners. He also has two PhDs.

Some, MP (1995) *Ritual.* Gateway Books. Explores ritual as a means of creating community and its importance in Western society.

Some, MP (1999) *The Healing Wisdom of Africa.* Thorsons: London. An excellent introduction to African Tradition.

Teish, L (1988) *Jambalaya: The Natural Woman's Book of Personal Charms and Practical Rituals.* Harper: San Francisco. Luisah Teish was born and raised in New Orleans. She is a priestess of Oshun in the Yoruba Lucumi tradition and teaches classes on African goddesses, shamanism, and the Tambala tradition.

Thompson, RF (1984) *Flash of the Spirit: African and Afro-American Art and Philosophy.* New York: Random House. A landmark book by art historian Robert Farris Thompson on how Yoruba, Kongo, Ejagham, Mande and Cross River cultures are reflected in the esthetic, social and metaphysical traditions of African Americans and Afro-Caribbeans.

Vega, MM (2000) *The Altar of My Soul: The Living Traditions of Santeria.* New York: Ballantine. An excellent introduction.

North-Eastern Europe

Dievturi Latvian Pagan Church, Elder Olgerts Auns, Kr. Barona iela 37–7, Ryga, Latvia. Information on Latvian Paganism is available on: www.pagan. drak.net/wwcrew/.

Romuva Vilnius, Elder Algis Jucevicius, Didzioji 11, 2000 Vilnius, Lithuania; http://www.romuva.lt. Represents Traditional religion in Lithuania. Romuva organizes summer camps and has information on the practice of Baltic religion today. Romuva USA can be emailed on: audriusdundzila@home.com and Romuva Canada on: ironwolf@idirect.com. Information on Lithuanian Tradition is also available on: www.lithuanian.net/resource/myths.htm.

Books on North Eastern European Traditions

Gimbutas, M (1963) *The Balts.* London: Thames and Hudson. Professor Marija Gimbutas was a Lithuanian feminist academic who inspired a re-evaluation of the roles of goddesses in early spirituality. Her archeological interpretations remain controversial but many women have been inspired by her work.

Gimbutas, M (1971) *The Slavs.* London: Thames and Hudson. Useful introduction to Slavic Tradition.

Löhnrot, E (1989 ed) *The Kalevala*, K Bosley trans. Oxford: Oxford University Press. Elias Löhnrot's collection of the myths and lore of Finnish Tradition provides an insight into this early shamanistic European Tradition.

Nelson, R (1999) *Finnish Magic: A Nation of Wizards, A World of Spirits.* St Paul's, Minn: Llewellyn. Dr Robert Nelson's book is a good starting point for people wanting to practice Finnish Tradition.

Shamanism

Foundation for Shamanic Studies, PO Box 1939, Mill Valley, CA 94942, USA: www.shamanism.org. Founded by Michael Harner to offer workshops and training in shamanic practice. There is also a quarterly newsletter for members.

Scandinavian Center for Shamanic Studies, Artillerivej 63/140, DK 2300 Copenhagen S., Denmark; http://www.shaman-center.dk. A small independent network, started by Jonathan Horowitz and Annette Høst, to teach and encourage the practice of shamanism.

Books on Shamanism

Eliade, M (1989 ed.) *Shamanism: Archaic Techniques of Ecstasy.* WR Trask trans. London: Arkana. The classic academic work that introduced many people to shamanism.

Jakobsen, MD (1999) *Shamanism: Traditional and Contemporary Approaches to the Mastery of Spirits and Healing.* New York and Oxford: Berghahn Books. Unique academic study of the ancient Inuit shamanism of Greenland with comparisons made with contemporary shamanic practice.

Maclellan, G (1999) *Shamanism.* Piatkus Books: London. Gordon Maclellen is a genuine shaman based in Britain and working in the European Tradition. His book and workshops are highly recommended.

Native American spirituality

Center for the SPIRIT (Support and Protection of Indian Religions and Indigenous Traditions), PO Box 17002, Oakland, CA 94601. A non-profit organization of American Indian people dedicated to the preservation and revitalization of American Indian spiritual practices and religious traditions. Seeks to address

New Age exploitation and expropriation of the sacred traditions of American Indian tribes.

Friends of the Native American Church, Box 307, Arcata, CA 95521, USA. A contact point for the Church.

Native American Organizations and Urban Indian Centers, website maintained by Lisa Mitten at the University of Pittsburgh; www.nativeculture.com/lisamitten/organizations.html.

Native American books

The University of Oklahoma has many excellent publications, some of which are listed here.

Allen, PG (1992 ed) *The Sacred Hoop.* Boston: Beacon Press, 1986. Paula Gunn Allen's book is a useful introduction, particularly with regard to women.

Crow Dog, M and Erdoes, R (1990) *Lakota Woman.* New York: HarperPerennial. Mary Crow Dog was an activist with the American Indian Movement during some of the most important episodes in the struggle for Indian rights in the 1970s that also saw the creation of a Pan-Indian movement for spiritual renewal of Native American Tradition.

Deloria, Jr, V (1994) *God is Red: A Native View of Religion.* Golden, CO: Fulcrum. Dr Vine Deloria is a Lakota academic at the University of Denver. His book is a fascinating and sometimes hard-hitting exposition on Native American spirituality. A newer book is Vine Deloria, Jr (1999) *For This Land: Writings on Religion in America,* London and New York: Routledge. An excellent collection of essays.

Gossen, GH ed (1997 ed) *South and Meso-American Native Spirituality: From the Cult of the Feathered Serpent to the Theology of Liberation.* New York: Crossroads. This is a collection of academic papers on spirituality as practiced today in the USA-Mexican border and further south. Illustrates how Native Tradition has survived the Christian era, often with a thin Christian veneer.

Fitzgerald, MO (1991) *Yellowtail: Crow Medicine Man and Sun Dance Chief: An Autobiography as Told to Michael Oren Fitzgerald.* Norman, Oklahoma: University of Oklahoma Press. Gives an insight into Native American spirituality through the life of a spiritual leader.

Leeming, D and Page, J (1998) *The Mythology of Native North America.* Norman: University of Oklahoma Press. A well-researched book on Native American sacred histories.

Locke, RF (1992 ed) *The Book of the Navajo.* Los Angeles: Mankind. Navajo writer Raymond Friday Locke gives an excellent account of Navajo Tradition.

Neihardt, JG (1988 ed) *Black Elk Speaks*. Lincoln and London: University of Nebraska Press. The life story and spiritual philosophy of the Lakota holy man Black Elk has inspired people of all races to honor and venerate the Divine through the Earth Traditions.

Zimmerman, LJ and Molyneaux, BL (1996) *Native North America*. Norman: University of Oklahoma Press. A good introduction to Native American Traditions.

Contemporary interpretations of Native American Spirituality open to non-Native Americans

Bear Tribe, PMB 223, 3750-A Airport Blvd, Mobile, AL 36608-16, USA; www.ewebtribe.com. Follows Sun Bear's teachings. It sponsors Medicine Wheel gatherings, training, apprenticeship, and vision quests; and publishes *Wildfire* magazine. The gatherings are child-friendly.

Storm, Hyemeyohsts and Swan, PO Box 11562, Santa Rosa, CA 95406, USA; www.hyemeyohstsstorm.com. Run workshops and other teaching sessions.

Contemporary books

Storm, H. (1997) *Lightningbolt*. New York: Ballantine Books; and Storm, H. (1970) *Seven Arrows*. New York: Random House. Offers a contemporary spirituality drawing on insights and practices from Native American spiritualities.

Bibliography

Books cited or used as sources that are not listed in recommended reading above.

Anderson, W and Hicks, C (1990) *The Green Man*. London: Collins.

Apuleius, L (1985 ed) *The Golden Ass*. Harmondsworth: Penguin.

Aswynn, F (1988) *Leaves of Yggdrasil: A Synthesis of Magic, Feminine Mysteries, Folklore*. London: Aswynn.

Auden, WH and Taylor, PB (1983 ed) *Norse Poems*. London: Faber and Faber.

Avalon, A (Sir John Woodroffe) (1978 ed) *Shakti and Shakta*. New York: Dover.

Awolalu, JO (1976) 'Sin and its removal in African Traditional Religion', in *Journal of the American Academy of Religion*, 44(2), page 275.

Bancroft, A (1996) *Women in Search of the Sacred: The spiritual lives of ten remarkable women*. London: Arkana.

Bloom, W ed (1991) *The New Age: An Anthology of Essential Writings*. London: Rider.

Bly, R (1991 ed) *Iron John: A Book about Men*. Shaftesbury: Element Books.

Bourne, L (1979) *A Witch amongst Us*. London: Hale.

Bray, O, trans (1908) *The Elder or Poetic Edda*. Viking Club.

Bullfinch, T (no publication date) *Bullfinch's Mythology*. New York: The Contemporary Library.

Campbell, J (1972 ed) *The Hero with a Thousand Faces*, Bollingen Series XVII. Princeton: Princeton University Press.

Carpenter, DD (1994) *Spiritual Experiences, Life Changes, and Ecological Viewpoints of Contemporary Pagans*. Unpublished PhD thesis, Saybrook Institute.

Carr-Gomm, P (1991) *The Elements of the Druid Tradition*. Shaftesbury: Element.

Chadwick, N (1970) *The Celts*. Harmondsworth: Penguin.

Cohn, N (1975) *Europe's Inner Demons: An Enquiry inspired by the Great Witch Hunt*. London: Sussex University Press in association with Heinemann Educational Books.

Crowley, A (no publication date) *Magick in Theory and Practice*. New York: Castle Books.

Crowley, V (1989) *Wicca: The Old Religion in the Age*. Wellingborough: Aquarian.

Crowley V (1994) *Phoenix from the Flame: Pagan Spirituality in the Western World*. London: Aquarian.

Crowley, V (1993) Women and Power in Contemporary Paganism, in Puttick, E and Clarke, PB, eds, *Women as Teachers and Disciples in Traditional and New Religions*. Lewiston, New York: Edwin Mellen Press.

Crowley, V (2000) *A Woman's Kabbalah: Kabbalah for the 21st Century*. London: Thorsons.

Crowley, V and Crowley, C (2000) *Ancient Wisdom: Earth Traditions in the 21st Century*. London: Carlton.

Currott, PW (1998) *Book of Shadows*. New York: Broadway Books.

Danaher, K (1972) *The Year in Ireland: Irish Calendar Customs*. Cork and Minneapolis: Mercier Press.

Dowd, GE (1992) *A Spirited Resistance: The North American Indian Struggle for Unity: 1745-1815*. Baltimore: The Johns Hopkins University Press.

Easwaran, E, trans (1988 ed) *The Upanishads*. London: Arkana.

Ellwood, RS and Partin, HB (1988) *Religious and Spiritual Groups in Contemporary America*. 2nd ed, Englewood Cliffs, New Jersey: Prentice-Hall.

Emerson, RW (1985 ed) *Selected Essays*. Harmondsworth: Penguin.

Farella, JR (1984) *The Main Stalk, A Synthesis of Navajo Philosophy*. Tucson: University of Arizona Press.

Farrar, J and Farrar, S (1981) *Eight Sabbats for Witches*. London: Hale.

Farrar, J and Farrar, S (1984) *The Witches' Way*. London: Hale.

Fenton, W (1991) *The False Face Society of the Iroquois*. Norman: University of Oklahoma Press.

Fortune, D (1976 ed) *The Sea Priestess*. London, Star Books.

Fortune, D (1978 ed) *Moon Magic*. York Beach, Maine: Samuel Weiser Inc.

Frazer, Sir JG (1957 ed) *The Golden Bough: A Study in Magic and Religion*, Abridged ed London: Macmillan. (First published 1922.)

Gantz, J trans (1976 ed) *The Mabinogion*. Harmondsworth: Penguin.

Gardner, GB, (1949) *High Magick's Aid*, Atlantis Book Shop.

Gardner, GB (1954) *Witchcraft Today*. London: Rider & Co.

Gardner, GB (1959) *The Meaning of Witchcraft*. Wellingborough: Aquarian Press.

Gimbutas, M (1989) *The Language of the Goddess*. London: Thames and Hudson.

Ginzburg, C (1991 ed) *Ecstasies: Deciphering the Witches' Sabbath*. 4th ed, Raymond Rosenthal trans, New York: Penguin.

Green, M (1988) *The Path through the Labyrinth: The Quest for Initiation into the Western Mystery Tradition*. Shaftesbury: Element.

Green, M (1991) *A Witch Alone*. Shaftesbury: Element.

Griffin, W ed (1999) *Daughters of the Goddess: Studies in Healing, Identity, and Empowerment*. Lanham, Md: Altamira Press.

Koppana, K-M (1990) *Snakefat and Knotted Threads: An Introduction to Finnish Magic*. Helsinki: Madragora Dimensions.

Koppana, K-M (1991) *The Finnish Gods*. Helsinki: Madragora Dimensions.

Hardy, J (1989) *A Psychology with a Soul: Psychosynthesis in Evolutionary Context*. London: Arkana.

Harner, M (1980) *The Way of the Shaman*. New York: Harper & Row.

Harvey, G (1997) *Listening People: Speaking Earth: Contemporary Paganism*. London: Hurst & Co.

Harvey, G and Hardman, C, eds (1996) *Paganism Today: Wiccans, Druids, the Goddess and Ancient Earth Traditions for the Twenty-First Century*. London: Thorsons.

Harvey, G ed (1999) *Indigenous Religions: A Companion*. London and New York: Cassell.

Heelas, P (1996) *The New Age Movement: The Celebration of the Self and the Sacralization of Modernity*. Oxford. Basil Blackwell.

Hillman, James, ed (1987) *Puer Papers*. Dallas: Spring Publications Inc.

Hollander, LM, trans (1962) *The Poetic Edda*. Austin: University of Texas Press.

Hoyle, F (1965) *Of Men and Galaxies*. London: Heinemann.

Hirschfelder, A, Fairbanks Molin, P and Echo-Hawk, WR (1999 ed) *Encyclopedia of Native American Religions: An Introduction (Facts on File Library of American History)*. New York: Facts on File, Inc.

James, W (1982 ed) *The Varieties of Religious Experience*. London: Collins.

Jung, CG (1967 ed) *The Collected Works of C.G. Jung*, Vol 5, *Symbols of Transformation*. London: Routledge & Kegan Paul.

Jung, CG (1968 ed) *The Collected Works of C.G. Jung*, Vol 9, Part 1, *Archetypes of the Collective Unconscious*. London: Routledge & Kegan Paul.

Jung, E (1957) *Animus and Anima: Two Essays*. Zurich: Spring Publications.

Krech III, S (1999) *The Ecological Indian: Myth and History*. New York: WW Norton & Co.

Leland, CG (1974 ed) *Aradia: The Gospel of the Witches*. London: CW Daniel Company.

Levine, MP (1994) *Pantheism: A non-theistic concept of deity*. London and New York: Routledge.

Lewis, JR ed (1996) *Magical Religion and Modern Witchcraft*. Albany: State University of New York.

Lorimer, D (1990) *Whole in One: The Near-Death Experience and the Ethic of Interconnectedness*. London: Arkana.

Macalister, RAS trans (1938—56), *Lebor Gabala Erenn*. Dublin.

MacCrossan, T (1991) *The Sacred Cauldron: Secrets of the Druids*. St Paul's, Minn: Llewellyn.

Matthews, C (1989) *Elements of the Celtic Tradition*. Shaftesbury: Element.

Matthews, J (1991) *Choirs of the God: Revisioning Masculinity*. London: Mandala.

Mbiti, JS (1991 ed) *Introduction to African Religion*. Oxford: Heinemann Educational.

McNeley, JK (1981) *Holy Wind in Navajo Philosophy*. Tucson: University of Arizona Press.

Meadows, K (1990) *The Medicine Way*. Shaftesbury: Element.

Meyer, K trans (1909) *The Instructions of King Cormac mac Airt: Royal Irish Academy Todd Lecture Series, XV*. Dublin: Hodges, Figgis & Co.

Morgan, LH (1962 ed) *League of the Iroquois*. Seacaucus, New Jersey: Citadel Press.

Murray, MA, (1921) *The Witch-Cult in Western Europe: A Study in Anthropology*. Oxford: Clarendon Press.

Murray, MA (1970 ed) *The God of the Witches*. Oxford: Oxford University Press.

Murray, WH (1951) *The Scottish Himalaya Expedition*. London: JM Dent & Sons.

Nelson, R (1999) *Finnish Magic: A Nation of Wizards, A World of Spirits*. St Paul's, Minn: Llewellyn.

Odinist Committee (1983 ed) *This is Odinsim: Guidelines for Survival*. London: Raven Banner Editions.

O-hogain, D (1988) *Fionn Mac Cumhail*. Dublin: Gill & Macmillan.

Pagan Federation (1992 ed) *The Pagan Federation Information Pack*. London: Pagan Federation.

Page, S and Page, J (1995) *Navajo*. New York: Abrams.

Pearson, J, Roberts, R and Samuel, G (1996) *Nature Religion Today*. Edinburgh: Edinburgh University Press.

Pennick, N (1989) *Practical Magic in the Northern Tradition*. Wellingborough: Aquarian.

Perry, M (1992) *Gods Within: A Critical Guide to the New Age*. London: SPCK.

Puttick, E (1997) *Women in New Religions: In Search of Community, Sexuality and Spiritual Power*. London: Macmillan.

Rees, A and Rees, B (1961) *Celtic Heritage: Ancient Traditions in Ireland and Wales*. London: Thames and Hudson.

Roberts, WH (1998) *Celebrating Her: Feminist Ritualizing comes of Age*. Cleveland: Pilgrim Press.

Silver Ravenwolf (1993) *To Ride a Silver Broomstick: New Generation Witchcraft*. St Paul's, Minn: Llewellyn.

Slater, H (1978) *A Book of Pagan Rituals*. New York: Samuel Weiser Inc.

Spiegelman, JM and Vasavada, AU (1987) *Hinduism and Jungian Psychology*. Los Angeles and Phoenix: Falcon Press.

Starhawk (1982) *Dreaming the Dark: Magic, Sex and Politics*. Boston: Beacon Press.

Starhawk (1990 ed) *Truth or Dare: Encounters with Power, Authority and Mystery*. San Francisco: Harper.

Stewart, RJ (1991 ed) *Living Magical Arts: Imagination and Magic for the 21st Century*. London: Blandford.

Stewart, RJ (1991) *Celebrating the Male Mysteries*. Bath: Arcania.

Stubba (1991) *The Book of Blots: Ceremonies, Rituals and Invocations of the Odinic Rite*. London: Odinic Rite.

Sturluson, S (1987) *Edda*, Anthony Faulkes, trans, London: Everyman Library, JM Dent.

Stutley, M (1990) *Hinduism: The Eternal Law*. Wellingborough: Crucible.

Tacitus, C (1990 ed) *The Agricola and The Germania*, H Mattingly trans. Harmondsworth: Penguin.

Thoreau, HD (1863) 'Walking' in Robert Finch and John Elder eds. (1990 ed) New York: Norton.

Tooker, E ed (1988 ed) *Native American Spirituality of the Eastern Woodlands*. Mahwah, New Jersey: Paulist Press.

Trikunas, J (1992) *Romuva USA, 8*, Sambariai.

Valiente D (1975) *Natural Magic*. London: Robert Hale.

Valiente, D (1973) *An ABC of Witchcraft Past and Present*. London: Hale.

Wallis, RT (1972) *Neoplatonism*. London: Duckworth.

Water, F (1977 ed) *The Book of the Hopi*. New York: Penguin.

Wehr DS (1988) *Jung and Feminism*. London: Routledge.

Wilde, Lady, (1971 ed) *Ancient Legends, Mystic Charms, and Superstitions of Ireland*. Galway: O'Gorman.

Worthington, Vivian *A History of Yoga*. Arkana, London, 1982.

Wyman, LC (1970) *Blessingway*. Tucson: University of Arizona Press.

York, M (1995) *The Emerging Network: A Sociology of the New Age and Neo-Pagan Movements*. Lanham, Md: Rowman and Littlefield.

Zimmerman, LJ and Molyneaux, BL (1996) *Native North America* Norman: University of Oklahoma Press.

Index